THE MADISON WOMEN

The
Madison
Women

*Gender, Higher Education, and
Literacy in Nineteenth-Century
Appalachia*

Amanda E.
Hayes

WEST VIRGINIA UNIVERSITY PRESS / MORGANTOWN

ISBN 978-1-959000-25-9 (paperback) / 978-1-959000-26-6 (ebook)

Library of Congress Cataloging-in-Publication Data

Names: Hayes, Amanda E., 1981– author.
Title: The Madison women : gender, higher education, and literacy in
    nineteenth-century Appalachia / Amanda E. Hayes.
Description: Morgantown : West Virginia University Press,
    2024. | Includes bibliographical references and index.
Identifiers: LCCN 2024009295 | ISBN 9781959000259 (paperback) |
    ISBN 9781959000266 (ebook)
Subjects: LCSH: Madison College (Antrim, Guernsey County, Ohio) |
    Women college students—Ohio—Antrim (Guernsey County)—
    History—19th century. | Women—Education (Higher)—Appalachian
    Region—History—19th century. | Women in public life—Appalachian
    Region—History—19th century. | LCGFT: Biographies.
Classification: LCC LC1569.O55 H39 2024 | DDC 378.008209771/92—
    dc23/eng/20240318
LC record available at https://lccn.loc.gov/2024009295

Book and cover design by Than Saffel / WVU Press
Cover image: Drawing of Madison College at its peak, from the 1854 Madison College
catalog.

Contents

Acknowledgments

Where do I begin? Thank you to all my family, those who are, those who have been, and those who will be. To my mom, who traveled with me to archives, museums, and graveyards. To my dad, who was with us when this book started but didn't live to see its end. I'd give anything to have him here to pretend he read it.

Thank you to all the colleges and professors who nurtured my interest in Appalachia and recognized its value. To Mary Ellen Ontko (my aunt Meem), who took me on my very first college visit when I was little. Thank you to the dedicated volunteers at the Franklin Museum in New Athens for keeping its flame alight. I also owe great thanks to all the librarians and archivists who helped me muddle my way through historical research, including the knowledgeable and kind staffs of the following: the Guernsey County Genealogical Society, the Guernsey County District Public Library's Finley Room (thank you, Lori Mitchell, for all the obits!), the Muskingum and Marietta College archives, the Ohio History Connection archives, and the Western Reserve Historical Society archives. Also thank you to my colleagues who supported this project with their interest and encouragement, especially to Dr. Nicole Willey, whose leadership of the faculty writing group kept me on track. Thank you as well to Clara Totten, who kindly shepherded me through the book proposal process, as well as everyone at West Virginia University Press for believing in this project. Thank you to Kate Babbitt for her careful copyediting that saved me from many embarrassments. And thank you to Sara McKinnon, genealogical researcher extraordinaire.

Most of all, to Dale and Emily, who are our family's past, present, and future all rolled together.

Introduction

————

In the tiny village of Antrim, in rural Appalachian Ohio, there is a Presbyterian church and an adjoining cemetery. My great-grandparents and my great-great-grandparents are buried there. The gravestones are a mix of old and new, sometimes with the worn and unreadable beside the fancy and finely cut. Among these stones, however, two stand out. Dwarfing nearly all the other headstones are two tall monuments standing near the church. One is dedicated to the Rev. Dr. Samuel Findley Sr., a man now largely forgotten who founded Antrim's Madison College, a school that flourished and then floundered in the 1800s. Beside his grave, and even taller, is the stone dedicated to his wife, Margaret Ross Findley. The inscription reads:

> *A Tribute of filial affection*
> *to our departed mother*
> *from her sons &*

The rest is unreadable. Perhaps it is fitting that the word "daughters" has been erased by time from her gravestone, just as Madison College's daughters have faded from history.

I know very little of Margaret, her education, or her views on her husband's educational endeavors. Her children loved her, as indicated by her epitaph. While some of Samuel's story has been preserved, though not as much as I would like, it is her story, and the stories of those like her, that I've been looking for these past years.

While the men in the Findley family are impressive by any measure, Margaret has recently captured more of my interest. Few concrete facts of her life remain, beyond the information that she was born in County Antrim, Ireland, in 1793, and died in Antrim, Ohio, in 1846. Her gravestone is hard to miss: a large odalisque that towers above Samuel's own (fig. 1). This caught

Fig. 1. Memorials for Margaret (*left*) and Samuel Findley (*right*), in the Antrim, Ohio, Presbyterian churchyard. (Photo by the author.)

my attention. As did the epitaph, which is more personal than Samuel's. Whereas his states that it was erected by the church parish, hers was done by her children. It's a fitting monument to the ideal of separate spheres that Margaret would have recognized: while men were expected to operate in the public world, a woman's life was meant to be lived privately, her concerns to be home and hearth.

My sense of who Margaret was and what her life was like has been pieced together largely through tangential evidence. I don't know what Margaret's educational experiences were or what she thought about women's place in higher education. I can, however, surmise that she must have posed no opposition, given that at least one of her own daughters and multiple granddaughters were college educated. Even if she had no formal education herself, Margaret was vital to Madison College's success in ways that were not recorded, as was true for many women. If nothing else, Samuel Findley almost certainly couldn't have gotten his endeavor off the ground if he had been responsible for child-care and domestic management, as Margaret would have been. She also had a son who supported women's education and worked to make such education possible. And while there is no evidence that she served as an instructor to her own children, there is also no evidence she did not. There is, however, great evidence for the love and esteem those well-educated children bore her in the form of her towering monument and affectionate epitaph. That love means something.

When I think of Margaret, I think of my grandmother Alberta. She never completed high school, dropping out to find work, which she quit when she married my grandfather. She then took up full-time housekeeping, a profession that required more thought, care, and hard, hard work than it has ever truly been given credit for, especially for a woman in rural Appalachia. Every element of domestic life fell within her purview, often without the conveniences many today take for granted. Trips to town for supplies happened at most once per month, and even then funds were limited. Anything else the family needed, she had to produce. This included one of the things I most remember her for: preserving food. There was nothing we could eat that she didn't know how to seal in a jar, or so it seemed to me as I marveled at the rows of pink, yellow, and green mason jars lined up in the root cellar. More than that, she was responsible for our emotional needs as well—it was often grandma we cried to, discussed worries with, and turned to in sickness. When she died, I was tasked with writing her obituary. I faltered, because I knew then, as now, that conveying her life, how much she meant to so many people, was impossible. The words simply failed me.

But hers was a complicated life, too. I know that she was unsatisfied, that she felt isolated at times. And she absolutely *hated* canning all those jars of food that I adored. She did it, as she did many things, because it was her job, her duty, and because she loved us more than she hated canning. As Sarah LaChance Adams succinctly put it, "Mothers do not always revel in the self-forgetting and sacrifices that frequently characterize motherhood."[1] Yet in part because of this, and because of the daughter Alberta raised who became my own mother, I grew up fed, cared for, and encouraged when I showed an interest in academics.

How much this resembles Margaret's story, if at all, I don't know. But in that shared love for and from their families, I see women whose lives were important, even if they weren't the type of figures we typically see recorded in histories. My grandma didn't get much schooling, but because of the life she helped give me, I could. This is a book about women who also chose education, but never forget that it's also about many other women, whose names and stories we may never know, who made those choices possible, far earlier in our history than I'd ever realized.

Madison College and Personal History

I had a dream awhile back that I uncovered the foundation stones of a long-disappeared college in my backyard. Everything but these stones was gone, and I was shocked to realize that I'd never known of the existence of something so amazing so near my own home. It was a bit on the nose as far as dreams go. By that time, I had been investigating Madison College for some months.

On the nose, but not entirely accurate. I didn't really discover a former college in my backyard. In reality, it was about ten minutes down the road. Nor did I really "discover" Madison College. There are still those who know it existed. There are far fewer, however, for whom that knowledge matters as much as it does for me.

Most books establish early on what their purpose is and who they hope to reach. Mine is slightly complicated on both points because I'm writing from an Appalachian context. Culture can affect our writing just as it can influence so much about how we live and think. In my experience of Appalachian rhetoric—by which I mean the ways I learned to interpret, create, and share meaning—stories play an integral role. You can't know fully how to hear and understand a story without knowing something about the teller—their places, their peoples, the experiences that have shaped them. For me, these matter not only in terms of how I listen to stories but also in terms of how I tell them. My place, the people who have shaped me, my educational background, all of these are part of how I write and why I think the stories about the early women students of Madison College matter.

For example: my brother was a Cub Scout at the Antrim Presbyterian Church. Mom took me along to the scout meetings. Even though I was a year younger and a girl, I got to be included in some activities—I remember pizza parties, soap carving, games of hot potato, and the like. During the parts where I was excluded, one of the other scout moms sat with me on a bench in the church basement and taught me to crochet. It is knowledge that I treasure even to this day. But what I remember that is more significant for my purpose here is that we took a tour of the church cemetery one Halloween. I don't remember much of what was said during the tour—I was only about six or seven years old—but I remember being interested in those two tall triangular monuments standing near the cemetery's edge. This was my first introduction to Samuel and Margaret Findley. I wouldn't think about them again for many years.

I was good at school, but I didn't like it. I read what I was told to read, I wrote what I thought I should, and I filled in the bubbles on tests, but not because I was ever particularly interested in what we were supposed to learn. I did it because I didn't want to make waves. I followed the path of least resistance. School was, for me, both academically and socially a place where I kept my head down and tried not to get it smacked down. This isn't to say I didn't have some great teachers—I had some *great* teachers. But the whole way that school *worked* . . . well, it didn't work for me. What I learned in school seemed so abstract and disconnected. I never felt like it had much bearing on my life once the final bell rang.

I wasn't the first in my family to feel this way. My grandparents quit school early to find jobs, and neither of my parents chose college over work. (I don't think they would have, even if they could afford to.) Going to college wasn't relevant to the lives they expected to lead. I suspect some of this feeling, maybe even most of it, had to do with the systemic inability of local schools to incorporate local realities into curriculums. I may have been exposed to the periodic table of elements and other scientific concepts, for example, but never once were we asked to apply these to the ways mining runoff was affecting local streams or the ways soil composition influenced the success or failure of crops on local farms. We didn't even learn about gardening and food preservation, something that could have been helpful for many of us in a district with high poverty levels. And I certainly didn't learn about local history or the ways local stories could affect how we thought about who we were or wanted to be. If we got any of this, it was informally, through our families. I was one of the lucky ones who did; fewer and fewer of us, it seems, do.

I was so ambivalent about school and so riddled with social anxiety that I wasn't sure college was something I wanted to do. But by my day, there weren't many options for a livelihood without it. In fact, it was my mother who made sure I went. She packed me in the car and drove me to class at the nearest regional college, where I shocked myself by falling in love . . . with *school*.

In college, I was asked to think as much as, in fact more than, I was asked to memorize and repeat. It was at college that I started to think about who I was, where I came from, and what that could mean for how I moved through the world, including through school.

Yet this is an experience I don't think many of us, especially in my region of northern Appalachia, are taught to expect or embrace. Attitudes toward college in general, toward its purposes, benefits, and costs, are far from universally positive where I grew up. This knowledge makes what I'm learning about our educational history—specifically, that we were a region that once embraced college—particularly meaningful for me. My identity, my ways of thinking and writing, are shaped by my regional upbringing and my experiences with higher education. Once, I thought that made me an oddity. Now I'm learning that it makes me fit in my home region's history better than I ever knew.

Purposes and Audiences

One of the first things we are taught in college-level academic writing courses is to always think about your audience and purpose. These can shape what you want to say and how you say it. This is pretty good advice for writers in all contexts, but my situation with this book is more complicated. When I write, I envision myself as having multiple purposes and audiences.

Specifically, I want this book to have relevance for the people in my community, those figurative and literal descendants of the Madison founders and students who might not even remember its existence or know their ties to it. I want them to know this part of our history, to know that we were, and still can be, people who have chosen education and used it to benefit, not to belittle, our communities.

I also want it to matter for people outside northern Appalachia, or even Appalachia as a whole—perhaps specifically for the academic communities that produce the teachers responsible for our formal education at all levels. I want them to know, too, that we are not what we are traditionally presented as in films and stereotypes: determinedly ignorant, living in the land that intellectualism (and feminism) forgot. The truth, as is often the case, is so much more nuanced.

Far from being the educational backwater it is largely considered to be today, Appalachian Ohio (as well as northern Appalachia more broadly) was a higher education powerhouse in the 1800s. A partial list of regional colleges founded during the nineteenth century includes the following:

Now closed:

Madison College, Guernsey County, Ohio
Franklin College, Harrison County, Ohio
Sharon College, Noble County, Ohio
Beverly College, Washington County, Ohio
Richmond College, Jefferson County, Ohio
McNeely/Hopedale Normal College, Harrison County, Ohio
McCorkle College, Muskingum County, Ohio
Scio College, Carroll and Harrison Counties, Ohio
Steubenville College, Jefferson County, Ohio
Wheeling Female College, Marshall and Ohio Counties, West Virginia
Storer College, Jefferson County, West Virginia
Washington Female Seminary, Washington County, Pennsylvania
Madison College, Fayette County, Pennsylvania
Woodburn Female Seminary, Monongalia County, West Virginia
Morgantown Female Seminary, Monongalia County, West Virginia
Lewisburg Female College, Greenbriar County, West Virginia
Chillicothe Female Seminary, Ross County, Ohio
St. Clairsville Female Seminary, Belmont County, Ohio

Still going:

Muskingum University, Muskingum County, Ohio
Marietta College, Washington County, Ohio
West Liberty University, Ohio County, West Virginia
Bethany College, Brooke County, West Virginia
Allegheny College, Crawford County, Pennsylvania
Washington and Jefferson College, Washington County, Pennsylvania
Marshall University, Cabell County, West Virginia
Slippery Rock University, Butler County, Pennsylvania
Waynesburg University, Greene County, Pennsylvania

It's likely that there were even more than this, that there are schools that have fallen so far off the historical record that I've missed them entirely. However, their existence was part of a larger phenomenon carried through the Appalachian frontier by Scotch-Irish Presbyterians, who brought with them a perception of higher education as almost a religious duty.[2] Although they are certainly not the only immigrant group or religious denomination in the region, they do seem to have made an important, albeit undervalued, mark in our nation's educational history. Many of the schools on the list above were established by Presbyterian congregations that have since largely disappeared, but other schools, such as Princeton University (another school founded by Presbyterians) certainly have not. Most of these schools were at least nominally Presbyterian or otherwise Protestant in denomination, but they offered a variety of nonreligious subjects of study, often to both genders. These private colleges were mostly founded before public universities or even in some cases before public schools were available.[3] This would ultimately make their survival more difficult, because without public funding, they were vulnerable to the vagaries of economic downturns and population losses in the communities they served.

Despite its current obscurity, Madison College and the other often-forgotten local schools I've learned of in the counties surrounding mine—Franklin, Hopedale, Sharon, and Scio Colleges, to name a few—are case studies whose histories stand as sentinels against the stereotypes of Appalachian people as anti-education. Yet Madison College's stories are nuanced, as were the students who attended it. Together, they produced complex effects on their families and the communities around them before their scant record trails faded into the silence of history.

These nuances make writing about this history complicated, particularly because it isn't easy to specify who might be reading it. In *Rhetoric of Respect: Recognizing Change at a Community Writing Center*, Tiffany Rousculp also struggled with the question of readers and how she wanted to write her book. While she initially hoped to reach audiences from both within the academic community and outside it, she ultimately decided that this was not feasible. She concluded that "my envisioned audience of academic and nonacademic readers was a fantasy. The only people likely to want to read such a book were compositionists, and as much as I wanted to open access to anyone, I couldn't expect that 'anyone' would be interested in it (unless they were members of my family)."[4] Because of this, she decided to use a more standard academic writing approach.

I understand this decision—and I especially understand the feeling that nobody beyond my family will be at all interested in what I write anyway. Nonetheless, my own way of writing isn't, and possibly can't be, limited to solely academic style—not if I want to tell these stories the way I feel they ought to be told. My choice to use a more braided form, by incorporating both academic and more colloquial narrative styles, isn't only to do with potential readers but also with me as a writer, alongside the women I'm writing about.

I am, and they were, part of an Appalachian cultural context. We both had experience with Appalachian storytelling traditions as well as academic writing. To blend these is to be true to myself and to them.

So what, then, is this book about? Let me put it as concisely as possible. This book is about the history of higher education in Appalachian Ohio in the 1800s as told primarily, but not exclusively, through the history of Madison College and its women students. I'm focusing on the women because they more than anyone complicate the stereotypes of Appalachian culture's attitudes toward both gender and education. I want readers from outside my home region—perhaps especially those who think they know what being Appalachian means—to reconsider those definitions. I want readers from within—particularly those who have internalized the idea that we are a small-minded people that is hostile toward higher education—to reconsider their own definitions.

I will be looking at the lives of the people involved with the college, but also more specifically at how they learned to write and speak through their college education. According to the stereotype of the silenced, beaten down, barefoot mountain woman, they shouldn't have been doing any of these things. Their rhetorical and literacy instruction, more than anything, can tell us something about what their education was meant to (and what they did) achieve. Many teachers today would say that they hope their students learn to be thoughtful, engaged citizens in their local and national communities. Did the Madison women's education have a similar purpose? Did they learn to be active contributors to their communities at a time when women in general weren't expected to have strong public voices? On the other hand, did their educators treat them as savages whom education would civilize—a view that Appalachian scholars often perceive in educator attitudes even today? Did education allow them to rethink what women could do and be—something feminists have long seen as one of the possibilities of education? To answer these questions—to tell this history in a way that feels right for me as a writer and at least hopefully right for the people(s) I hope to read it—requires something beyond a straightforward approach.

I therefore invite you as a reader to read this book in the ways that make sense for you. If you are an academic reader who is interested in traditionally academic features—methodology, for example—I'm including a chapter on that. However, if you are reading this more for the regional and human history it contains, feel free to skip through. I am including throughout what I'm calling, for lack of a better term, "small stories." These are the stories of individual women who attended Madison as best as I can tell them from the often-scant records they've left behind, narratively streamlined with fewer notes. (Their names are given as they appeared in the original sources, which include the 1854 Madison catalogue or subsequent Madison reunion articles.) I feel a commonality with them in the sense that given our shared places and peoples, they too were likely immersed in both a storytelling and an academic writing culture. My hope is that the style, organization, and aims of this book can reflect both of these traditions.

This, then, is my tribute of filial affection to the geographical, cultural, and educational foremothers I hadn't known that I had.

CHAPTER 1

Place, Culture, and Imagination

A Discussion of Methods

———

Introductory chapters on methodology are common in academic books because it isn't enough to hear what the author has to say. Academic audiences want to know how the author has drawn their conclusions. Where did they get their information from? By what means did they decide to interpret those ideas . . . and are they means we would agree with? Academic readers want to know, or at least be able to consider, other ways that other interpretations might be possible. It's an admirable ethic, especially given the ways that social media is changing how we get our information. More than half my life as a teacher has been spent showing, helping, admonishing, and/or begging students to think carefully about where they get their ideas and what the strengths and weaknesses of those sources are. Analyzing methodology forces us to think not only about where our information comes from but also about how that information tumbles around in our minds to be shaped into ideas. In other words, telling the story I want to tell about the Madison women isn't just a matter of unearthing facts; it's about how those facts became the story I believe and want to share.

Methodology becomes particularly significant when shaping and telling the stories of marginalized peoples, those whose stories are less likely to be told or whose lives go undocumented. How do we learn about people who have left few traces for us to follow? They are the people who don't immediately spring to mind when many of us think of history. Often they are the people who are or have been pushed to the edges of society because of gender, race, culture, religion, or national origin. However, as cultural and social historians have long shown, it is these marginalized groups whose lives reflect and resist the inequalities of our societies. Their lives teach us how to live in harsh conditions and, often, how to make those conditions better.

In my case, the Madison women make for difficult research subjects not only because they were women living in the United States in the nineteenth century but also because most were poor, rural Appalachians and many were the children of immigrants. These aspects of their identities led me to interpret their stories in specific ways that may not be the only valid interpretations possible.

For example, my tendency is to read in the Madison women's interest in higher education a mix of motivations and pressures. A great deal of research has been done in more recent years on the pressures first- and second-generation American students feel to both maintain their home cultures and assimilate into more mainstream ones. Those pressures are shared by many marginalized populations in their encounters with school. Higher education in the nineteenth century had a vested interest in "correcting" students' languages, tastes, and ideals to make them fit mainstream molds. This kind of "civilizing" mission was particularly prevalent in institutions seen as serving marginal or frontier populations.[1] However, the fact that many Madison students were the children and grandchildren of immigrants was not the only facet of their identities that would have likely made college education a complex experience for them. Other elements of their identities are ones I share, such as (at least for the women) their gender and their upbringing in northern Appalachia. I know, or at least surmise, some of the pressures they faced and some of the ideas they valued.

These connections compelled me to make educated guesses about some aspects of their lives and motivations. Those guesses were particularly necessary in this case because surviving records of Madison College's students and faculty, especially for the women, are very scant. Without drawing what conclusions I can based on the records that survive, this history would continue to go unwritten. By necessity, this book is a constant negotiation between tenuous analysis and silence. Ultimately, my greatest sources of information about the specific women who attended Madison College came in the following forms:

- The Madison College 1854 catalogue and various college flyers and advertisements
- Newspaper clippings
- Obituaries
- Genealogical research and census data
- County historical compilations
- Gravestones

I was not able to locate surviving journals, writings, or school essays. This, unfortunately, is not uncommon in the study of women in history because women's literary outputs were often seen as less significant. The lack of surviving writing from their school days may be attributable to multiple factors, including the passage of time or the perception that these documents lack importance for their family histories. However, this doesn't mean that Madison women didn't value their college experiences and learning. In fact, discovering what they learned and how they felt about their access to higher education has been a central focus of my research. But finding these answers has required me to rely on something other than their own first-hand accounts.

To draw conclusions or at least ideas about what the Madison women thought, experienced, and valued, I have had to think deeply about the ways my experiences intersect and diverge with theirs. In other words, sharing regional, cultural, and gender experiences with the Madison women has helped me understand something of their points of view. However, at a remove of over 150 years, our perspectives are certainly not identical. Walking this fence line between what we do and do not share provided me with some insight into their lives but still allowed me to be surprised and confused by much of what I encountered.

Using a shared background in order to make educated guesses about historical subjects is not a new methodology. The concept, which is called critical imagination, was pioneered in *Traces of a Stream*, Jacqueline Jones Royster's groundbreaking exploration of African American women's literacy practices. Royster describes critical imagination as "a commitment to making connections and seeing possibility . . . a critical skill in questioning a viewpoint, an experience, an event."[2] Critical imagination allows possibilities and meaning to arise from ephemeral evidence. Researchers can use critical imagination as a methodology to "think between, above, around, and beyond this evidence to speculate methodologically about probabilities, that is, what might likely be true based on what we have in hand. We use critical imagination as a tool to engage, as it were, in hypothesizing in what might be called 'educated guessing,' as a means for searching methodologically, not so much for immutable truth but instead for what is likely or possible, given the facts in hand."[3] In Royster's case, educated guessing is rooted in her shared context with the women she researches. As she says, "the story of African American women and literacy is my story too."[4] Like Royster, I applied critical imagination to the trace evidence available about the women attending Madison College, in the sense that my speculative understanding of them is filtered through my understanding of our shared cultural contexts in the same rural farming community. Therefore, for me, critical imagination became critical *localized* imagination.

A critical localized imagination helped show me how to read the scant evidence that exists in more productive ways. For example, when I was seeking to understand how deeply these women valued their experiences in higher education without their own recorded statements, one of my impulses was to seek out information about their children's educational experiences. Did the Madison women have children, including daughters and granddaughters, who sought out higher education too? Many of them did, and as those experiences occurred in our more recent history, they were more likely to have been recorded or remembered. Likewise, many of these daughters and granddaughters pursued careers in education. This, in my mind, is a strong indicator that these women deeply valued and prized their own college experiences. My instinct to look for these records and my belief in what they tell me is based on a shared cultural experience in a shared regional context. My sense that the value these women placed on writing and education might be made visible through their children is a deeply cultural one reflected by other Appalachian scholars. Katherine Kelleher Sohn has discussed the role maternal relationships play in Appalachian culture; it is, she argues, a significant factor in children's attitudes toward education.[5] Likewise, Amy Clark has written about the influences Appalachian mothers and grandmothers have on their children's literacy uses and expectations.[6] Because I grew up in the same place and among similar people as the Madison women, I was able to speculate that educational attitudes could be transmitted through families, via a mother's stories about her own schooling and the expectations those stories engendered in her children. Looking for evidence of these stories through maternal lines is a strategy born from localized imagination.

This shared regional/cultural context also influenced my sense of what kinds of things could serve as sources of information. Gravestones, for example, have formed a central part of my life since long before I ever considered their archival value. Each year, my family would put flowers on the graves of ancestors from multiple family branches in multiple cemeteries across two counties. When my grandparents passed, the family came together to decide what their stones would look like and what they would say, based on what we believed they would have wanted. This experience is not unique to our family. My archival research unearthed a letter (sadly, not written by or to a Madison woman but by a nearby resident) from the late 1800s in which the writer discussed approvingly how well a deceased cousin's gravestone represented her. This understanding of the importance of gravestones in one's personal and family story led me to seek these out as a possible insight into the Madison women's lives and identities. Therefore, graves became particularly important to my research process. (See Sarah McKittrick's story at the end of this chapter for more information on how gravestones can convey messages about literacy, values, and voice.)

Similarly, I rely on my sense of cultural understanding to interpret how these past college students would have responded to the educational ideologies of their day. Because my interest lies primarily in how these students experienced writing and literacy instruction as well as how this instruction potentially shaped their wider outlook and actions, I have been particularly interested in reading the books they would have read as college students. The 1854 Madison College catalogue shows that their academic instruction in rhetoric—that is, formalized writing and speaking—would have come via Richard Whately's text *Elements of Rhetoric*. In reading this book, I have asked myself how Madison's students might have responded to Whately's injunctions. What would have meshed and what would have clashed with the cultural knowledge they learned in their upbringing, as rural Appalachians, about how to best create and share knowledge? My answers to these questions are by necessity tentative, as one could argue much historical analysis is. However, those tentative answers are not shaped in a vacuum; they are built upon a foundation of place, culture, and gender. Even if these foundations have been battered somewhat by the winds of time, they still hold.

Creative imagination as a methodology is not one that all scholars accept. Some go so far as to argue that it merely fictionalizes the past in the form of unprovable stories concocted without concern for provability. However, I would argue that the alternative of not considering at all what the lives of obscured past figures might have been like is by far the more damaging methodology. This view may in part be linked to a cultural sense of what rhetoric is and can achieve. Stories, in my experience, are how people of the past are kept alive and how their lives convey meaning in the present. Appalachian writer Sharyn McCrumb explores a regional tradition of intermixing historical fact and narrative as a means of gleaning and passing on knowledge from the past. The point of this form of storytelling, she explains, is to make audiences care about and think about the past as a potential resource for mediating the present, to "make sense of the inexplicable."[7] This tradition as she describes it does not seek to falsify the past or the peoples who inhabit it but rather to enliven it in a way that makes them memorable, instructive, and enduringly human. McCrumb links this tradition of conveying the past through people's stories to Scotch-Irish cultural traditions that would have been deeply familiar to many of Madison College's students, whose families shared this cultural background.

This is not to say that I have a perfect understanding of these students' lives and ideologies. Arguably, that isn't possible even between two people living at the same time, let alone between people removed by almost 200 years of time and social change. Royster cautions against "overreach[ing] the bounds of either reason or possibility" in the application of critical imagination as a method of analysis.[8] This opens the question of how to understand instances of difference between my subjects and myself—in other words, how to interpret ideals and actions that are outside my own experiences and expectations. Lisa Blankenship raises the concept of rhetorical empathy, a practice of engagement with difference that requires deep listening and consideration of another person's motives so we can "consider our own motives, our blind spots, and our prejudice."[9] For example, I must consider that fact that I want the Madison women to exhibit empowerment and self-actualization in ways that they themselves likely did not or would not have recognized. Rhetorical empathy as a methodology requires me to meet these women where they are in order to avoid overestimating the power they had in their societies. I can look for ways the Madison women pushed at social limits without being disappointed or finding their stories less than valid because none of them ran for political office or even, seemingly, campaigned for the vote. Rhetorical empathy asks that I question my own sense of what empowerment means, what voice and education mean, and what stories are worth remembering. I can't change the world for the Madison women, but they can still enrich ours. Ultimately, I don't see myself as "fictionalizing" the Madison women's stories. Rather, I am telling them in the ways that seem most logical and empathetic, based on the data available to me and guided by my sense of the localized realities of their lives. My choice was to do this or to consign them back to the fragmentary silence from which they emerged to me.

The inclination to tell our history through people's stories has influenced my decision to organize this book in what are, for me, distinct but linked sections: an academic exploration of past attitudes and ideals interspersed with the "small stories" of individual students and places. I use the term "small stories" to describe these narratives that, though perhaps brief and incomplete, can also shed light into the darkened corners of history. I weave between chapters the stories of individual Madison College students, at least as fully as I can tell them from my readings of the surviving evidence. These stories may be small in terms of length and the women in them may not have had the effects on the world that we traditionally look for in figures deemed historically relevant. Yet they are what bring this history to life, make it real, and I owe them my greatest responsibility in telling their stories in a way they would have recognized. This incorporation of both traditional chapters and shorter narratives of former students might seem disjointed. However, it allows me to address aspects of local history that didn't fit within the more academically traditional text.

The story that Madison College tells is one that needs to be told because it challenges some of the deepest and most damaging stereotypes about Appalachia: specifically, that its people are ignorant, hostile toward difference, and disinterested in education. Folklorist Amy Shuman has discussed the narrative concepts of "storyability" (what gets told) and "tellability" (who gets to tell it).[10] Sara Webb-Sunderhaus applies these concepts to stereotypes as the dominant narratives of Appalachian identity: they are the stories that get repeated and accepted because they confirm what an audience is willing to accept.[11] The stories that currently pass for tellable about Appalachia as a whole are deeply negative, especially as concerns our literacy and our educational values and abilities. Madison College and its students demand that we expand our sense of what is tellable: that both men and women in Appalachia have historically sought out higher education when it was available to them, and that they valued the experiences it provided. Neal Lerner argues that the power of archival research is that it allows us to "construct histories—if only partial ones—that speak to the continuing challenges of current times."[12] In this way, the women who attended Madison College have many stories to tell us.

However, there might be questions about my description of the Madison women and their regional/cultural contexts as Appalachian, if for no other reason than a consideration of the time when they lived. "Appalachian" as an identity marker was not prevalent in the nineteenth century. Even today, many in the region do not immediately see it as a primary descriptor for their identities. However, as early as the mid-nineteenth century there was a growing perception that people living in the Appalachian region were a cultural "other" to a more mainstream America. For example, in 1869, writer Will Harney described Appalachia as the "strange land" of "a peculiar people."[13] By the late nineteenth century, wide coverage of the Hatfield and McCoy feud was solidifying a negative image of rural Appalachia and its people in the public consciousness. So whether or not students at Madison College thought of themselves in those terms, their regional context was already being positioned as geographically and culturally unique.

That uniqueness has often been presented negatively, in the shape of an identity that presents Appalachian people as poor and uneducated (if not violent, lazy, and/or drug addled). However, even the arguably "positive" perception of Appalachian identity, one redolent of *Waltons*-style simplicity, doesn't offer a full or fair picture of who we are. Chimamanda Ngozi Adichie's powerful TED talk on "The Danger of a Single Story" explains far better than I can how critical it is to speak, hear, and accept more than one story about who or what a nation, a culture, or a people are. In his book *Appalachia North*, Matthew Ferrence brings similar concerns to bear on the idea of northern Appalachian identity. When we are told that we don't "accurately" reflect the culture or place we belong to, we can come to feel like we have no identity to claim, no stake in the health of our own communities or own skins. The reality, Ferrence argues, is far richer: "Appalachia exists today as the overlapping scribbles that create not a meaningless but a new totality. Hollers, banjos, split-levels, Run DMC, flowing streams, strip malls, dulcimers, electric guitars. . . . I fear and resent, of course, the ways that certain definitions are declared as *real* or *true* or *authentic*, particularly since so many of these definitions leave me out: weirdo Northern Appalachian, former pro golfer, highly educated and nonaccented Maritime-loving me."[14] Like Adichie and Ferrence, I want us to listen to more than a single story. In my use of the term Appalachian to describe the students of Madison College, what I mean is this: they lived and were educated in Appalachia. Their lives and experiences here force us to widen our sense of what Appalachia can be and has been.

Likewise, my sense of kinship with the Madison women as well as with others in northern Appalachia leads me, at times, to refer collectively to us throughout the book as "we." This is a tricky move, one that needs explanation. My usage of we, which I mostly did without even thinking, is not meant to collapse any differences between me and my readers and/or subjects. The last thing I want to do is insinuate that we all think or act alike or that I am qualified to speak for anyone beyond myself. However, there is an inclination I've discovered in my experience with Appalachian rhetoric that compels me to identify with, rather than set myself apart from, my audience. When I say "we," then, I'm not trying to talk over or for you; I'm trying to connect with you, to create or reflect a kinship.[15]

By claiming some cultural kinship with the Madison women, I am not saying that I have a perfect understanding of the realities of their lives or the lives of all other peoples in Appalachia. Such a claim would deny the distinctions that exist throughout the region as squares in a broader Appalachian cultural quilt. What I can claim is that Madison College's students were raised in an Appalachian culture that was heavily influenced by their Scotch-Irish heritage, in the hill country of Antrim, Ohio, just as I was. Times may be different, but here . . . here, sometimes things get held onto. As for what has been let go or lost, well, perhaps what is lost can be reborn. In fact, in forming my pictures of who these women were and in bringing the legacy of their time at Madison College back to our attention, I'm hoping for that.

Small Stories, Part 1

While each of the "small stories" of individual Madison students has its own unique elements, I've clustered them based on connecting threads that illuminate some shared experience or interest among them. In my mind, the following stories are linked by the ways they demonstrate the value Madison women placed on their education and on the people who provided it.

Sarah McKittrick

Sarah McKittrick lived and died in rural Guernsey County, the child and grandchild of farmers. She was born in 1830 and died in 1860. In 1854, she attended Madison College. Beyond these facts, she left behind very little written evidence of her life. How, then, can we know anything about a woman whose life has gone sadly unrecorded? Her story is an example of the methods I used to research and draw conclusions about the Madison women, because my picture of Sarah is based on factors beyond her own words—of which I have none. What I have instead are details about her family and a sense of how family interests get shared regionally. In the case of the McKittricks, those interests were both literary and progressive. They were willing to step outside society's restrictions in order to stand up for their ideals, whether that meant supporting abolition through the Underground Railroad or seeking access to higher education for their children at Madison College.

While children don't automatically end up agreeing with their family's interests (in any culture anywhere), they at least grow up knowing what these interests are. The progressive social values Sarah's family demonstrated don't necessarily mean she shared them, but the power that family affiliation has in shaping regional identity would make it a good possibility.[1] This, coupled with the fact that she sought a college education as a woman in the nineteenth-century United States, indicates that Sarah had some progressive attitudes as well.

Progressive for the time, anyway. The family values Sarah grew up with are ones many of us today can get behind. Her grandfather Alexander was a documented figure in Guernsey County's Underground Railroad. Given the nature of this work and the fact that Alexander lived close to his children and grandchildren (including Sarah), the support of his family would have been necessary if he was to succeed in this in this dangerous and illegal undertaking. At the least, it would have been nearly impossible for him to hide these activities from them. This opens the possibility, though unfortunately not the certainty, that Sarah participated in (or at least agreed with) abolitionism and assistance for enslaved peoples escaping to the North. This is a family that was willing to defy even the law when what was legal contradicted what was moral.

There is also evidence that Sarah's interest in higher education came from her family. Her father, Joseph McKittrick, had a personal library that he insisted be split equally among his children, which included both sons and daughters (although because Sarah predeceased her father, she didn't receive this bequest). Sarah's near and extended family also included multiple teachers. Another exciting indicator that hers was a very educationally progressive family is the fact that her second cousin was none other than William Holmes McGuffey. McGuffey was a college professor best known for authoring the McGuffey Eclectic Readers, a collection of reading textbooks aimed at various ages and grade levels.[2] From 1836 to 1960, these books influenced the literate lives of millions of readers. Today they are collectors' items. I first encountered the McGuffey Readers as a child through my aunt, a former teacher and collector herself. Little did I know then that they would connect me even more deeply to the family of one of my county's academic foremothers.

Another indication of Sarah's interest in education comes from her gravestone. These stones were often the last ways that a person's identity or values could be reflected and preserved. Often a family's financial means limited how much a stone could say or even if there was a stone at all. The dearth of information many stones give about women reflects their subordinate position in society; it's not at all uncommon to see a husband's full name followed by only the wife's first name. Sometimes her affiliation with her husband's family is the only identity marker she gets—something that underscores the perceived importance of family groupings in conveying our identities. When a woman married, her husband's family identity overtook her own, although in practice her personal relationships with her birth family may have remained unchanged. As an unmarried woman, Sarah didn't have to forgo this element of

Fig. 2. Sarah McKittrick's gravestone features a carved book, perhaps a reflection of her interest in literacy and education. (Photo by the author.)

her identity on her gravestone. Gravestones as a genre can be used to read local social values and identities, especially when those stones buck normal trends.

Sarah's stone most certainly does that (fig. 2). She was buried in Londonderry, Ohio (a couple of miles away from Antrim), and her stone is adorned with a large carved book. This isn't unheard of, and often books carved on gravestones represented the Bible.[3] However, the choice to adorn the grave of a single woman with this image was unusual. As a fascinating 2019 study of eighteenth- and nineteenth-century Appalachian gravestones attests, this style of carving was largely read as masculine.[4] In fact, Sarah's is the only grave of an unmarried woman I've found who had one. Even most married women whose shared stones have carved books are far less ornately done than this one. Either Sarah herself (if she had planned ahead) or her family consciously chose a grave marker that went against convention. To me, this says that the book reflected something about Sarah that they or she wanted to be remembered. In short, the image of the book on this woman's gravestone says much about the role literacy played in her life. Her stone also has a written epitaph, which not all stones did. It is from Psalm 17:15: "As for me, I will behold thy face in righteousness: I shall be satisfied, when I awake, with thy likeness."

Understanding her epitaph is harder for me. I think back to another way that Sarah defied common expectations: she died unmarried. By the age of 30, she would have been solidly in spinster territory. Yet the fact that her family commissioned this lovely and ornate gravestone seems to indicate that they were not embarrassed by her and her single state. Why, then, select an epitaph that notes the search for satisfaction, specifically a satisfaction that can be found only in death? Did Sarah see her life as one lived in pursuit of mental and spiritual wisdom—something that higher education could offer her and the duties of marriage could not? Was she not able, due to the daily vicissitudes of rural life for her time and gender, to pursue learning to the degree that she would have wished? Did she have desires that her community and cultural context did not allow her to fulfill? The answers to these questions are ultimately unknowable. Yet the fact I am able to ask them, that I know that someone like Sarah lived and learned in my own community at all, is a legacy I'm grateful for.

Eliza Carpenter

Eliza Carpenter was born in 1830 in Londonderry, Ohio. Londonderry is Antrim's nearby neighboring town. Today, the only real business in town is the funeral home that held the calling hours for two of my grandparents. Several Madison students came from Londonderry and quite a few are buried there.

Eliza, however, did not remain in Londonderry. She married a fellow Madison alumnus named Joseph Porter, who became an attorney. Together, the family moved to Kansas, where Eliza bore at least two daughters. The 1870 census shows that one daughter, Zillah, became a teacher; another, Sarah, married one. Eliza also gave one of her sons the middle name Findley, although I've found no evidence that she was related to Madison College founder Samuel Findley. Traditionally, children's middle names were places where women could preserve their maiden or family names (since keeping their own after marriage was rarely done). The fact that Eliza chose a nonfamily name, specifically the name of her college president, for her son bestowed a high honor on a man she must have admired.

What speaks to me the most, though, about the interpretation that Eliza valued her time at Madison and the education it gave her is her gravestone inscription. Upon her death, either Eliza or a loved one chose the exact same inscription as that of Samuel Findley. It is from Revelation 14:13: Their works shall follow them. We may never know what works Eliza believed would follow her or perhaps even continue after her death, but her value and respect for her college's founder remains, written in stone.

Martha Lindsay

Martha's story exemplifies the immigrant roots of many Madison students and Antrim citizens more broadly. She was born to Irish immigrants, Martha and Samuel, who made their living as farmers. She married an Irish immigrant farmer named Robert Madden, with whom she lived, farmed, and raised a family; they spent their entire lives in the Antrim area. Like many of the other immigrants in my research, the Lindsays and the Maddens were seemingly not interested in further travel. Having found a community and good land, they established farms that lasted for multiple generations.

However, their attachment to place was not synonymous with a lack of interest in ideas or education. Place attachment as a social value—in other words, seeing one's "homeplace" or lands with familial connections as being part of personal identity—is a common Appalachian cultural trait that Appalachian writers and cultural scholars have frequently examined. However, the modern attitude in the wider United States seems to say that an attachment to place equals backwardness, that a desire to remain connected with ancestral lands signals a lack of sophistication, curiosity, and, of course, education. (I speak as someone who has seen horror on my non-Appalachian colleagues' faces when students say they plan to stay in the area after graduation. One even claimed that if he hadn't inspired his students to hit the road after college, he'd failed them.) Martha's story, like other Madison graduates, shows that having place connection does not equate to being uneducated or disconnected in the ways it is too often perceived to be.

Despite apparently having no ambitions for further travel, the Lindsay family was very invested in education and sent multiple children—sons and daughters—to be educated at Madison College. (The shared obituary for Martha's siblings Eliza and Robert, who later in life died within weeks of each other, praises their intelligence and learning.) Martha and her husband also contributed to education in their community after Madison was gone by providing room and board for schoolteachers. Martha and her family show us an interesting dynamic: although they were provincial in the sense that once they arrived in Guernsey County these families mostly stayed put, they sought out formal education even though farming didn't require it. Education must have meant something to them beyond being a means to an end. And the fact of their education casts doubt on the easy association popular culture makes today between a dedication to place, rural lives, and anti-intellectualism.

CHAPTER 2

The Advantages
of Education

A History of Madison College

———

Many might think of Appalachia in the 1800s as a hostile ground for growing something like a college, but was that actually the case? In this chapter, we will explore the geographic and institutional history of Madison College to see what kind of soil it sprang from and what traces it left after it withered.

Such an analysis may well begin with the community of Antrim, Ohio. Plenty of people, I'm sure, wouldn't even bother to call Antrim a town. With a couple dozen houses on either side of the one thoroughfare, two churches, and a volunteer fire department, it no longer houses even the tiny general store where you could buy dusty cans of baked beans or a pack of gum. There was once a brick high school just down the road called Madison where my mother graduated. At some point it was downgraded to a middle school, then to an elementary school (which I attended), and then torn down altogether as the Madison district merged with nearby Zane Trace to form the East Guernsey Local School District. Few even of Antrim's current residents know that Madison High School was not the first educational institution in the town to bear that name or that its predecessor was a respected college whose reputation extended beyond the state in an age when travel was not so simple as it is today. Travelers on State Route 22, which passes through Antrim, will certainly not know that this town once housed not only a college but also a bookshop, a hotel, and offices for doctors and lawyers. Never a wealthy region, it was nevertheless much different than it appears today, a difference largely attributable to the presence of Madison College and the students it attracted.

Regional History

The land that would later be known as Guernsey County was once the home of the Mound Builder peoples. Little record of them survives, although William Wolfe's *Stories of Guernsey County* records eleven known mounds in the area. Likely more existed but were obliterated by European immigrants—something that is known to be the case in other parts of Ohio. Later, the Mingo, Lenape, and Shawnee peoples lived in this area. While no permanent towns have been recorded for these groups, Native people's presence is undeniable. Any average corn field in Guernsey County turns up arrowheads during plowing season. I know this because my grandfather scoured fields in this and neighboring counties searching for them. He brought home pockets full of finds that I could spend hours looking through. His hobby, though perhaps problematic from an archeological standpoint, resulted not only in arrowheads but also tomahawks, hammerstones, and pieces of what appear to be pipes and jewelry. There's a little spot alongside the dirt road not even a mile away from our farm that regularly turns up so much flint, some of it seemingly in the early stages of being worked, that I can't help but wonder if it was a home or campsite at one time. Even more intriguingly, on the border between Guernsey County and neighboring Belmont County is a place called Track Rock, a collection of massive stones, hidden from the road by trees, with carvings of human footprints and animal shapes for which no one knows an explanation or origin.[1] By the 1840s, the Native population of Ohio had been largely decimated and displaced by violence, disease, and coercive treaties.[2]

The beginnings of Guernsey County, at least as a regional or political entity, lie with later European immigrants. Its name comes from a group of settlers from the Isle of Guernsey, who initially planned to continue moving westward. According to the story, those plans were changed by the group's women, who found these hills too beautiful to leave. Another immigrant group came from Ireland to live in what is now known as the town of Antrim on Guernsey County's eastern side. The earliest, arriving in the late 1700s and continuing into the 1800s, often clashed violently with Native people, as the "Indian Stories" in Wolfe's county history attests. Many of these newcomers were Scotch-Irish Protestants seeking to escape from violent religious and cultural clashes in northern Ireland.

In simplest terms, the Scotch-Irish were initially Scottish Presbyterians. In an effort to convert the Catholic Irish to Protestantism, England began a program called the Plantation of Ulster, moving poverty-stricken Scottish and northern English Protestants to the northern provinces of Ireland. Relations were initially cordial between many of the inhabitants and the incomers, likely because the native Irish and incoming Scots had cultural and historical similarities.[3] Both were Celtic peoples, and in fact much of Scotland could trace its ancestry to early medieval Irish immigrants. In some ways this would have been a homecoming. The incomers soon came to view their own identities as Irish rather than Scottish; many of the records I've uncovered show that local immigrants described themselves as Irish despite their Protestant Scottish roots. However, intercultural harmony was not what England intended with the Plantation project, and policies were soon instituted to exacerbate religious divisions and conflicts over land ownership, with legal superiority granted to Protestants. Likely the plan was that the native Irish would convert to gain those same benefits (whether they would have done so is debatable). Instead, the plan sparked mutual distrust and bloody sectarian violence in northern Ireland that continues, in waves and ebbs, to this day.

Many Scotch-Irish people emigrated from Ireland because of these conflicts. They tended to settle in the parts of the United States that were both more widely available and geographically reminiscent of their homeland. Appalachia fit that description.[4] The early influx of Scotch-Irish people is sometimes used to essentialize Appalachia as a wholly or inherently white space, a space representing the "pure Anglo-Saxon" roots of the United States.[5] Of course, those making this assertion don't seem to care that it is inaccurate on multiple levels. For one thing, the Scotch-Irish were a Celtic, not an Anglo-Saxon, people, and their historical relations with the Anglo-Saxons were not at all happy. Likewise, describing Appalachia as predominantly either Anglo-Saxon or Scotch-Irish erases the region's *many* other peoples and influences, not least of all Native Americans, African Americans, and Southern and Eastern Europeans.[6] While many of the people I discuss in conjunction with Madison College had Scotch-Irish origins, this is not generalizable to all of Appalachia. Such a generalization, I would argue, causes us more harm than good.

Antrim's particular origin, though, can be read in its very name:

> In the county Antrim, Ireland, is the "Giants' Causeway" where in the days of the giants, as the old story went, they walked about singing; "Fee Fie Foe, Fum, I smell the blood of an Irishman." But they did not kill them all, these north of Ireland Irishmen, and their descendants, having "known that there were giants in those days," were of that sturdy class fitted to battle with the giant oaks that capped Irish Ridge (the later name of the ridge near where Antrim [Ohio] was founded).[7]

From a remove of many years, I can be disturbed by the fact that my predecessors saw themselves as battling rather than coexisting with the land around them. Yet I say this as someone who has never had to cut down a giant oak or fight a giant. Although my land ethics have been shaped by different circumstances than theirs, I can't help but love that some of the first things they built from that timber was schoolhouses.

As the above quote illustrates, the peoples of Antrim, Ohio, identified with their Irish origins. However, they also held tightly to their identities as Protestants. The nearby town of Londonderry attests to that. Also named for a city in northern Ireland, the name itself encapsulates the region's religious conflict. Originally, and even today among Irish Catholics, the town in Ireland is called Derry. Calling it Londonderry was a way that Protestant residents signified their religious and political loyalty to the British Crown. The immigrant group who named their new villages Antrim and Londonderry doesn't seem to have identified politically with Britain, so much as it did religiously, in the sense of having a shared Protestant identity.[8] (I have yet to find any early Antrim or Londonderry settlers who described themselves as English or British, but many called themselves Irish.) Yet even though they were not aligned politically with England, in founding their own town, these early settlers chose Londonderry, rather than Derry, as its name. These were a people whose origins reveal a complex interweaving of cultural and religious identification. However, the multiple strands shared a uniting thread: a high value placed on literacy and education.

Samuel Findley

Madison College's founder, Samuel Findley, was not unique in his passion for education. That feeling seems to have been an outgrowth of, rather than a rival to, regional religious threads. In his 1882 *History of Greene County, Pa.*, William Hanna noted the correlation between the Presbyterian populations moving into northern Appalachia and the growth of schools: "One of the most conclusive arguments in favor of the perpetuity of [Presbyterianism] is the attention they have given to the subject of classical education. Scarcely were the great meetings at upper Tenmile, Concord, Milliken's, Jefferson, Hewitt's Grove, Hopewell, and Nixon's camp meeting, near Uniontown, over, when [they] began to agitate the question, 'Where shall we have an institution of learning?'"[9] Although this quote does not relate directly to Samuel Findley, it describes the cultural context that produced him. A Scotch-Irish Presbyterian from rural Pennsylvania, he connected the concepts of religion, citizenship, and formal education in ways that came to affect many communities in northern Appalachia.

In some ways, Madison College's founder came from illustrious stock. His immigrant grandfather, William Findley, attended Trinity College in Dublin before leaving Ireland's shores. His father, another Samuel, was a farmer and a judge (in the days when that combination wouldn't have been considered unusual) who was born in 1786 in the Appalachian region of western Pennsylvania. His uncle, William Findley Jr., was also a member of the legal profession, appointed by George Washington to arbitrate the Whiskey Rebellion. Will Jr. also served in the Pennsylvania delegation to ratify the Constitution, which he voted against because it didn't guarantee a right to education.[10]

In other ways, Samuel was the ideal of the rural scholar that is embodied in figures such as Abraham Lincoln. As a young teenager, Findley located a Latin grammar but had no time away from farm work to study. So he tied his book between the plow handles to read while he worked the fields. In this way, he taught himself Latin, Greek, and theology. By the age of twenty, he had made his way to New York for more formal schooling. According to a county history, "His last cent was spent to cross the Hudson River by ferry. He sold his pony for money to pay tuition, and then worked at odd jobs for enough to pay for his room and board. Having received his diploma, he walked home, a distance of 500 miles."[11] This might sound almost too mythologizing to be true were it not for similar stories in this country's history of people determined to reach for education against the odds.

Findley married Margaret Ross and took up preaching as a Presbyterian minister, crossing into Ohio by 1818. By 1824, he was organizing a church and a grammar school in Washington, Ohio (now known as Old Washington), as well as publishing a monthly magazine called the *Religious Examiner*. In the early 1830s, he took his ministry to nearby Antrim, where he moved his family into a log cabin.[12] By 1835, his family was sharing the cabin with eight pupils for whom Findley was providing education in the classical languages of Greek and Latin as well as theology. Interest soon outgrew the space, and in 1837, the school expanded into a two-story building built with local funds and labor, called at first the Philomathean Literary Institute. It was located, not by accident, on the highest hilltop in the village.

Wolfe's history and the "First Annual Report of the Philomathean Literary Institute" (1838) tell us a great deal not only about Findley's educational ideals but also about the high level of community support for his endeavors.[13] Far from rejecting formal education, as the stereotype about Appalachia would have us believe, the local populace readily invested in the school's founding: "So eager were the people of Madison township for such an institution to be established there that they contributed money, material, and work, many of them beyond their means."[14] Likewise, the 1838 report shows that the school already had 12 local men on its board of trustees.[15] In the report, Findley explained the purposes of his educational endeavor. Not content with the premise that education equaled "the mere acquisition of knowledge," Findley wanted students to learn habits of mind that encouraged "moral and mental training— the systematic regular exertion of his powers, and the habits of application."[16] He also articulated the value of a classical education, even for students who weren't likely to find a need for Latin or Greek in their daily professions: "Wherein for instance lies the profit of gaining an accurate knowledge of the latin language, even to a professional man? Is it in the ability to read it, or in the discipline of memory, of judgement, of reasoning, the accuracy of thought and precision of expression, or the rigid subjection of mental operation to fixed law? Is it not rather in the multiplication of its powers, the extension of its capacity, that the mind of the pupil has its chief acquisition?"[17] In other words, Findley encouraged thinking, not just memorization—an educational philosophy that many would be surprised to see in the past. He made the case that learning for its own sake matters, and he did so with the belief that sharpened minds would turn their powers of reasoning toward making positive contributions to society.

Findley positioned this ideology in the needs of both the local and national populace. By educating citizens to cultivate habits of mind and fulfill their responsibilities within a democracy, Findley hoped to see a greater participation in the issues of the day, including a local one he referred to in the report:

> It is in the general interest of these United States to have government; hence the demand that is made on every individual in the community to contribute their share in the support of Government. It is in the general interest of Antrim and Moorfield with their respective vicinities to have the Cadiz and Cambridge turnpike located on the route of the present grade, hence the obligation devolving on every citizen in the line of this route, to give their voice in petitions and their hand in action, to secure and effect the desired object. Not an individual will hold back in such a case that does not intend to be reputed a nondescript in society.[18]

In other words, Findley believed that educated people would exercise their voices about the issues that matter, both nationally and locally. He went so far as to postulate the need for a widely educated populace to stem the tyranny of an educated few:

Let a few possess themselves of the advantages of education, while the great mass is sunk in utter ignorance, and *this few* will quickly acquire all the elements of power, and thus subvert the liberties of the people. To prevent this, the people must be educated, to such an extent, at least, as to enable them to judge correctly, of the pretentions, demands, and conduct of those who aspire to instruct and rule them. . . . Let every American citizen, who is jealous of the civil and religious liberty he enjoys, consider well this important question; and not only see to it, that his own sons and daughters are educated, but cheerfully and promptly cooperate with the state, and with patriotic and benevolent individuals, in all feasible plans for diffusing the advantages of education throughout all ranks and classes of the community.[19]

There's a lot to unpack in this statement, but I want to focus in on a few ideas. One is the concept that when education is hoarded by an elite class, the educated elite will create inequality. The idea that widespread higher education is not only useful but necessary to the freedom of the nation is one that, again, is striking in its modern relevance. I speak from a time when the priority the state places on both public and higher education is decreasing and student debt and political attacks on voting rights are rising at an alarming rate. Findley foresaw these correlations.

However, I'm also intrigued by Findley's specific mention that both sons *and daughters* should receive this education. He described "the design of connecting with this Institute a Female Department" and he trusted that parents would recognize their "sacred duty"[20] to prepare their daughters for the kind of education he was offering and would send them to an institution where they could access such an education. While Findley did not precisely support full coeducation, he nonetheless advocated higher education for women at a time when few others, particularly few men, did. However, his own school did not formally incorporate a "Female Department" until the presidency of his son, Samuel Findley Jr., in the early 1850s.

The 1854 Catalogue

The single best piece of surviving evidence for Madison College is the *Catalogue of the Officers, Courses of Studies, Etc., of Madison College and Antrim Female Seminary for the Year Ending Sept. 27, 1854*. It isn't the only catalogue I've seen; besides the one for the college's early incarnation, the Philomathean Institute, I've found a partial Madison catalogue from 1853 as well as various notices and flyers. However, the 1854 catalogue provides by far the most detail about the college in its prime, including names of students and teachers, courses, text-books, regulations, and costs.[21] By that time, the board of trustees had grown to twenty men, most from Antrim and Londonderry but some from towns farther afield, including one from New Philadelphia, a county away. Samuel Findley Sr. remained on both the board and the faculty, but his son, Samuel Findley Jr., had become the college president.

Under Samuel Jr.'s leadership, the faculty had expanded and women had begun to enroll. Technically, they were in a separate department (the Antrim Female Seminary), but evidence indicates that this separation was largely nominal rather than actual. The women's course of study was identical to that of the male students, making it likely that those courses were being taught coeducationally. Although the seminary employed six women as faculty, four of them taught courses that seem to have been offered to women only, including instrumental and vocal music and French. Thus, in order to fulfill their other curricular requirements, the women students would have had to take their courses with male faculty. The catalogue confirms this; it directed women to take the "regular College classes" and complete "the classical course necessary for College graduation."[22] I take this to mean that Madison's female students were in fact receiving full college educations, not mere "ornamentations," as some have described the focus of women's academies at the time. (In fact, although the courses in "womanly" arts such as music and French were offered, they were not requirements.)

There are indications that the genders were not equally treated, however. The women were classified separately in the Antrim Female Seminary, even though they studied much of the same curriculum. The seminary's section of the catalogue is also separate, following that of the college (i.e., the men's pages). The sections were largely similar, but there were important distinctions. For example, the catalogue proudly described its library as containing upward of nine hundred volumes, but only in the seminary section were students warned that "novel reading is strictly prohibited, and all attempts to introduce such books into the Seminary will be promptly punished."[23] It is women who were seen as endangered by the influence of popular novels (novels, at the time, had a wider connotation with "romances;" literature was considered a completely different category), because women were considered more emotional and less logical by nature. This tracks with something Samuel Findley Sr. wrote in his common-place book prior to starting the college: "A woman is a creature of feeling[;] she acts from the impulse of the moment—as well may you think to stop the wind from blowing by reason as effect a woman who is under the impulse of her feelings."[24] It is this belief, in fact, that prompted his advocacy of women's education. He believed in the power of women's influence for good, specifically because they had an influence over their husbands and sons, but he also believed that women's nature was inherently given to irrationality and vice. This made it a matter of "the greatest importance" to educate women so they could "become fixed in virtuous habits" that could correct their natures and therefore have a beneficial, rather than a detrimental, influence over the men in their orbits. Given this frame of mind, it could be argued that Findley's impulse to educate women was born from sexism rather than the reverse. However, at some point, he or his son expanded their thinking. Were their only goal to train women's ostensibly faulty minds to embrace virtuous habits, they would not have needed to offer them a full classical education. In fact, others at the time argued that this kind of educational access for women was even more dangerous than reading novels.[25]

The 1854 catalogue offers more than just insights into the expectations surrounding women students. It specified that their tuition was $15 per term, with added costs for boarding. According to a Google search, this would equate to a tuition cost of approximately $465 today. This would be an excellent deal for a year's college tuition today but would have been a significant sum for parents at the time. This is especially true when we consider that that money was being spent on educating daughters, whose future prospects certainly didn't require higher education. (While women could become teachers, teaching was then, as it is now, a low-paying profession. In addition, female teachers were often required to quit when they married. Therefore, they couldn't expect to recoup these costs through future earnings.)

In terms of professional development, Madison offered some surprises. Perhaps *not* surprisingly, given its Presbyterian roots, it advertised itself as a training ground for future ministers (for men, anyway) and teachers (for men or women). Training to become a teacher in a normal school—a name derived from the French *école normale*, meaning a model school—was becoming popular in the United States. Such institutions combined a classical college education with the study of pedagogy and classroom management. The Madison catalogue said that special training was available in the college's Normal Department, "in which young ladies and gentlemen will receive such training as will qualify them for filling, honorably and successfully, the Teacher's profession."[26] What is more surprising is that Madison also billed itself, under a prominent, distinct heading, as providing what might be called a major in civil engineering and architecture. "Young gentlemen," the catalogue specifies, "who wish to devote themselves, in practical life, to Civil Engineering or Architecture, will find it to their interest to patronize this Institution."[27]

I find this surprising for a couple different reasons. On the one hand, Madison was on the cutting edge of higher education in offering not only the classical course, with its emphasis on Latin, Greek, and theology, but also "practical" subjects that could have professional implications for students in their lives after college. The emphasis on practicality doesn't shock me: the people I grew up with are deeply practical about education, uncomfortably so from the perspective of one who chose the so-called useless major of English. (I've known many girls who went to college for nursing—the most practical major of all, in that it requires a shorter time and a smaller financial commitment than medical school and the graduate emerges with a secure and well-paid profession. I've known far fewer who actually claim to feel a passion or a vocation for the field.) What surprises me is that I'm not used to seeing my region equated with anything cutting edge, yet Madison College was recognized for training students in civil engineering and architecture. These professions, which are implicitly tied with technological development, aren't what I expected to see emphasized here in the 1800s. The Findleys, however, saw no reason why they shouldn't be.

The catalogue specifically touts this region as being particularly fitting for an institute of higher education, though perhaps not in the ways we might think today. "Madison College is pleasantly located in the town of Antrim," the catalogue glowingly reported, "and possesses all the advantages that a healthy locality, and a moral, religious, and enterprising community can confer upon any literary institution."[28] Prospective students and parents were assured that "several denominations of evangelical Christians have churches and regular divine service in the town, so that the religious preferences of the student can always be accommodated."[29] My first inclination was to be charmed that although Madison was founded by Presbyterians, the college did not enforce denominational preference among students; though it is worth noting that the emphasis on *evangelical* did not extend the same welcome to students of other faiths, for example Catholic or Jewish students. Whether this was intentional bigotry on the school's part or simply an acquiescence to the realities of the region, I don't know. (Although Catholic churches existed in Guernsey County, they were father away, and to this day there are no Jewish synagogues in the county.) What the catalogue ultimately wanted its readers to know about Madison College, Antrim, and the surrounding region was that the area offered a mix of modern ideas and quiet rurality. The school's building, books, furnishings, and equipment were new and advanced. But "far removed from the vices of large towns and cities, and presenting to the student none of the inducements for squandering money, time, and character . . . this Institution affords advantages for study equal to any other in the State."[30] This is, again, a detail that delights me: no one else that I know of was making the argument in the mid-nineteenth century that rural Appalachia was *better* suited than other parts of the country to academic pursuits specifically because it was quiet and removed.

The 1854 catalogue provides a list of all the men and women in attendance that year and the town they came from. Lest we forget that this was 1854 and modern medicine was far in the future, occasionally names were followed by a small asterisk that indicated the student had died within the past year. (The principal of the female seminary, the delightfully named Miss Adelphia Powers, was also noted to have died just prior to the catalogue's publication.) The men's names are abbreviated to a first initial and a last name, which makes them harder to track down, although most of the surnames are ones I still recognize in the vicinity. Thankfully, the women students are named in full, and each student's hometown is listed next to their name. While most of the students were from Antrim, Londonderry, or other nearby villages such as Fairview or (Old) Washington, others were from another county or even another state. This data demonstrates the high level of support for Madison College from the local populace: in 1854, of the 136 students attending, nearly half were women, even though the cost of education was high and job prospects a college education would afford women were low. The same was true for men, many of whom went on to continue their family farms. Yet the number of students at Madison College in 1854 was higher than the number of students in my graduating high school class over a century later.

The End?

Wolfe's *Stories of Guernsey County* records that Madison College closed during the Civil War, when young men were leaving to fight rather than staying to study. This, however, is not entirely accurate. While the loss of students (and faculty, several of whom were drawn into military service) no doubt caused the college to stutter, it didn't end it. The Civil War spanned the years 1861 through 1865, yet a surviving flyer from graduate John McBurney's papers advertises the closing exercises of Madison College on July 4, 1867. It seems, then, that the college soldiered on for at least two years after the war. Among the students reading their essays for the public were two women, Zelima May and Alice Bracken. The coeducational Madison Literary Society, which also presented an exhibition during the event, include a female officer named Jennie Bell.[31] While literary societies had existed at Madison College before this point, they had previously been segregated by sex, something that had obviously changed. Admission to the society's event was 25 cents, which would be "used for repairing Madison College."[32]

What actually happened to Madison College? The answer remains somewhat of a mystery. The received wisdom, that Madison closed during and due to the Civil War, is not entirely without basis. Wolfe wrote that the loss of students happened at a uniquely bad time. Just before the war, the college had spent a great deal of money to expand its building (or perhaps to build an entirely new edifice; the sources are unclear), and therefore had no funds to pay creditors when attendance dropped so quickly. There are, however, hints that other factors came together into a perfect storm for Madison. An article in the *Guernsey Times* about a later reunion of Madison College's students states that "had there not been some mismanagement . . . Antrim would have been the seat of a great institution of learning today."[33] Whether this mismanagement refers to the building expansion or some form of financial dishonesty is not clarified. Another article that looked back at Madison's history shows a political breach between two of Madison College's prominent families, the Stockdales and the Mosses, in which a "secret midnight conclave" among the James Moss faction "planned the defeat of Esquire Stockdale" in an election for the justice of the peace for Madison township, a position in which Stockdale was the incumbent.[34] Both of these men and their families were tied to Madison's rise. Stockdale was the first teacher in the township, having organized a grammar school in his family's log cabin (as Samuel Findley would later organize a college in his own). James Moss was a close friend of Findley, who is listed in the 1854 *Antrim Almanac* as Antrim's bookseller.[35] (He was also the father of student Lizzie Moss, who went on to marry Madison graduate John McBurney, who contributed his papers on Madison College to Marietta College.) Both Moss and Stockdale served on Madison College's board of trustees. A breach between these two influential families could not have come at a worse time; a divided community would not have been best positioned to weather the financial crisis barreling toward the college. An 1893 article in a local newspaper also referred to a division within the local United Presbyterian Church "on some non-essentials in the church policy" around that time.[36] Despite the author's dismissive tone, a religious breach could also have affected Madison's survival. While Madison was not a Presbyterian institution in the strictest sense (it did not require Presbyterian adherence from students), the church was nonetheless deeply bound with Madison's founding, and most of the college's presidents, including the Findleys, were ordained Presbyterian ministers. A rupture in the church would have taken attention away from Madison's struggles at a time when there was none to spare.

Regardless of the causes of Madison's decline, that decline was much less abrupt than Wolfe seems to indicate. In 1864, a notice in another Guernsey County newspaper, the *Jeffersonian*, advertised the public auction of the college's land and property:

> Monday, the 16th day of May, 1864, between the hours of ten o'clock, A.M. and four o'clock, P.M. of said day, at the College, in the town of Antrim, Guernsey County, Ohio, the following described real estate, to wit: Lots Nos. 26 and 27 in Savage's addition to the town of Antrim, with the College edifice erected thereon. . . . Also the following personal property, to wit: 50 volumes of Books, Cabinet of Minerals, 4 Stoves and Pipes, 2 Globes, 3 Blackboards, 25 Marble settees, and 2 Clocks. . . . Terms of sale, one half cash, and one half in one year, with interest, to be secured to satisfaction of the undersigned.
>
> April 15, 1864
> J.W. White, Assignee of Madison College[37]

Books, minerals, globes, blackboards—a school, indeed, seemed to be disappearing.[38]

However, the flyer from John McBurney's papers clearly shows that the college was still functioning in 1867. This opens a few possibilities: that the sale never took place or at least was delayed by some years, that local people purchased enough of the college's materials that it could continue offering classes in another building, or perhaps that the college had been restarted from scratch. While there is no evidence that it continued beyond 1867, this does not mean that its influence was at an end.

The Afterlives of Madison College

It's difficult to imagine a bigger change from the ornate building of Madison in its heyday (fig. 3) and the bare hilltop today where it once stood (fig. 4). I've wondered if it's significant that nobody ever built on the site, not even a home to enjoy the views once afforded the college's classrooms. Evidence shows that the local community deeply hoped to reinstate Madison's former glory for decades following its demise. Speakers at the Madison College reunions, which occurred for decades after the closure, regularly noted the value the college had brought to the region and to their lives. One, Rev. Dr. C. J. Hunter, "said it was a suicidal act for the community to let [Madison] die."[39] A former Madison president, Rev. Dr. James Duncan, lauded Madison's contributions to both teaching and scholarship, which would "always compare favorably with that of

Fig. 3. This drawing of Madison College at its peak, from the 1854 Madison College catalog, may or may not reflect the building in its final iteration. Because no photographs of Madison College seem to survive, it's impossible to know if this building was ever completed. The closest to a surviving photo comes from the time of its final demolition in 1956, when only one corner of the building still stood.

larger schools."[40] In 1882, an unnamed correspondent from Antrim wrote in to a county newspaper: "the literary talent of this community lies dormant, being either dead or slumbering. If the latter, why not arouse it; if the former, resurrect it."[41] This tells us that at least one person once saw the Antrim community as a hub of literary endeavor, one they hoped to rekindle. As late as 1891, an article in the *Jeffersonian* pleaded for either the restoration of Madison College in Antrim or the founding of a new college.[42] Neither of these things happened. The next time Guernsey County had access to a college within county lines would be in 2001, when a branch of Zane State College (originally Muskingum Tech, a community college in neighboring Muskingum County) opened as a training center in Cambridge, the county seat. However, enthusiasm for Madison lingered after its closure; the last recorded Madison College celebration was in 1939, for the 100th anniversary of its founding.

Even without Madison, the local populace did not let the intellectual grass grow under their feet. Despite the claim in 1882 that literary interests lay

Fig. 4. Site of Madison College today. (Photo by the author.)

dormant, a 1913 article praised "the people of Antrim [for being] fully alive to the needs of public education and [being] abreast of the times in teachers, equipment, and methods."[43] The article attributed this community investment in education to the influence of Madison College, despite it having been closed for decades. Multiple examples also exist of the ways in which the community invested in adult education. For example, in 1886, citizens in Antrim organized a "Chautauqua reading circle" with the hope that it would become "a permanent organization."[44] The title of the reading circle indicates that its purpose was not merely pleasure reading, but rather active investigation of ideas about education or social issues. In another example of local engagement with education, in 1890, the "young folks" of Antrim organized a history class, independent of any school affiliations.[45]

Former Madison students were active as both founders of and participants in local teachers' institutes, continuing education programs designed to increase the skills and knowledge levels of local schoolteachers. John McBurney, a graduate of Madison College and later a professor at Muskingum College, became a driving force in promoting education in Guernsey County through his work with the teachers' institutes and with later normal school programs. Though McBurney was active in promoting further education for local teachers, he was far from the only participant with a Madison connection. A newspaper article shows that former Madison students Mary Sleeth, Jennie Moore, and Lizzie Boyd were active members of the Teachers Institute in 1867, alongside many other participants, both men and women, whom I can't directly tie to Madison but who share surnames with previous students (e.g., Hanna, Bell, McClenahan, Johnson, Wallace, Kennon, Hastings).[46]

Antrim's normal school likely grew as a more formalized version of the teachers' institutes. Whereas the institutes were often one- or two-day instructional programs, the normal school program ran for a six-week term in the summer with the goal of providing teachers with education in more advanced subjects and in the latest theories about pedagogy and classroom management. For educators who lacked easy access to higher education in the decades after Madison's closure, these programs provided brief access to the kinds of formalized higher education that they otherwise wouldn't have been able to receive. While some colleges operated full-time normal programs, Antrim's summers-only program was more flexible, although there was a call to change this. An 1884 article called for a "permanent Normal School" that would be "of value to the town and to the management," although this appears not to have come to fruition.[47] Regardless, the spirit of Madison College, as embodied in its graduates and their children, continued to influence the state of education in Guernsey County.

Though less directly connected with Madison College, another feature that appeared in the early 1900s demonstrates that the community promoted and desired further education, especially for adults. The Farmers Institute was a regular meeting of local farmers and agricultural experts to share knowledge about the latest methods and scientific advances related to farming. The programs also included music and recitations as well as discussions of political issues and aims that would benefit the community and the local environment. For example, in 1904 the Antrim Farmers Institute published a series of resolutions that included the following: "We favor the passing of such a law as will protect on quail and other insect eating birds for at least five years," showing the interest these participants had in environmental science and legal protections based on it.[48] (Environmental protection in postindustrial Appalachia seems to be a much more divisive issue today.) In 1902, the Farmers Institute included a meeting about "the improvement of local schools."[49] Participants also "heartily endors[ed] the Free Library movement and by unanimous vote resolved in favor of the granting of a site for the building by the county com-missioner. C.F. McBride presented the matter to the institute."[50] Antrim did not end up getting the library (Cambridge, the county seat, did). However, what these articles show is both the desire the community retained for educational opportunities and the continuation of the intersections of education, social engagement, and political activism that Samuel Findley endorsed in his found-ing of Madison College. And while teachers institutes, farmers institutes, and normal schools were not exclusive to Antrim—they were much wider phenom-ena throughout the country—their existence here and in the surrounding coun-ties shows that these rural people were as interested in education as people in other parts of the nation were.

Samuel Findley Sr., didn't see these afterlives, however. He left Antrim when Madison College closed, heartbroken by the demise of his life's work. Finding it too hard to remain in the community where his college had failed, he wrote in a letter to friend and former Madison trustee John Moss: "To abandon the sinking ship might not be the best policy, but I felt so locked up and my strength so much reduced. . . . I feel that I have still abandoned the great seat of my life-labor and buried myself out of being almost."[51] He died soon after in 1870 while living with a son in New Jersey. However, he chose to be buried in Antrim, the town to which he had dedicated so much of his intel-lectual and spiritual endeavors. The epitaph on his monument reads:

Erected by the U.P. Cong.
of Antrim to the Memory of
Rev. Samuel Findley, D.D.
Who was born June 11, 1786
And died Feb. 22, 1870
In the 84th Year of his Age

———

He was installed first pastor of
This congregation in June, 1824,
And faithfully served in this capacity
Till 1854

———

His works do follow him

The first time I really looked at this epitaph when I began my research on Madison College, I was surprised that it didn't mention the college. This isn't true for all those who were associated with it; the stone for college official Milton Green proudly reads:

First Secretary to Madison College
Guernsey County Whig Central Committee
Husband of Susan Moore
age 41 years 6 months

One might wonder how Susan felt about being third in this list of her husband's priorities, but given that their daughter attended Madison, perhaps she shared in his enthusiasm for its remembrance.

Maybe when the congregation planned Findley's epitaph, they were still too disappointed by Madison's closure to memorialize it in stone. Or perhaps they simply thought that a disappeared college carried less weight than a still-thriving religious congregation. Regardless, that final note—his works do follow him—has haunted me. Does it mean that the works he began still continue in the world? Or that they followed him to the grave? Arguably, both could be true.

The Works That Follow

While Madison College seems to have permanently succumbed around the same time as Findley, not everything he did immediately disappeared. One way it could be argued that Findley's works continued to echo in the world is through the impressive work of his former students, including his son, Samuel Jr. The younger Samuel took over the presidency of Madison College in 1853, after having served as the head of the Chillicothe Female Seminary in Ross County, Ohio. He immediately began to formally admit women to Madison through his founding of the Antrim Female Seminary (later they would enroll coeducationally in Madison College with equal standing). Each of the women who studied at Madison, and all the ways they encouraged the spirit of inquiry in their children, stem from the Samuel Findleys, Sr. and Jr.[52]

However, there are even more direct ways that Samuel Sr.'s works carried on after him. Among Madison's alumni were teachers, ministers, lawyers, and doctors. Two would become presidents of neighboring Muskingum College, now Muskingum University, which exists to this day. In fact, Muskingum partially owes its existence to David Findley, a cousin of the Antrim Findley family, who first surveyed and donated the land that became Muskingum's campus. When Madison closed, it transferred its charter to Muskingum College, officially merging the two institutions. However, given the physical distance between the schools during a time when travel was a much longer and more difficult activity than it is today, many who would otherwise have attended Madison no doubt found college beyond their grasp.[53]

One other concrete and lesser-known way that Findley's work continues is in a different college and through a different family altogether: the Wallace family of nearby Fairview, who went on to found Monmouth College in Illinois. David, Nancy, and Eliza Wallace were born to Irish immigrants who operated a mill in Fairview. Fairview is a tiny town—smaller even than Antrim is today—and the Wallaces had few economic means. David Wallace, like his sister Nancy, began his career in higher education at Madison College. He later attended other Ohio colleges before becoming the president of Muskingum College in 1846. While in New Concord, he married Martha Findley, a distant cousin of Samuel Findley. David went on to become the first president of Monmouth College in Illinois, which admitted women and minorities from its beginning in 1856. He is famous in Monmouth history for proclaiming that "We must educate in war as well as in peace" and for keeping the college going during the Civil War with a class largely made up of women while their male classmates served in the military.[54] His sister Eliza studied at Monmouth and later taught mathematics at a time when very few women taught in coeducational institutions. Since then, Monmouth has forged a national reputation for educational excellence. It is an example of what I imagine Madison could have become if only circumstances had been different.

By serving as the starting point for the Wallace family's educational journeys, Madison is arguably a contributor to the lives of every student who has benefited from Monmouth College in the years since. Among the alumni in the later 1800s are names that Antrim residents would have recognized, including Stockdale, McBride, and of course Wallace. It seems likely that in the absence of Madison College, at least some Antrim students were pulled toward its offspring, even though by then that meant leaving their homes, possibly forever. Among a people for whom place and family connections are prized, there is no better illustration of their value for higher education than that.

Appalachia, then, was not such a poor place to plant a college such as Madison, even if it couldn't flower for long. In fact, it proved so fertile that its seedlings sprouted as far away as Monmouth, Illinois. In contrast to every stereotype popular culture thinks it knows about Appalachia, this region produced teachers and thinkers who went on to change lives.

Small Stories, Part 2

***

While many of the Madison women's stories show the ways that a desire for education traveled within and among families, the following stand out most strongly for me. They show not only that an interest in education for women trickled down through generations but also that the women who sought educations were valued by their families and communities for doing so—something that contradicts many Appalachian stereotypes.

Elma Brashear

Elma was born in 1833 to Hannah and Otho Brashear. Her father, Otho, was a trustee of Madison College, which tells me that her family cared deeply about higher education. Elma's attendance says that this concern extended to women.

Elma is noted in the catalogue's 1854 student list as having died shortly before the list was published, one of several Madison faculty and students who died around 1854. At least two, the seminary principal Adelphia Powers and student Nancy Wallace, are recorded elsewhere as having died of consumption, better known today as tuberculosis.

If there was a tuberculosis outbreak at Madison College in 1854, it was kept out of the official historical record, including notice in the county newspapers. However, I wonder what effect potential contagion would have had on Madison's survival. (We only need to look at what the COVID pandemic has done to colleges today to see that it wouldn't have been good.) While no doubt the Civil War played a huge role in draining Madison of students, even the rumor of Antrim as a location with high levels of contagion could have been a significant blow. Given that one of the most persistent arguments against women's education was that the mental exertion would harm their physical health, who is to say that parents wouldn't have become even more hesitant to allow it for their daughters?

Elma's death must have been a blow for her family. However, it is once again through her family that I can begin to picture the kind of person Elma may have been, or at least to see how valued her education was. While I don't know what Elma's life would have been like if she had lived, I have a much clearer view of her niece, Imogen Brashear Oakley. Imogen was the daughter of Elma's brother, Basil, who also attended Madison. Dr. Basil Brashear became a physician in New Philadelphia, Ohio, where he married Catherine Whitacre. During the Civil War, he served as a medical officer for the 16th Ohio Infantry, while Catherine served as a nurse and surgical assistant. (She was dubbed by the soldiers "The Mother of the Regiment," which fits with the contemporary view that women could play a significant role in their husbands' professions.) Basil later became a professor of medicine at the University of Wooster. Imogen, like her aunt Elma, went on to attend a school that believed in the benefit of educating women: Bethlehem Female Seminary, also known as the Moravian Young Ladies' Seminary, and today better known as Moravian College.

Bethlehem prided itself on being modeled after "the best [i.e., male] institutions in the land," noting in their 1862–1863 catalogue that "the reputation and character of a *fashionable school* are designedly avoided." This was a school for girls in which "solid learning, the discipline and development of the mind . . . are considered of paramount importance. No effort shall be spared to impart such an education to the pupils as will fit them for the highest usefulness in this life."[1]

And useful Imogen became. Her obituary notes that as a young woman in Pittsburgh, she "organized the first society in this State for civic improvement, The Health Protective Association," which she used to create and successfully advocate for local laws regarding garbage and smoke pollution control. Later, after moving to Philadelphia while her son attended the University of Pennsylvania, she became chair of the Civil Service Committee of the Pennsylvania Federation of Women's Clubs, working toward civil service reform. She published a book on that topic that became "recognized as a work of reference by both the United States and Canadian Governments."[2] She visited Japan in order to establish its first Women's Club, and then went to Rome to discuss public health education reforms with Mussolini. (How successful she would have been in advocating civic reform movements to Mussolini, I don't know.) Her other publications include a work of poetry, a book on early American architecture, and an article titled "The Prohibition Law and the Political Machine" in the *Annals of the American Academy of Political and Social Science*. Her work continues to have relevance; she was quoted in a 2000 *New York Times* article titled "The Nation: Pulling Strings; Invoking the Moral Authority of Moms."[3] Motherhood as a position of authority and power is a concept whose cultural roots the Madison women would have recognized.

This was a woman whose family's educational roots grew from a small Appalachian college and who went on to have a strong, effective public voice. Whether her aunt Elma would have done the same . . . she is one of the many women whose stories were ended too soon to tell. But I can't help but wonder how many of these women's gravestones could potentially have mirrored the inscription on Imogen's:

Beloved Wife
Incomparable Mother
Tireless Worker for the Public Welfare

Austa M. Porter

Austa Porter is yet another woman for whom there is little remaining evidence, but what exists hints at a more fascinating, brave, and human story.

She was born in 1834 to farmers Jane and Luke Porter. She is the only Madison woman I've found so far who came from out of state to attend the college—she came from Greenville, Pennsylvania, along with her sister Mary. After her education, she returned to Greenville to spend the rest of her life there. Her mother had died and her father had remarried soon before his young daughters appeared in Antrim. Did this remarriage perhaps lead him to send young Austa and Mary away? (I can't confirm whether Mary also attended Madison, but their close ages and move to Antrim makes it a logical deduction.) Or was it their own choice?

There's no way of knowing whether family tension or a desire for education (or something else entirely) led the sisters to move to Antrim. However, the records show that neither sister ever married. The reasons for this remain likewise obscure. Did family tensions make them wary of marriage? Were one or both of them simply not sexually attracted to men? Did they, as opponents of women's learning argued at length, find that education made them dissatisfied with the inequalities they'd face as wives? Or, as was also argued by opponents of women's education, did men find them "too smart" and thus unattractive? Again, I don't know the answers to these questions. I do know that remaining single was not the norm. This was an era in which roughly 90 percent of women married at some point during their lives.[4] Remaining single would have had uncomfortable consequences. (Though, to be fair, the consequences of marriage could also be uncomfortable.) Single women had few methods of financial support, and their social status as spinsters left them open to stigma and ridicule. Even today, unmarried women in this region are looked at askance. Austa and Mary's choice to remain single, particularly to live alone as single women unattached to the households of male relatives, was a brave one, a choice that speaks to a desire for self-determination.

Austa and Mary remained close, living together for most of their lives. Mary's obituary, like her life, bucks some contemporary trends. When Mary died in 1917, her obituary in the Greenville newspaper—written, perhaps, by Austa— said that she loved reading. This is not an attribute I've found in many women's obituaries of the time. If they mention any interests, they are much more likely to praise women's "feminine" homemaking skills. The obituary also notes, with what I imagine is no little pride, that Mary was "mentally bright." I don't doubt that Austa could claim the same.

M. Kate Wiser

M. Kate was likely born Mary Catherine Wiser, the daughter of Maranda and tailor/silversmith D. R. Wiser. Like many Madison women, there is little further mention of her in the historical record, but what does exist shows her as a woman who used her education in ways that benefited her home community— exactly the effect that Samuel Findley imagined when founding the college.

According to Wolfe's *Stories of Guernsey County*, Wiser went on to a teaching career. In fact, she taught the first class at Cambridge High School. Cambridge remains Guernsey's county seat and commercial hub—when I was growing up, "going to town" was understood to mean Cambridge—and its high school has flourished ever since Wiser began it. Her obituary in the March 15, 1867, edition of the *Jeffersonian*, praised her "highly gifted mind"—an attribute that would have been enhanced by her time at Madison College. Not many women's obituaries discussed intellectual interests; it says a lot about her and the esteem of those around her that this one did.

Mary Smith

Mary's story illustrates the ways that a Madison education connected people in the Antrim community. There's a fear I've heard tell of again and again from local people, including some in my own family, that education will disconnect students from their homes. It will make them think less of their families and disavow them as a result of that disdain. Yet far from alienating students from their families and communities, it seems that for some, Madison forged relationships between them that continued into successive generations.

Mary was the daughter of Wilhelmina and Mayberry, whose first names seem designed to make up for the commonality of the surname "Smith." Mayberry was a respected local figure; he was both a tanner—certainly an important trade at this time—and a member of the college's board of trustees. Mary married a local farmer named John Wherry, whom she certainly must have loved in order to be willing to take on the name Mary Wherry. (I couldn't determine if John was also a Madison student, but his family may well have valued reading; his father's tombstone includes not one but two carved books.)

Whether or not John was educated at Madison, we know that the couple remained in the Antrim area and raised their family there. Mary kept close ties with fellow Madison women, as evidenced by the fact that her daughter Myrtle went on to marry Josiah, the son of another Madison woman, Eliza Giffee. Eliza was also a proud alumnus of Madison; she is listed as a speaker at a Madison College reunion in 1896. Thus, the connections between students carried on to the next generation.

Mary Catherine Stockdale

Born Mary Hixon in 1834, Mary Catherine married John Stockdale, the brother of another Madison woman, Elizabeth Stockdale, a move that further attests to close community bonds between Madison students. Although there is no definitive evidence that John also attended Madison, it seems likely, given the Stockdale family's deep ties with the college.

Mary's children certainly valued education: her daughter Henrietta became a schoolteacher, while her son attended Muskingum College and became a lawyer. Mary herself was appointed the Antrim postmaster in 1893, a position that, from what I can tell, she was the first woman to hold. This was a position of responsibility, especially since post offices served as unofficial community centers and gathering places where political thought was frequently shaped and debated.[5] It's easy to suppose that Mary's rhetorical training would have been useful in that situation. Her tenure as postmistress opened the door for more women to work in the postal system, including her successor, another woman named Kate Crumbaker. Mary was obviously well respected in the Antrim community, where she lived her entire life; she died there in 1918. Her position of power speaks well not only of her but also of the long-ranging effects Madison had on its students and on the region.

CHAPTER 3

Divided Arguments

Rhetorical Instruction at
Madison College

———

Two premises underlie this book. The first is that academic literacies can adapt to fulfill individual and community needs rather than just to "correct" or subsume them. And the second is that to some degree, at least, Madison College did this. Many students whose histories and identities have not traditionally found favor in academia face pressure to conform to a standardized set of behaviors. This pressure is played out most often in the writing classroom, the space where we most often consider how literacies shape us and what the ramifications are when those literacies are not valued. How did Madison's teachers and students encounter these issues? This chapter looks at how writing was taught at Madison College in order to consider these questions. What did educators at Madison take for granted about academic literacy? About students' home literacies? What can I, as a teacher today in Appalachia, learn about how my predecessors felt about their roles and abilities?

I've always been fascinated with writing. When I was little, I'd push the alphabet magnets around on the refrigerator in random patterns, asking grownups if I'd spelled anything. Eventually I came to view writing's greatest importance in my life as a way to think about and preserve stories—especially family and community stories, which I've learned hold meanings far beyond the surface.

It took me time to come to this conclusion. My view of writing isn't echoed in most writing textbooks, which tend to privilege academic argumentation. I randomly discovered one textbook during my time as a master's student that looked at writing as something more akin to my original sense of it: as a meaningful form of shaping and sharing stories. The Ohio University

English Department office kept an entire wall of shelves filled with textbooks that publishing companies had sent in the hope that they'd be adopted. In one of my frequent perusals of these shelves I found Gary Colombo, Bonnie Lisle, and Sandra Mano's *Frame Work: Culture, Storytelling, and College Writing*. The correlation between writing and quilting alluded to in the title (and on the cover image) first drew my attention. Quilting is a prized ability in my region, where many people learn their artistry from mothers, grandmothers, or great-grandmothers. (Mine tried to teach me when I was young, but I was too impatient to get very far.) The book focused on the idea that our identities are quilted together by stories and that those stories—those we tell and are told within our own communities and cultures—are intellectually valid:

> We all possess a wealth of cultural stories, stories that shape our ideas, values, and tastes—stories that we inherit from the many different cultures we participate in. In effect, we don't create stories so much as they create us. Our stories come to us: we hear them around kitchen tables, at holiday gatherings, on neighborhood streets, and on the job. The readings and the writing assignments you'll encounter in *Frame Work* encourage you to become critically aware of the way these cultural stories shape your own ideas, attitudes, and beliefs.[1]

This echoes a premise that I've come to recognize in my own experience of Appalachian culture: our stories are how we make and share knowledge. That textbook, unfortunately, didn't find a wider audience among college writing teachers; it went out of print after only one edition. It has, however, continued to influence my own teaching and strengthen my belief in the power and relevance of storytelling. In writing, I tell my students, we can shape, preserve, and interrogate the stories that create us. In some ways, that is what I'm doing now—interrogating the story of Madison College, what it means, and why it has not been told.

It was because of my professional focus on writing that I was interested in knowing more not only about who the Madison women were and what they did with their lives but also what they were taught to see as (and reproduce as) good writing. Did they find a place for their stories in the college classroom? Without having any of their written academic work available, these are tough questions to answer. However, surviving evidence gives us clues about what shape writing instruction took in the classrooms they sat in. The 1854 college catalogue doesn't list a specific course in writing or composition; instead, all students took a required course in rhetoric.[2]

The most likely reason why composition per se wasn't a requirement at Madison is that it wasn't commonly defined as a specific course, at least not during the mid-nineteenth century. Instead, writing would likely have featured broadly across courses, with essays assigned in multiple disciplines.[3] It wouldn't be until later in the century that composition as a course would begin to establish itself in college curriculums, influenced by Harvard's composition program. However, the rhetoric course as Madison's students would have known it incorporated a good deal of what came to be characterized as college writing or composition. At the time Madison's students were studying rhetoric, the discipline itself was in a state of flux. Rhetoric instruction had for centuries focused on oral delivery as opposed to writing, but that status was rapidly changing by the mid-1800s. Robert Connors attributes this shift in large part to the influence of women in higher education. Male students were commonly taught rhetoric as antagonistic oral debate—a verbal wresting match. However, this was not seen as appropriate for women: "Such a rhetoric was dangerous, and it could be fed to women only in harmless bits and pieces, stripped of its popular uses. The situation of rhetorical instruction for women mirrored the attitude that women's proper sphere was private, minimizing traditional agonistic oral forms and maximizing analysis and composition. . . . This sort of analytical rhetoric—*ars* stripped of praxis—was a way of avoiding what male college administrators feared: the bringing together of women and the agonistic arena of debate."[4] If oral argumentation was too "masculine" for women's sensibilities (or men's safety), writing could be made appropriately academic while still preserving enforced feminine silence.

This is not to say that all writing was considered particularly more feminine, at least not the forms of argumentative writing women were likely to encounter in the classroom. This kind of writing, too, could be dangerous in the hands of women. In the article "A History of Male Attitudes toward Educating Women," Gary Cabaugh collected statements from prominent male figures across the centuries. As early as fourth-century Greece, boys were practicing their writing skills by copying out the sentence, "He who teaches a woman letters feeds more poison to the frightful asp," a statement attributed to the playwright Menander.[5] In more recent history, Immanuel Kant decreed that "even if a woman excels in arduous learning and painstaking thinking, they will exterminate the merits of her sex," and renowned American intellectual Ralph Waldo Emerson opined in his journal that "women should not be expected to write or fight or build or compose scores; she does all by inspiring men to do all."[6] He eventually changed his mind and became a supporter of women's rights and women's enfranchisement. However, the idea that women should be satisfied with providing "inspiration" rather than accomplishing their own goals proved powerful enough to keep women from college classrooms for centuries. Even many of the women who advocated for access to higher education shared the idea that a woman's primary value was that of inspiring, rather than producing, wisdom and virtue in others, particularly in her children and her husband. Institutes, normal schools, and colleges therefore tended to shy away from encouraging women to write in ways that could have public repercussions—a reality that would affect how female students studied writing and rhetoric. As Connors notes, "Women's colleges and the coeducation schools turned increasingly to a form of discourse that no one found threatening from women: written composition . . . purg[ed] of its public and oratorical elements in order for it to become a safe subject."[7] Instruction in written composition for women could incorporate an epistolary style, as letter writing was one of the primary traditional uses of women's literacy. Jane Donawerth has explored the rhetorical style this compositional focus supported, a "conversational rhetoric" that was seen as suitably feminine and as responsive to women's expected roles as domestic correspondents.[8]

However, there is no evidence that women at Madison College were limited in their rhetorical education or that they were allowed to study rhetoric only through non-argumentative letter writing. In fact, the evidence indicates that they were studying the same style of rhetoric as their masculine counterparts. The 1854 Madison catalogue specifies that all students of rhetoric, regardless of gender, were taught using Richard Whatley's *Elements of Rhetoric*. (A class on logic also used Whately's text *Elements of Logic*.) Knowing that the Madison women were provided rhetorical instruction through the lens of Richard Whately tells us something about what was expected from their written work, but it also opens up questions. It tells us that their rhetoric instruction incorporated elements of both oratory and composition. However, the ways Whately's text conveys this instruction makes it worth questioning why he was being taught at Madison. Whately's text in particular meets Connors's criteria of masculine rhetoric, which makes the choice to teach it to women extremely noteworthy.[9]

In fact, there are multiple ways that Whately seems a less likely candidate for Madison College than his rival, Hugh Blair. Instruction in rhetoric in higher education during the early to mid-nineteenth century was dominated by the texts of a trio of authors: Hugh Blair, George Campbell, and Richard Whately. Blair was by far the most popular author of the three. However, it isn't only that Blair was the biggest seller in the United States that makes him, on the surface, a more likely candidate for the Madison curriculum.[10] Blair shared a cultural background with many of Madison's students and founders, including Samuel Findley. Born in Scotland in 1718, Blair received a classical education at the University of Edinburgh. Findley's family roots extend back to a famous Scottish university town (St. Andrews), and like Blair, his education was dominated by Protestant theology, Latin, and the rhetorical heritage of the Greco-Romans.[11] Like Findley, Blair was a Presbyterian minister who also became a university professor. Blair's popular *Lectures on Rhetoric and Belles Lettres* was first published in 1783 and was very popular in Britain and Europe as well as in the United States. It went through many editions to satisfy demand. However, despite his popularity and the cultural/religious similarities Blair and Findley (as well as much of the population around Madison) would have recognized, Blair's was not the voice that educated Madison students in rhetoric.

Richard Whately, at least at first glance, might have seemed less familiar to Madison's students for multiple reasons. Whately was born in London, England, in 1787, and was educated at Oxford, which, at the time, was actually not known for academic rigor.[12] He became an Anglican clergyman and returned to teach at Oxford in 1825. His *Elements of Rhetoric* developed during a time when he was working to reinvigorate intellectual life at the university. In addition to differing from Findley and the majority of Madison's populace by national origin and religious denomination, Whately was also overall a less popular author than Blair. Consideration of why Whately and not Blair was in use at Madison College requires a deeper look into what each was actually trying to teach and how Madison's professors might have perceived the student population and its needs. Even though both authors focused on rhetoric, their approaches were markedly different.

Blair looked at rhetoric more holistically in a way that, from a modern perspective, seems laudable. What I mean by this is that Blair advocated seeing the connections between reading, writing, and speaking that continue to be valued in modern classrooms. He also acknowledged the value in "disorder and irregularity" in writing.[13] In other words, he didn't insist that students limit their writing to prescribed rules; sometimes successful writing and rhetoric mean being flexible about the accepted standards. This seems to open a door through which Appalachian students could have made the writing classroom their own by bringing their dialects and stories into the academic realm. This does not mean, however, that such digressions from "the rules" of accepted rhetoric would have been accepted by their professors; comparative forms of multicultural rhetoric were not widely valued at this time. Still, Blair's approach could have allowed a somewhat wider scope for students to explore writing on their own terms.

Whether or not such an exploration would ever have been considered in a mid-nineteenth-century classroom, it would have been far less likely to occur in a classroom that used Whately's *Elements of Rhetoric*. Whately focused on rule-based argumentation rather than writing as a means of self-discovery and thinking through ideas. In fact, he specified that "the *ascertainment* of the truth," a process he called "inferring," was separate from rhetoric, which should only involve proving that truth to others. In essence, rhetoric was about persuading others to accept your ideas, not about using writing to explore those ideas.[14] Whately held that writing should occur only after the student had worked out a clear idea of what they wished to say—a method that certainly would have saved on ink and paper expenses, but not one that seems like it would have allowed the most intellectual exploration.[15] Additionally, he argued that rigidly rule-based writing was not, in and of itself, what led to the "cramped, meagre, and feeble" writing often seen from students; rather, the dryness of student essays was more likely because the students had not yet mastered the effective use of those rules.[16] The fact that Whately felt compelled to specify this indicates that the kind of argumentative writing he advocated was not known for producing the most enthralling work.

In the essay "Thinking Like *That*: The Ideal Nineteenth-Century Student Writer," Kathleen Welsch points out that "the ideal of Whately's *Elements* is correctness: of argument and arrangement, of managing the passions and influencing the will, and of style. The management of the writer's passions as a means of swaying the reader's will—the use of language as an instrument of correct reasoning—is the characteristic which distinguishes Whately from other rhetoric texts of the time."[17] The lack of allowance for a writer's emotion and passion in Whately's rhetorical ideals makes me question its relevance and effectiveness for many students, not just those with whom I share cultural connections. In teaching a system that subsumed emotion beneath a disciplined logic, Findley and the other professors at Madison may have been making a commentary on the perceived character of the "rustic" local population. The perception that Appalachian peoples are volatile, even illogical, persists to this day. Likewise, women have for centuries been perceived as more inherently emotional than men, given to hysterics rather than calm, logical thought (an attitude inherited at least in part from the enduring philosophical influence of Greco-Roman culture). It is likely that Madison educators intended Whately's system to train these traits out of their students, whether they existed in reality or merely in perception.

This is not to say that Whately's rhetoric was an entirely antiquated, unnaturally strict ideology of writing that was completely out of step with modern methods of teaching, or even that Blair speaks more strongly to modern teachers. There are elements of Blair's rhetoric that would raise eyebrows in a modern writing classroom. In fact, considering why Madison educators might have chosen *not* to use Blair can be as thought provoking as considering why they ultimately chose to use Whately. A possibility lies in Blair's biggest difference from Whately: his dual focus on argumentative rhetoric and belles lettres.

Belles lettres incorporated what we might today think of as literature or literary study; in other words, the study of "fine writing." It included the types of writing intended to be appreciated for emotional or aesthetic qualities, including poetry and fiction. It was his appreciation of belles lettres that helped Blair see the value of writing that is occasionally "disordered" or that breaks the rules. Those practices could lend an aesthetic quality to the work that it wouldn't have otherwise. However, this emphasis on aesthetics left Blair concerned about the cultivation of taste among his students.

Blair defined taste as "the power of receiving pleasure from the beauties of nature and of art."[18] In his view, students needed to be taught how to appreciate the art of literature: what specifically made it beautiful and why certain styles did not meet the criteria of good taste. To do this, Blair sought to bring "to its most improved state" his students' senses of "delicacy and correctness."[19] From a modern perspective, it isn't difficult to see the potential problems inherent in this ideology. It assumes that one definition of "delicacy and correctness" is shared by all, when that definition is, of course, a matter of culture rather than nature. When the validity of cultural differences is overlooked, the result can be a powerful degrading of the students' cultures and identities. "Taste" becomes something that is dictated by others, and when that definition is accepted without question, the message is conveyed that any differing opinions or styles are inherently inferior. This is why many modern classrooms are working to foreground texts from a variety of authors outside the accepted Euro-American cannon. When you learn that what constitutes "literature" is only what comes from the dominant culture, what does that say about the literatures of cultures on the margins? Nothing good, or even fair.

It is unlikely that Samuel Findley had a prescient sense of the cultural colonization that can happen when qualities of taste or correctness are dictated by others. The person doing the dictating in this case, Blair, was after all someone with whom Findley had a good deal in common. There's every reason to believe they would have shared a general definition of good taste that was based in the norms of an Anglo-European elite. Blair's Scottish background doesn't mean that he was any less susceptible to English cultural influence than the rest of Scotland. In promoting his ideals of taste, Blair wasn't promoting an appreciation of native Scottish literatures so much as he was accepting English ideas of what constituted artistically relevant writing. Winifred Bryan Horner argues that Scotland and the United States at this time shared "colonial inferiority complexes" where England was concerned:

> Students from these countries, so recently provincials, felt that they were basically second-rate and spoke a dialect inferior to the London standard. To become more "English" they wanted to know and understand the literature of England and speak and write the London standard. Their English courses, which included both composition and rhetoric, were a way to reach this goal. The concept of taste reinforced this attitude. . . . Hugh Blair's concept of taste was zealously adopted by the provincials.[20]

The idea that Blair was so popular because he provided a means by which "provincial" students could "correct" their aesthetic taste opens up an interesting question. By using Blair's rival Whately, were Madison educators rejecting the notion of their own inferiority?

In one sense, maybe, but the selection of Whately for students' rhetorical education indicates other perceived needs—specifically, in terms of the proper way to compose and deliver arguments. Whately rejected the incorporation of belles lettres in the rhetoric/writing classroom. In his mind, that space was reserved entirely for argumentation. He rejected the belletristic school of thought as a superficial focus on style over substance.[21] In contrast, he described argumentation as a public good:

> It seems generally admitted that skill in Composition and in speaking, liable as it evidently is to abuse, is to be considered, on the whole, as advantageous to the public; because that liability to abuse is neither in this, nor in any other case, to be considered as conclusive against the utility of any kind of art, faculty, or profession;—because the evil effects of misdirected power, require that equal powers should be arrayed on the opposite side;—and because truth, having an intrinsic superiority over falsehood, may be expected to prevail when the skill of the contending parties is equal; which will be the more likely to take place, the more widely such skill is diffused.[22]

In Whately's view, rhetorical argumentation was much more important for the public good because it was so easily abused. Society needed honest people with the skills of rhetoric who could stand up for truth against those who used their argumentative skill to "misdirect."

Madison's choice to utilize Whately, then, indicates a few possibilities. One is that Madison's professors believed that the students had arguments that were worth making, or in other words, that the local populace was not so devoid of taste, values, and intellectual ability that they needed to be completely overhauled before students could write anything worth reading. While Blair would have focused at least in part on correcting students' sensibilities and ideologies before teaching them how to convey them, this inclination is less evident in Whately. By not addressing the idea that students' sensibilities are inherently deficient, Whately at least somewhat allowed students to value their own ideals. Another aspect of Whately's text indicates that the teachers at Madison approved of the world views and ideologies the students brought into the classroom: Whately argued that writing projects should be directly relevant to students' lives. Students should choose subjects for writing that fit their interests, skill levels, and sentiments. In fact, forcing students to write on topics outside their interests and abilities was no different than "the absurdity of dressing up children in wigs, swords, huge buckles, hoops, ruffles, and all the elaborate full-dress finery of grown-up people."[23] By adopting this text, Madison educators were at least tacitly acknowledging that their rural, provincial students could choose topics to write about that were worth addressing. Their lives could provide suitable topics for college writing.

However, Whately's rhetorical standards were very different from what students at Madison would have known. These standards indicate what their educators perceived as a deficiency in regional discourse. There is an undeniable strain of standardization in Whately's rhetoric that can very easily convey that writing instruction should "correct" students' home dialects and discourses, if not their sensibilities and tastes.[24] For example, while Whately advocated that students choose their own writing topics based on their sensibilities, interests, and needs, he felt that that would be acceptable only if the teacher took "sedulous care in correction" of the students' language, grammar, and adherence to his rules of argumentation.[25] The dialects that Madison's students brought into the classroom, influenced by their regional upbringing in northern Appalachia and likely by their parents' and grandparents' Irish accents, would not have met the standards of academic grammar. Today, many rhetoric classrooms operate with a greater sense of the intersections between dialect, identity, and forms of rhetorical expression. These were not ideas available to Whately or the students at Madison College who were learning from his texts. Their ideas about how to logically and effectively persuade others probably bore little resemblance to what they encountered in the classroom.

My own experience of local rhetoric likewise bears little resemblance to what Whately described. I have written a good deal about the ways Appalachian storytelling traditions work to make arguments in ways that are engaging and non-adversarial, so I don't want to delve too deeply into the topic here.[26] In short, the rhetorical tradition I grew up with in this region is one in which family and place-based narratives work not only to share experiences but also to argue for the values and ideas implicit in those stories. The "rules" of a rhetorically functional regional narrative are more fluid than the rules of academic argumentation even today and would have been very unlike the structured arrangements favored by Whately. For example, he specified the need to state a direct and clear point early on in the argument, something that modern academic writing still values in the form of the introductory paragraph and thesis statement.[27] In my experience of local storytelling traditions, a specific point may not come until late in the narrative or may not even be present. The argument a story conveys can sometimes be left up to the reader or listener to infer. This also has the effect of keeping the argument from becoming adversarial. The focus is on how the teller/writer has formed a conclusion or come to value an idea they invite the audience to share.[28] The lack of a specific thesis doesn't make the telling of the story less of a potential argument in the sense that the telling/writing is done with purpose to convey a rhetorical message. I'm not sure Whately would have agreed.[29] This isn't because he specifically said that narrative cannot be a form of argument; he didn't address narrative writing in any meaningful way at all. He did note that an "indirect" method of argumentation is possible and at times useful, but he saw its utility mostly in "holding up an opponent to scorn and ridicule, by deducing some very absurd conclusion from the principles he maintains," a technique that would be most effective if the reader was "unlearned . . . ignorant of Logic."[30]

The idea that family- and place-based narratives can make a type of non-adversarial argument doesn't appear in Whately's text, but in my local experience, it's the predominant way that people share the truths that matter to them. For example, my grandparents often told me stories about the "Old House." It was a tiny ancestral house across the yard from where I grew up. By the time I was born, no one had lived in the Old House for quite some time. I never knew its last inhabitant, my great-grandmother, personally, but I knew her through stories. I knew that the Old House had been built by my three-times great-grandparents just after the Civil War. I knew which of my ancestors had been *in* the Civil War. I knew that my two-times great-grandmother, who had also lived in the Old House, was a midwife and herbal healer, what in some parts of Appalachia is called a granny woman. I even knew the names of some of the herbs she hunted well into her old age. These types of stories, from what I can see, are not rare in Appalachia. They carry in them arguments about who we are and what our relationship to our homelands should be, about the value of familial and personal connections with places and with history. Stories don't get told over and over for generations unless there is power and purpose in them. However, these types of stories wouldn't have passed muster in Whately's rhetoric classroom.

Categories are at the heart of Whately's text, which could have made its concept of writing difficult for students whose home discourses defy easy categorization. Early in his text, Whately explained his system: "Arguments then may be divided, First, into Irregular, and Regular, i.e. Syllogisms; these last into Categorical and Hypothetical; and the Categorical, into Syllogisms in the first Figure, and in the other Figures, &c. &c. Secondly, They are frequently divided into 'Moral' (or 'Probable,') and 'Demonstrative,' (or 'Necessary.') Thirdly, into 'Direct,' and 'Indirect,' (or *reductio ad absurdum*,) the Deictic and the Elenctic of Aristotle. Fourthly, into Arguments from 'Example,' from 'Testimony,' from 'Cause to Effect,' from 'Analogy,' &c. &c."[31] Each of these categories comes with specific definitions, purposes, and guidelines. Maybe it's just me, but I'm breaking into a sweat just *thinking* about how to fit my writing into these categories. However, a student learning about rhetoric and academic literacy from Whately could easily get the sense that such a fit was necessary—that good writing is, at its heart, a matter of proper categorization. The danger of categories, however, is that they exclude those who don't fit, people whose regional or familial ways of communicating and writing are judged to fall more on the side of the unlearned, the ignorant, and the illogical.[32]

This leads me to wonder if Madison's students found Whately's approach to writing and rhetoric jarring or disorienting. Several modern Appalachian and writing scholars have examined the disjunction students can feel in the academic writing classroom.[33] As an undergrad, I was confused about the expectations and norms of academic literacy, even though I was an English major. A great deal of retrospection and introspection have led me to a realize I have a differing sense of what academic writing can address and what forms it can take. I believe that one of the most powerful things writing can do is help us preserve family stories, like that of the Old House and its residents, while also helping us think through the arguments, values, and limitations implicit in those stories. Whately may have advocated letting students choose their writing topics, but his textbook doesn't encourage writing about those topics in the ways they were told, the ways that might have felt most natural to his students.

Maggie Boyd, the first woman student at Ohio University in 1868, was also a northern Appalachian woman with Scotch-Irish roots, like most of the Madison students. According to Ohio University's 1871–1872 catalogue, she likely took a rhetoric course that used Whately's text.[34] Amazingly, her diary of experiences as a student still exists. In it, she wrote that "it seems to me that I cannot write as well now as I could one year ago. . . . I am getting so I fairly dread to write."[35] Boyd didn't specify what it was about her writing that her professor found so objectionable, although her diary itself provides evidence that she was not, in fact, an unskilled or unenthusiastic writer. How much of this alienation from writing, I can't help but wonder, came from being thrust into a system of "correct" writing and rhetoric so different from her own?

Of course, the opposing perspective, even today, is that by enforcing standardized rules of writing and language, students from marginalized populations are given access to the power implicit in these forms. If a student learns how to make arguments in the ways (and language) accepted in the dominant society, their chances of succeeding in that society are greater; they aren't limited to the community or the discourse of their birth. However, in the absence of a wider pedagogical discussion at that time about how to teach the discourse of power without harming students' identities, I have no reason to believe that this instruction was accompanied by the caveats that are at least somewhat more common in college writing instruction today. I doubt that many professors in the 1800s were teaching their students that while standardized forms of writing and language are powerful, they are not inherently more correct or intellectually valid than others. In fact, Maggie Boyd's assertion, her sense that she was getting worse as a writer, indicates that she saw standardized college writing as simply the correct way—a way of writing at which she felt a failure.

Because I haven't been able to locate surviving examples of the Madison women's writing or any examples of their professors' feedback on their writing, I have no way of judging what their experience was like. I can't help but wonder, though, if a similar sense of themselves as failures at "correct" writing and rhetoric, as stipulated by Whately, has something to do with why these writings haven't survived. Even if Whately's style of writing felt alienating to Appalachian students such as Maggie Boyd, we can't assume that those students were less likely to internalize his criticisms. Given the fact that many if not most of Madison's students were the children or grandchildren of immigrants, it is possible that they sought out the standardization and "correctness" of expression Whately offered. Social mobility outside their home communities could have depended on their ability to adapt to mainstream norms, a pressure that was becoming particularly prevalent as the ideals of middle-class society became more concrete. According to scholars Elizabethada Wright and S. Michael Halloran, "In the competitive middle-class society of the nineteenth century, speaking and writing 'correct' English took on new importance as a sign of membership in the upper strata."[36] On the other hand, as with the children of immigrants today, this pressure could have induced feelings of shame, either for failing to meet standardized requirements (as was the case for Maggie Boyd) or for "turning their backs" on the communities that raised them. Literacy instruction was a complicated proposition for peoples on the margins.

Whately believed that his categorized system of rhetoric promoted logical thought and expression as students were taught to manage their passions. Both women and Appalachians have been perceived (and perhaps are still perceived) as peoples whose reasoning relies far too little on logic and far too much on passion. Because these stereotypes were held up to less scrutiny then than they are today, it makes sense that rural schools such as Madison College and Ohio University utilized Whately's text for their students. The rhetoric that Whately conveyed to Madison College's students would have been both empowering and inhibiting. It could have limited their sense of what was correct in both the language they used and their style of communication. This continues to be the case for many Appalachian students encountering college writing instruction today. When they are taught that there is one "correct" way, it is very easy for them to get the sense that there are right ways and wrong ways to speak, write, think, and even *be* in the world and that the ways they bring with them often fall into the wrong category. On the other hand, Whately would have taught students how to make standardized arguments in ways that the wider American culture was coming to accept, ways that were categorized and focused on clarity and directness. He would also have taught them the value of choosing their own topics for writing, validating the relevance of their interests in the classroom. As instruction for women, this was potentially revolutionary. By providing women with the same training in rhetoric as men, Madison was opening a gateway for women's participation in issues that mattered to them, even if those issues had not previously been recognized as academically valid.

It is also possible that Madison's students, or Appalachian students at a variety of schools more broadly, learned to integrate styles of rhetoric in ways that worked for them and their audiences. My great-great-grandfather William was a preacher at the church near where I grew up. He and my great-great-grandmother are buried in the church cemetery, where we bring them flowers every May. There are no records or family stories about William's formal schooling, but he undoubtedly had some form of literary and rhetorical training. There survives in our family archive a faded, crumbling journal of sermons handwritten by him, dating to the 1880s. I don't know if he ever read Whately's *Elements of Rhetoric*, but his writing does at times have a directness that Whately would have valued. However, he also integrates narrative, experience, and regional dialect in a way that most definitely didn't come from Whately. For example, in one oration he described the day that he and his parishioners learned that Fort Sumter had been fired upon, when they felt the sinking understanding that war was now inevitable—that their world was about to change forever. He didn't attach a thesis statement to this story, but based on the text that follows, this story was meant to illustrate the importance of gratitude for our lives, communities, and freedoms. William's sermons blended different styles at different times: sometimes beginning with a specific premise followed by a logical arrangement of textual, biblical evidence and sometimes followed by personal narratives based on a shared sense of values. Both styles work to make a point, to compel agreement in the audience . . . in other words, to argue. William obviously saw value in braiding these forms. Given how many students sought out an education from Madison College (and the other colleges throughout the region), it's not a stretch to believe that they found substance and value in their rhetorical training. And as we will see in upcoming chapters, the women who attended Madison College found ways to use their education beyond the classroom.

In her 2007 essay "'Our Life's Work': Rhetorical Preparation and Teacher Training at a Massachusetts State Normal School, 1839–1929," Beth Ann Rothermel quotes a student composition written by a woman in the 1880s who noted that the "skill of composition . . . thrills and animates the mind to noble action."[37] Given that this student author was from New England, perceived then and arguably still now as the academic capital of the United States (one need only peruse *US News and World Report*'s college rankings to see that the most prestigious and expensive colleges cluster there even to this day), it's difficult to know if she experienced the same type of "culture shock" in the composition classroom that Maggie Boyd did. However, she made an important point: feeling a sense of control and skill in one's ability to communicate the ideas that matter most can be deeply empowering. Whether or not Whately helped the Madison students feel this empowerment is unclear. However, he was only one voice that would have influenced the Madison women in their own literacy journeys. Their status as women in academia led them to encounter other voices that will be explored in the next chapter.

Small Stories, Part 3

———

Popular culture paints Appalachia as a region that is hostile to education, a place that is often incomprehensibly anti-intellectual. The following stories offer a counternarrative: they illustrate that education was valued in this region and that students, far from being shunned for their "book learning," went on to play influential roles in their families and communities.

Sarah and Lizzie Jamison

I know very little about Sarah or Lizzie from official records, beyond the facts that they are siblings who were listed as students in 1854 and, according to census data, were born to farmers Mary and John. (John's father Robert, an Irish immigrant, was a schoolteacher in Londonderry in 1820—one of the few immigrants I've found who wasn't primarily a farmer and whose own education must have happened in the old country.) I was able to find a photo of Sarah and Lizzie's mother, Mary—a rare find for Madison's students or members of their immediate families. An elderly, bespectacled woman in a sensible black dress, she holds an opened book on her lap. She looks up and to the left of the camera, as if she has just been interrupted in her reading.

This would perhaps have been the only photo ever taken of her, as photography was still uncommon (in her youth, it would have been unheard of). In it, she chose to be pictured with a book. If a picture is worth a thousand words, I'm not at all surprised this is a woman who sent two of her daughters to college when she had the chance.

Her daughters weren't the only ones to embrace education; her sons were just as keen on learning. This is shown in a surviving letter from Mary's son (Sarah and Lizzie's brother) Robert. It was written to Sarah in 1857, and it was quoted in the *Guernsey County Community & Family History Book*. Robert, who had moved to Illinois, described his homesickness, but he was also proud to announce to his sister that "we have a school here almost as large as Madison College and I will try to procure you a situation [teaching job] in it." (Given his location and the timing of the letter, he was likely referring to the Geneseo Seminary. It is unclear if Sarah took him up on his offer to seek employment, but it is noteworthy that he had no doubts that his sister could and should be a college-level teacher.) He went on to note that despite their newly founded school, "we can beat Old Guernsey at everything, except education."[1] The Jamison family not only recognized the value of education for women, they also believed the region to be educationally unmatched by other parts of the Midwest. That, to me, is a history well worth preserving.

Violet Scott

Named as a former student in an article about a Madison College reunion, Violet Scott is one of the Madison students who most defied the common ideas about women in her time. Women were not encouraged to engage in public speaking in most of the United States. There were, of course, notable exceptions to this; some women spoke out anyway on important social issues of the day, such as Sojourner Truth's and the Grimké sisters' public addresses on slavery and women's status. However, their choices to speak were not met with wide social approval—a town hall where Angelina Grimké Weld spoke was burned to the ground by an angry mob the next day. This probably had a lot to do with her topic—anti-slavery—but many men spoke out against slavery as well without quite as violent a response.

Even educated women were often discouraged from public speaking, as we will see in the chapters discussing Emma Willard and Lydia Sigourney—figures Violet would certainly have been familiar with through the Madison women's literary societies. However, Violet ignored this prohibition and seems to have been supported by her community for doing so.

Her academic abilities are recalled in the family record; a book on the Scott family refers to her as a storyteller of family history who was educated at McNeely Normal College (which would later become Hopedale College) in neighboring Harrison County. There are two possibilities to explain this attribution. Perhaps she attended both Madison and McNeely. She wouldn't have been the first Madison student to bounce between local colleges; at least some attended both Madison and Muskingum or Franklin at various times. In the nineteenth century, college was not necessarily a clear four-year pathway so much as it was a piecemeal endeavor undertaken during times when the student had available time and funds. Alternatively, the book's author, a distant cousin, might have misremembered the name of Violet's college after forty years. Even if this is the case, there was no shame or attempt to hide her academic experience, whether or not the specific school is named correctly. In fact, she was described as "a very sensible and excellent woman," despite standing outside the norm for most women at this time.[2]

Violet used her education to become a teacher, one who took an active part in community projects and issues. In 1892, the *Jeffersonian* favorably mentioned Violet's public speaking work. Specifically, she trained young people, including girls, to take part in Demorest Contests.

These contests were begun in 1886 by William Jennings Demorest in order to popularize the temperance movement. The contests, which occurred in communities around the country, required young participants to memorize and deliver speeches by temperance leaders. The *Jeffersonian* noted that "Miss Violet Scott gave much time and patient care to drilling and training the contestants and [is] to be congratulated for their success. As [an] educator, [she is] far in advance of any other such project introduced into the community."[3] In other words, Violet was training young people to speak publicly on a prominent social issue. Not only was her participation noted, it was also held up as exemplary.

The degree to which Appalachia is described as patriarchal and anti-woman is complicated by the undeniable existence of strong women's voices throughout its history. Far from being silenced by her community, Violet found a way to use her voice to influence public thought—and she had her community's respect while doing it. Perhaps this was entirely due to approval of her topic (though, knowing what I do of this region, not everyone supported prohibition) . . . or perhaps women's voices in our culture have not always been as constrained as many would claim.

A lifelong Guernsey County resident, Violet Scott remained unmarried, dying in 1897.

Amelia J. Matthews

When I began searching for Amelia Matthews, I went down a wrong path—an experience that anyone who has done genealogical research will understand.

I thought she was the Amelia/Parmelia who was the daughter of Dr. Samuel Matthews, a graduate of the Western Reserve College (today Case Western Reserve University) from Cleveland, Ohio. "Oh," I thought, "this is another case of family influencing a child's educational aspirations."

I think my assumption was right, but not in the way I'd imagined. A closer look at dates, combined with the lack of definitive evidence tying her to the Antrim locale, showed that that Amelia was almost certainly not the one I was looking for. A new search located another Amelia Matthews, this one also from Ohio but located in Antrim. She was raised by her widowed mother, who worked as a seamstress to provide them a living. This Amelia's mother is noted in the census as being illiterate. However, in a time when not all children got any formal education, she had Amelia in school by the age of four.

That Amelia continued her education past the point of basic literacy is telling, especially because she could have been put to work early as a seamstress or washer to contribute to her family's finances. Amelia's mother was a prime force in her daughter's education, not because she came from a family that valued it but because it was something she herself lacked. Given the number of first-generation college students I see in my own classes, this is a story that has very real local relevance even today.

Amelia married into the Stockdale family, many of whom were students or trustees of Madison College. Her husband Moses went on to earn a living as a carpenter who, according to the local paper, was noted for building local schoolhouses. That he and Amelia had impressive literary interests is also shown in the name of one of their sons: Ralph Waldo Stockdale. Since neither Ralph nor Waldo seem to have been family names, he was almost certainly named for famed writer and transcendentalist Ralph Waldo Emerson.

Amelia and Moses lived their entire lives in the Antrim community.

Sue Craig

Sue Craig was born in 1838 to Nancy and William Craig, a merchant. Her parents were active members of the Underground Railroad. According to William's entry on the Find A Grave website:

> Before the Emancipation Proclamation was put into effect by President Abraham Lincoln in 1863, those individuals participating in the underground railroad were also at risk for potential prosecution for harboring

fugitives, thus assisting any fugitive slaves was a well concealed practice. William H. Craig (the original owner of the house on Church-Goodrich Street in Newcomerstown) was a former Cadiz merchant. He and his wife later moved to Newcomerstown and built the home in 1860. It was said that the fugitive slaves, either "stowaways" on a passing canal boat, or traveling along the canal locks by foot at night, were secretly ushered to the Craig home, where they were given refuge in the cellar which also had a door that led outside, in the event a quick escape became necessary.[4]

The degree of their daughter Sue's participation in these activities is unknown, but as with Sarah McKittrick, she was almost certainly aware of them and protected the secret. Sue has one unique claim to history that also interests me: she is one of the few Madison women whose picture as a young woman survives. People at this time didn't have their pictures taken as often as we do today. A photograph involved a visit to a professional photographer's studio, which meant an expense of both money and time. That Sue had a photo taken of herself at a young age hints at a level of status, resources, or even self-worth that was not available to all women in the mid-nineteenth century.

Sue married Peter Spader Suydam, who is described in the census as a lightning rod manufacturer. However, he also had some connection with academia; he is recorded as having business ties with Ohio State University's Greek Department (though what those ties were is not recorded).

Like many of the Madison women, her views on education are indicated not by any remaining evidence of her own, but from that of her daughter. When Sue's daughter Margaret died in 1956, her obituary described her as an intelligent woman with interests in politics, the arts, and the sciences. She "maintained a keen interest in world affairs. . . . Nearly every afternoon friends dropped in to chat with her about world and local events." She also "did a lot of painting, in oil and pastels."[5] These do not necessarily prove that Margaret believed in the value of higher education or that this was a value she took in from her mother's example. However, it is noteworthy that she believed in her right to have a voice in the politics of both her community and the wider world. Higher education has long held as part of its purview the education of engaged, informed citizens of the world. We know from Samuel Findley's address to the Philomathean Society (Madison's precursor) that he saw this as part of the college's own mission—though certainly not all educational institutions saw this as important for women. Artistic interests were more associated with feminine virtues. At Madison College, Sue Craig would have had the option of learning arts and music. Perhaps Margaret's artistic interests were created or nurtured through her mother Sue's experience at Madison College.

The same might be said for Margaret's scientific interests, which were less traditionally feminine at the time. Margaret's obituary notes that she developed a new form of a "delicious-tasting wine-colored peach" from her own garden, an accomplishment that would have required some sense of the science of botany. Her mother Sue would have studied botany while a student at Madison. Science was given a prominent role in the Madison curriculum. In fact, a surviving Madison catalogue shows that by 1858, students could choose a "Classical" or "Scientific" focus and the number of women in the scientific department outstripped the number of women in the classical department. This defies our modern gendering of the humanities as "feminine" and the sciences as more "masculine" in nature.[6] While gardening was acceptably feminine at the time, Margaret took it one step further, as she did with her political and artistic interests. I can't help but suspect that this step began with a nudge from her mother.

CHAPTER 4

Madison College and Women's Education

Acceptance and Resistance

———

This chapter has two aims: to consider what higher education, specifically education in writing/speaking/rhetoric, was like for women in the mid-nineteenth century and to look for the ways the Madison women either upheld or challenged these norms. I'm coming to see that they did both—and that the reason why they might have accepted and resisted larger American cultural norms has a lot to do with the ways those norms intersected or clashed with regional Appalachian culture.

To begin, Madison was unusual in providing higher education for women at all. By 1870, less that 2 percent of people—men or women—in the United States attended college, putting the Madison women solidly in a minority.[1] However, my research indicates that northern Appalachia as a whole had its foot in the door of women's higher education, as demonstrated by the number of women's seminaries in existence in southern and eastern Ohio, western Pennsylvania, and northern West Virginia.

Some may dispute whether women's seminaries should be seen as providing higher education to women on a par with the education provided at contemporary men's colleges. The women's seminary movement began when the concept of coeducational colleges was unthinkable; educators believed that any access women would have to higher education would have to come in gender-specific institutions. The first of these was begun by Emma Willard, who selected the term "seminary" rather than college to avoid stirring misogynistic feelings against her endeavor.[2] However, from the very start the "women's seminary" was intended to provide a classical higher education, albeit one tailored to a woman's "separate sphere." In essence, the separate sphere ideology held that women's energies and influence belonged in the private home-and-family circle, whereas men were meant to exercise these in the public realm. Too often, historians dismiss women's seminaries as lacking intellectual rigor, based more on assumptions than on reality about what a women's school would provide. If women were being taught only to serve as wives and mothers, how intellectually advanced could their educations be? This rests on a presumption that these are inherently nonintellectual roles or that the women fulfilling them would lack intellectual interests. While undoubtedly some seminaries saw greater value than others in providing classical educations to women, the belief that seminaries by their nature were intellectually inferior is demonstrably false.[3] Surviving catalogues for the seminaries I've focused my investigations on in Appalachian Ohio, Pennsylvania, and West Virginia proclaim their desire to provide a rigorous education. Those statements are backed up by curriculums that match those of single-sex male colleges. Many seminaries believed in the importance of educational rigor specifically because they saw women as meant for the home sphere. Early advocates of the seminary system, including Emma Willard and Mary Lyon, argued that because as mothers women would be the educators of future leaders, it was extremely important to provide the highest levels of intellectual training.[4]

The concept of separate spheres was deeply entrenched as a reason against coeducation, at least at the college level. However, the separate spheres ideology surprisingly also provided a prominent argument for giving women access to education. As Patsy Parker notes, "conservatives claimed it would destroy the role of women in the household as homemakers, wives, and mothers. Liberals, on the other hand, claimed that a college-educated woman would be a better homemaker, wife, and mother."[5] Both camps positioned women's destinies as so distinct from men's that some degree of separation was warranted. Women's seminaries existed to allow access to higher education, albeit in a gendered context that maintained separation.

Women's seminaries therefore provided many women with their best chance at higher education, even though some seminaries adjusted their curriculums and approaches to fit the expectations of women's options. This makes Madison College's approach to educating women particularly interesting. Despite being considered, technically, part of the Antrim Female Seminary rather than Madison College, they studied the same subjects as the men. In fact, the women's curriculum at Madison was identical to the men's, with the optional addition of courses in what were seen as the more feminine pursuits of music, art, and modern languages. The catalogue specifically states that coursework in the classical curriculum was being taught to both men and women, ostensibly by some of the same professors: "As thorough mental training is essential to the full development of the female intellect as well as of the male, we cannot too strongly urge upon the young ladies the importance of entering the regular college classes, and completing the classical course necessary for College graduation."[6] The women at Madison College were, then, receiving educations as rigorous as that received by the men, often taking the same courses. At least some of the women insisted on their status being seen as coequal to their male classmates: the obituaries of Sarah Owens and Lizzie Moss said that they were graduates of Madison College, *not* of the Antrim Female Seminary. Arguably, the women were receiving better educations than the men because in addition to the shared classical curriculum, the women could also study art, languages, and music.

However, the concept of women's "separate sphere" remained the social norm in wider American society, and it did have an impact on how students in women's seminaries learned. Because women were seen as being inherently more tied to home and family, the style of teaching pioneered at the women's seminaries attempted to echo the maternalism girls were expected to adopt with their own families.[7] In other words, teachers were encouraged to see themselves as maternal, nurturing figures in relation to their students. This shift in educational philosophy would, in fact, come to be hugely influential in education at all levels in the United States, making the ideal teacher more of a parental figure than a drillmaster.[8] Likewise, some seminaries, including Emma Willard's pioneering Troy Seminary, also included courses in the domestic sciences that were meant to make women more successful in the home sphere. However, the pedagogy and course offerings should not be taken as indicators that students received less valid or rigorous educations in seminaries in general. Seminaries continued to provide students with subjects in the sciences, mathematics, history, languages, and, significantly for our purposes, rhetoric. My reasoning for perceiving these northern Appalachian women's seminaries as colleges is ultimately based not on how they differed from men's colleges, but rather on how they resemble them through their core curriculums.

The same analysis applies to the more famous offshoot of the women's seminary: the normal college. Popular in the later nineteenth century, normal colleges focused specifically on the education of future teachers and were therefore popular options for women, whose career choices were largely restricted. Like women's seminaries, normal colleges have suffered from the retrospective belief that they were less academically inclined. However, because the perception was that a liberal arts degree was good preparation for a teaching career, these schools also provided a solid college education.[9] In fact, some women's seminaries and normal colleges might have provided a better education in written composition than what men received in single-sex colleges because writing was seen as a somewhat more feminine form of communication than public speaking. Ultimately, I would argue that the ubiquity of women's seminaries and normal colleges in addition to traditional (i.e., male-focused) colleges shows that higher education mattered in nineteenth-century northern Appalachia for both men and women.

Of course, not every seminary or educational institution was a site of resistance to patriarchal gender norms. However, Madison was ahead of the curve for women's education in some significant ways. Robert Connors points out that until the later 1800s, even when women were provided a rhetorical education, it was presented in gendered ways.[10] Men were encouraged to use rhetoric as training in argumentation and take part in debate, but it was considered socially unacceptable for women to do the same. He looks at the case of Oberlin College, the oldest continually operating coeducational institution of higher education in the United States, which began admitting women in 1837.[11] Although Oberlin, like Madison, based its rhetoric courses on Whately's *Elements of Rhetoric*, only men were permitted to apply his rhetoric to oratory; women were limited to writing essays. There is no evidence that the women in Madison's classes were limited to instruction in writing and not speaking. We know that at least one female student was trained in oratory because she put her training to use. Violet Scott is recorded in an 1892 *Jeffersonian* article as providing oratorical training to students competing in a local Demorest Contest. The speakers she trained were described as "pure in tone, and elevating in character . . . present[ing] the principles and purposes of temperance in a most pleasant, interesting, and attractive form, and if the voters will take the interest in the conquest that is manifested by the youth in the contest, the result will be a grand advancement of the temperance cause."[12] In other words, a former Madison student was not only taking part in a public issue in the community, she was also training both boys and girls to speak publicly. If she received this training during her time at Madison, then the Madison women are not only a significant example of early women receiving rhetorical training, they are also a significant example of women learning to speak publicly at a time when very, very few women in the United States had that possibility. This would be a feat that places them beyond the scope even of celebrated early women's colleges such as Vassar, which promised in its 1865 catalogue to provide a properly "womanly" education, with "no encouragement . . . given to oratory and debate."[13]

Violet Scott's experiences teaching oratory don't conclusively show that women were educated in this aspect of rhetoric at Madison. However, there is evidence that these women were writing, speaking, and performing public debates as members of student groups, making it likely they also received formal training in the classroom. A flyer for an 1856 public event sponsored by Madison's Sigourney Literary Society shows that women were both publicly reading their essays and staging debates—in this case, whether "the fashions of the gentlemen are more absurd than that of the ladies."[14] On the surface, this may seem like a fairly lightweight topic for debate, but depending on what the arguments were, it could have undercut a major source of condemnation against women: that they were too focused on their appearance (especially given that an interest in fashion has never been exclusively female). However, the main point is that this shows these women were engaging in public writing, oratory, and debate—something that wider society at the time deemed unsuitable for women at all. Not even all women's seminaries would have sanctioned such a move. Yet this small rural college in a corner of the Appalachian hill country, dominated by immigrant farmers, was doing just that.

Even later in their lives, Madison women chose to speak in public events, at annual Madison College reunions, for example.[15] Newspaper reports of reunion events show that women were giving public speeches about their reminiscences of attending Madison alongside male graduates. An article about the 1896 college reunion noted that the college's alumni include "many of our noted men *and women*."[16] While I can't know exactly what the Madison women's classes looked like, I do know that their community appreciated that they had them.

A more concrete sense of what the women themselves thought about their education can be found through their student literary societies. This discovery came about from the papers of Dr. John McBurney, which are housed in the archives of Marietta College. McBurney was a Madison College graduate who went on to have a distinguished career, both in Guernsey County public schools and at neighboring Muskingum College. He married a fellow Madison student, Lizzie Moss. While the papers in the Marietta archive are listed only under McBurney's name, I strongly suspect that the fliers it includes of the Madison women's literary society events are her contribution.[17] Lizzie, after all, is the one who would have been directly involved with the women's literary societies.

Literary societies are a now largely forgotten yet hugely significant aspect of early college life in the United States. Students joined college literary societies in order to gain additional training in reading, writing, and speaking in a less formalized, more social atmosphere than the classroom. In a literary society, students could expect to read and discuss ideas with their fellow students. Male literary societies in particular were associated with debate and practice in oratory. Many college literary societies had their own meeting spaces and libraries. In his article "College Literary Societies: Their Contribution to the Development of Academic Libraries, 1815–76," Thomas Harding describes these groups as featuring "jolly companionship, long and heated orations and debates, dramatic 'productions,' and comparatively large libraries."[18] Even though they offered "jolly companionship," literary societies were far from merely being social clubs. These societies were "a standard feature of nineteenth-century higher education in the United States . . . that was primarily the preserve of men. College students often received more practical experience in writing, speaking, and debating in the societies than in the classroom."[19]

The ways that women experienced literary societies would have been somewhat different because of their socialization as part of the "separate sphere" and because of the perceived danger of women learning argumentative writing, speaking, and debate. Echoing the familial, maternal ideology promoted by the seminary movement, members of women's literary societies were, according to scholar Catherine Hobbs, "often centered on creating community rather than differentiating their selves, an emphasis that contributed to an alternative model of literacy."[20] In other words, women's literary societies were often intended to focus on sharing and discussing ideas rather than on debating them, as was the ideal in men's societies. Of course, to say that all men's literary societies functioned as debate clubs while all women's looked like peaceful salons is too simplistic to reflect reality.[21] However, the names the Madison women chose for their literary societies indicate that they too approved of the ideals of separate spheres and believed that the nature of women was inherently maternal. At Madison College, the two women's literary societies were dubbed the Willard Society and the Sigourney Society.

Even before I did any deeper research into literary societies, the flyers shown in figures 5 and 6 provided me with a wealth of information. The women at Madison took their literary societies seriously, enough that they publicized their events and had promotional materials professionally printed. They also told me that the Madison women were composing and publicly reading their writing—an indication of their pride in their learning and their right to speak in public venues. Also, they were writing and reading on topics that might have been seen as publicly controversial. Rather than limiting their work to personal essays (which, again, would have been seen as slightly more acceptable for women), they appear to have been making arguments—at least it seems so, from what I can tell by the titles, including an essay titled "Woman: Her Sphere

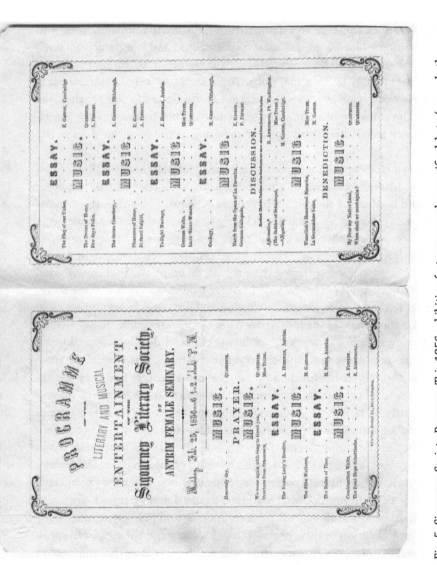

Fig. 5. Sigourney Society Program. This 1856 exhibition features a gender-specific debate (over whether men or women wear more "absurd" fashions). An 1855 exhibition debated the notion that women are intellectually inferior. Given that the Madison women named their literary societies for famed female intellectuals, it seems likely that this wasn't a notion they held. (From the John McBurney Collection at Marietta College.)

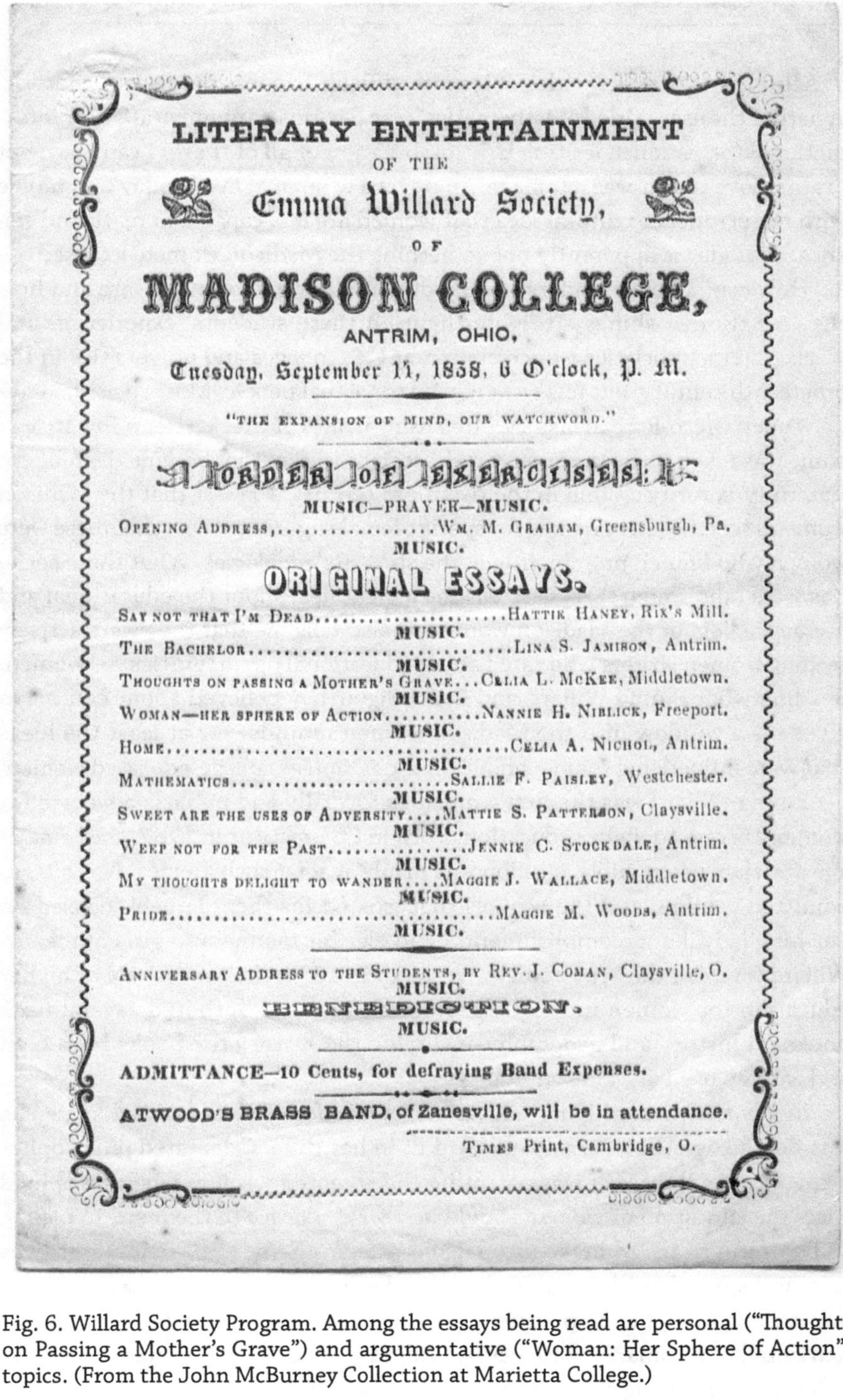

LITERARY ENTERTAINMENT

OF THE

Emma Willard Society,

OF

MADISON COLLEGE,

ANTRIM, OHIO,

Tuesday, September 14, 1858, 6 O'clock, P. M.

"THE EXPANSION OF MIND, OUR WATCHWORD."

ORDER OF EXERCISES.

MUSIC—PRAYER—MUSIC.

OPENING ADDRESS,..................Wm. M. Graham, Greensburgh, Pa.

MUSIC.

ORIGINAL ESSAYS.

Say not that I'm Dead.....................Hattie Haney, Rix's Mill.

MUSIC.

The Bachelor...........................Lina S. Jamison, Antrim.

MUSIC.

Thoughts on passing a Mother's Grave...Celia L. McKee, Middletown.

MUSIC.

Woman—her sphere of Action..........Nannie H. Niblick, Freeport.

MUSIC.

Home.................................Celia A. Nichol, Antrim.

MUSIC.

Mathematics.....................Sallie F. Paisley, Westchester.

MUSIC.

Sweet are the uses of Adversity....Mattie S. Patterson, Claysville.

MUSIC.

Weep not for the Past...............Jennie C. Stockdale, Antrim.

MUSIC.

My thoughts delight to wander....Maggie J. Wallace, Middletown.

MUSIC.

Pride.............................Maggie M. Woods, Antrim.

MUSIC.

Anniversary Address to the Students, by Rev. J. Coman, Claysville, O.

MUSIC.

BENEDICTION.

MUSIC.

ADMITTANCE—10 Cents, for defraying Band Expenses.

ATWOOD'S BRASS BAND, of Zanesville, will be in attendance.

Times Print, Cambridge, O.

Fig. 6. Willard Society Program. Among the essays being read are personal ("Thoughts on Passing a Mother's Grave") and argumentative ("Woman: Her Sphere of Action") topics. (From the John McBurney Collection at Marietta College.)

of Action."[22] With other titles, it is more difficult to guess the style of rhetoric. Whether the essay titled "Mathematics" was personal, argumentative, or informational (or, as much writing is, a combination of all of these) I can't say, but I rather love that it was a topic taken up by a woman.[23] Even today we grapple with the erroneous cultural idea that women are less capable in math and science. That idea is apparently not something the Madison women accepted.

However, a better understanding of what literary societies were and how they functioned shines a brighter light on these students' experiences and ideals. Literary societies were common at U.S. colleges and universities in the nineteenth century, but few were named for actual people. Most society names drew upon Greco-Roman history, often using names of Greek letters. This style of name was taken up by the later "Greek" social societies that became the modern fraternity/sorority system in the twentieth century. The fact that the Madison women's societies were named for specific female figures tells me that these were women who figured prominently in the students' ideologies. What these societies were (and weren't) named tells me a great deal about the educational and literacy beliefs of the Madison women. It also tells me that they were actively reading women writers who cared about educational opportunities for women. Reading what Emma Willard and Lydia Sigourney believed about education gives me a window into the Madison women's minds—or at least the ideas that were influencing them—about their position as college-educated women.

Emma Willard was the first woman to formally and publicly advocate for women's access to higher education. Born in Connecticut in 1787, she came of age at a time when public opinion was firmly against such an idea. No colleges admitted women, and the schools that existed for them largely focused on teaching ladylike "accomplishments" and elegant manners to girls of means. Willard founded the Troy Female Seminary in 1821, the first school of higher education for women in the United States. She also authored several textbooks on history and geography, including the history textbooks both men and women used at Madison College.

In advocating for higher education for women, Emma Willard knew she was doing something largely unheard of in her time. Celebrated philosopher Jean-Jacques Rousseau was parroting the accepted wisdom when he opined that "the education of women should be always relative to the men. To please, to be useful to us, to make us love and esteem them . . . to render our lives easy and agreeable."[24] So deeply ingrained was this concept that women who had serious thoughts on politics, government, or education were seen as fundamentally unwomanly.[25] However, Willard turned women's injunction to be helpful and pleasing to men to her advantage. In her 1819 "Address to the

Public Particularly to the Members of the Legislature of New York Proposing a Plan for Improving Female Education," Willard said: "Barbarians have trodden the weaker sex beneath their feet. . . . Nations, calling themselves polite, have made us the fancied idols of a ridiculous worship. . . . But where is that wise and heroic country, which has considered that our rights are sacred, though we cannot defend them? that tho' a weaker, we are an essential part of the body politic, whose corruption or improvement must affect the whole? And which, having thus considered, has sought to give us by education, that rank in the scale of being, to which our importance entitles us?"[26] In asking these questions, Willard revealed some of the main reasons for her advocacy of women's education. She argued that because women are essential components of society, the degree to which they are educated, or not, would inevitably affect society.

There are multiple points in Willard's treatise that I can imagine the Madison women finding particularly compelling. For one thing, she advocated education for women as an element of religious responsibility. She wrote that because "our highest responsibility is to God," education could and would allow women to better understand and fulfill their spiritual duties. Willard then made a rhetorical link between women's spiritual duties and motherhood—another element of her ideology that I suspect the Madison women would have been predisposed to accept.

In fact, Willard argued that the ultimate reason women should have access to higher education was rooted in their roles as mothers. As mothers, women "have the charge of the whole mass of individuals, who are to compose the succeeding generation; during that period of youth, when the pliant mind takes any direction. . . . How important a power is given by this charge! Yet, little do too many of my sex know how, either to appreciate or improve it."[27] It's a complicated idea, in that it could be read as saying that women who are not college educated are inferior mothers. However, it also allows women a path to power and recognition that was otherwise lacking. Arguably, Willard was saying that women deserve far greater respect in society at large for the value their domestic work brings to the nation: the "prosperity (of the nation) will depend on the character of its citizens. The characters of these will be formed by their mothers."[28] She even went so far as to posit that past democracies had failed because they hadn't adequately educated women, leading to a populace of male offspring who were unable to sustain the mental and moral burdens of such a form of government. The fate of the still-young United States, in Willard's estimation, rested on its willingness to accept higher education for women, the mothers of the nation.

In seeing the power of motherhood, Willard was making a case that I imagine the Madison women would have recognized. As I discussed in the chapter on methodology, multiple Appalachian cultures, including my own, stress the importance and potential social power of motherhood, including the ways mothers influence their children's educational goals. Many of the Madison women had children who sought out higher education or became teachers. In one of the most poignant stories I've unearthed about the Madison women, Elizabeth Stockdale reportedly risked her life to run home from a neighbor's farm during Morgan's Raid, refusing the offer of shelter by saying, "I want to die with Mother."[29]

It's a sentiment I understand, personally, culturally, and academically. *Mom* is the root of the emotional and social power structure in many local families. Educationally, too, in my own family: my mama was an insistent bedtime story reader when we were young, and she made sure we had a head start on our letters and numbers before we started school. Despite the fact that she never attended college herself, she knew and used her power as our first teacher.[30] The Madison women, in short, could have been culturally predisposed to accept motherhood as a powerful position, making them particularly receptive to the idea that higher education was therefore not only a right but a duty they owed their future children. More recent research in the field of Appalachian literacy studies shows that mothers and motherhood continue to play a hugely influential role in how children experience education at multiple levels. In *Whistlin' and Crowin' Women of Appalachia*, Katherine Kelleher Sohn shows that many of the women in her college composition classes not only saw their mothers as powerful literacy sponsors but also justified their own attendance at college in terms of serving as role models for their children.[31] The emphasis on motherhood as both the means and gateway to education is an aspect of Willard's ideology that no doubt found fertile ground among the Madison women.

Willard extended the benefit of educating women as future mothers to also allow for women's professional opportunities in at least one field: education. Not only would college-educated women make wiser and better mothers, but they would also by extension be more fitted to the role of teachers in the nation's expanding common school system. Unfortunately, her argument for women as teachers is based on an idea of inherent femininity that many today would question: "That nature designed for our sex the care of children, she has made manifest, by mental, as well as physical indications. She has given us, in a greater degree than men, the gentle arts of insinuation, to soften their minds, and fit them to receive impressions; a greater quickness of invention to vary modes of teaching to different dispositions; and more patience to make repeated efforts."[32] In this view, because women are inherently gentler and more patient, they are naturally the more sensible choice to be classroom teachers. As such, they must themselves be allowed the benefit of higher education.

This argument was being made at a time when women were still the minority of classroom teachers. As a way of according women both educational and financial opportunities, it is laudable. However, the credit I'm able to extend to Willard for this is undercut from a gender equality standpoint by her assertion that women teachers wouldn't need to be paid as much as men. Also, by taking over the classroom, women would free up men for "any of those thousand occupations, from which women are necessarily debarred."[33] Although Willard's address to the legislature arguably provided a pathway for women's greater freedoms, the scope of those freedoms was still extremely limited, a fact that Willard accepted as simply natural and necessary.

Much of Willard's text is a combination of (for the time) radical and (for now) problematic arguments. On one hand, she took umbrage to the idea that women's only education ought to be ornamental, for the purpose of pleasing men. On the other, she argued that a more equal education would not and should not be a threat to men because it would not change women's fundamental natures as "the weaker" and more subservient sex. She pointed out the unfairness of treating women as the more flawed or ignorant sex when they had not been allowed the education needed to give them other options. However, she stopped short of putting women's access to higher education on an entirely equal footing with men through coeducation. Her ideal was for a proliferation of publicly supported women's seminaries that would educate women, separately from men, to fulfill their narrowly defined purposes in society.

Of course, it is unfair to expect modern gender ideologies from a historical figure. Emma Willard was raised in a society that largely saw the higher education of women for *any* purpose as radical and undesirable. To argue for perfect educational and occupational equality would have been hopeless, even if she believed in it. (There is no evidence that she did, and quite a bit of evidence to the contrary.) Even the argument that she made, which positioned women's education as important mostly for the benefit it could give men, was largely unsuccessful at the time. And we cannot say with certainty that the women in Madison's Emma Willard Literary Society agreed with her every idea. However, they were at least familiar with and likely influenced by these ideas—most notably, that the right and responsibility to seek higher education was theirs to claim.

Their positive response to Willard appears not only in the name they chose for their society but also in my sense of what gender politics looked like in that place and time. Motherhood would still have been seen as a woman's primary, and potentially empowering, role in life.[34] However, there was at least a thirty-year gap between the publication of Willard's treatise in 1819 and the time when the Madison women would have been reading it. It's possible that some of Willard's ideas on women's limitations might have been called into question, specifically regarding women's right to participate in public action. The later participation of several Madison women in public advocacy groups such as the Women's Christian Temperance Union certainly raises the question.

The members of Madison's Sigourney Literary Society would have wrestled with similar questions about their roles. Lydia Sigourney was a figure who, like Emma Willard, wrote about women's right to higher education. When we look at Sigourney's pedagogical work as what the members of the literary society read, we are left with a sense of the beliefs and values the Madison women had about literacy, education, and their roles as women in society.

Lydia Sigourney was a far more literary figure than Emma Willard. Whereas Willard's reputation was based largely on her work as an educator and proponent of female higher education, Sigourney was primarily thought of as a poet, albeit one who represented a style of women's literature that male critics often disparaged.[35] (Anyone who has ever heard the term "chick-lit" knows this is still a reality many women authors face.) One possibility is that members chose the Sigourney Literary Society over the Emma Willard Literary Society because their writing preferences were more artistic or literary. However, Lydia Sigourney was not just a poet. She was also a cultural critic whose words had powerful effects on what women were expected or allowed to do in society.[36] As an educator, she left behind two books of her thoughts on teaching, gender roles, and women's education. Therefore, she left us an even clearer sense of her pedagogical ideals than Willard did.

Like Willard, Sigourney's viewpoints combine the progressive and the conservative in ways that today might seem incompatible but for her time were revolutionary. More so even than Willard, Sigourney sought to remove the class divide inherent in access to education, praising most the "children of the log-cottages" whose fight for education could change the course of society.[37] The Madison women, as well as the Madison students as a whole, were exactly those children, and Madison College itself had begun not long before in a log cabin. Sigourney understood the power education had to affect the people's views and abilities, as every interaction one has can influence those around them. How much the better if that influence came from a populace of educated citizens?[38] She also saw a scope for women's greater participation in the field of education at higher levels: "Our grandmothers had only the simple training which suffices for 'household-good.' Our grand-daughters may have an opportunity of becoming professors."[39] As the metaphorical granddaughter of the Madison women, I did.

However, some of Sigourney's other social views are just as problematic as Willard's. Sigourney argues that women should find pleasure and privilege in being the "subordinate" sex, cared for and protected by men.[40] (The racial blinders this opinion required are appalling but not surprising from the viewpoint of a nineteenth-century middle-class white woman.) She also advocated education for the purpose of cultural homogenization, writing that "the influx of foreign population renders it doubly important, that some features of our native character and customs, should be preserved for our descendants."[41] Given that many of Madison's students were the children and grandchildren of immigrants, this point seems particularly pointed—it was their "foreign" ways that Sigourney wanted education to combat. And, in an issue that would come to the foreground during the lifetime of many of the Madison women, neither Sigourney nor Willard believed that women should vote. According to Sigourney, women's influence on the political stage should come through their influence on husbands and sons in the home. Voting was anathema to both Sigourney and Willard because it would take women into the male preserve of the public sphere. Sigourney saw the debates over the "rights of woman," including the right to vote, as dangerous to women's "congenial duties" because it would "[leave] the sweet home guardianship to desolation."[42] I came to find that some of the Madison women did take action on social issues (such as temperance, which as I will discuss in a later chapter, had a feminist element that bled into the suffrage movement), but I haven't seen anything indicating that they fought to gain the vote.[43] Perhaps this evidence has been lost, or perhaps Sigourney influenced their sense of what women's empowerment should, and should not, include.

Regardless, Sigourney's pedagogical ideals can say something about how the Madison women thought about education, specifically in literacy and writing instruction. Again, her ideas strike me as both regressive and sometimes startlingly modern. Like Whately, she believed that writing exercises should be guided by student interests and the genres that mattered to them. For example, she pointed out that women traditionally serve as the dominant household correspondents in the domestic sphere; therefore, she had students practice writing "in the epistolary style" to her—and she answered those letters.[44] This method for addressing subject, genre, and audience (as well as lowering writing anxiety by both personalizing the assignment and decreasing its formality) in her teaching is a far cry from the skill-and-drill methodology that would have dominated much writing instruction then and since. She also encouraged her current and former students to keep journals as a mental exercise for the purpose of recording "the reflections of a mind in search of knowledge and truth."[45] It would be hard to believe that none of the Madison women accepted this advice, though none of those journals, if they survive, have come to light.

On the other hand, she also espoused ideas that make me, as a writing teacher, occasionally cringe. For example, she discouraged her students from taking notes, arguing that this "excuses the memory from its trust."[46] Sigourney even advised against making notes in the margins of textbooks. (This is particularly tragic to me, as I would give anything to have academic notes taken by Madison students.) This clashes with the modern advice given to most first-year college writers: that taking notes is an essential component of active, critical reading and writing.

However, Sigourney does provide a glimpse into what the literary society named for her at Madison would have looked like. Sigourney advocated not only reading works of history and social commentary but also sharing ideas about them and discussing their importance:

> Weekly societies . . . should comprise but few members, and those of somewhat congenial taste and feeling, that no cause of restraint or reserve may impede the action of the mind. Three or four young ladies, with one or two older ones, will be found an agreeable and profitable number. Let the system to be pursued, and the authors to be studied, be a subject of mutual arrangement, and at the stated meeting, let each compress the substance of what she has read during the week, relate the principal events with their chronology, and as far as possible mention what was taking place at the same period of time, in the annals of other nations. Opinions dissenting from those of the historian should be freely given, and the reasons for such variation. . . . If to read, each of the same era or people, produces monotony, the history of different nations may be studied, or one can pursue a course of biography, another of mental philosophy, the natural sciences, or theology, and thus vary the mental banquet. From this partnership in knowledge, great increase of intellectual wealth will be derived.[47]

Given the number of women attending Madison, it's unlikely that the society was as small as Sigourney recommends. However, other elements of Sigourney's advice could easily have been followed, ideas that were revolutionary for women's education. She encouraged students in a literary society to form a community and operate via mutual consent. She also encouraged them to talk back to (most likely male) authority figures by questioning the authors they read. Additionally, she encouraged them to reach beyond the narrow limits of accepted "feminine" reading material, seeking out and comparing viewpoints on history from multiple perspectives and nationalities. These are actions I require from my students today for their research writing; to know that my academic foremothers in my own community were also taking up such activities is a feeling I'm hard-pressed to describe.

I am both elated to discover the Willard and Sigourney Literary Societies and, on reflection, surprised that I would be. Knowing that these women were reading and discussing what can be called, at least in some ways, early feminist texts, is on one level mind blowing, given how new the women's movement was at that time. However, I also see why Willard and Sigourney would have appealed to my Madison foremothers because I can still see elements of their philosophy in Appalachian culture. I would argue that the belief in the importance and power of motherhood—and the demand that others respect it—is a form of feminism that still flourishes locally, but it receives little recognition in wider feminist philosophy today. Willard and Sigourney encouraged women to see higher education and the intellectual benefits it afforded as intersecting with maternal power. It gave them the right to demand education on a par with that of men and it provided an ideological backing on which to make those demands. The Madison women were fully aware that their gender was more widely perceived as an intellectual deficit. This is demonstrated by one of the Sigourney Literary Society's public exhibitions in 1855. According to the event flyer, two members debated the question: "Are the mental abilities of males superior to those of females?"[48] Although the nature of the event—a debate—necessitated that one of the members, Maggie Hyatt, argued in the affirmative, the very fact that she was in college and a member of a literary society named for Lydia Sigourney indicates she did not, in fact, agree that they were. However, in knowing that such as question was a matter of debate in society and choosing to take the reins of the argument into their own hands, the Madison women were demonstrating an intellectual agency that many would have denied them.

On that note, while it's significant that the societies were named as they were, I also find it very significant to consider the names that were *not* chosen, the feminist voices that were not honored in these selections. For example, Margaret Fuller's *Woman in the Nineteenth Century* was published in 1843, only ten years prior to the Madison women's entrance into higher education. However, its ideology advocated a breakdown of the separate spheres ideal, encouraging women to be self-sufficient independent of men and of the social conventions of being wives and mothers. This, I suspect, was a step too far; it doesn't surprise me that there wasn't a Margaret Fuller Society or a Mary Wollstonecraft Society. One need only look to the number of women, even former Madison students, who don't even have their maiden names on their gravestones—who are very often described only as the "wife of" their husbands—to see that marriage still had a powerful influence on local women's identities. This isn't to say that none of the Madison women would have read or even agreed with these more radical works. (In fact, quite a few Madison women remained single, a state Margaret Fuller advocated. They were also capable of independence; Ester Stockdale is recorded in the 1860 census supporting herself independently as a "farmer gal.") I simply have no evidence whether they did or did not embrace the ideas of the radical feminists of their time—although I can't tell you how delighted I would be if one or both of their literary societies had extensively read early feminist theory. Given that Sigourney advised these societies to read and discuss the ideas circulating in the world, perhaps they did.

Ultimately, what I perceive in the Madison women's adoption of Willard and Sigourney is a mix of radicalism and conservatism that is still familiar to me, if not entirely explicable. Willard and Sigourney demanded educational access for women and a respect for their power as mothers, but neither believed that women should vote or take part in public affairs, activities would have taken them outside the domestic sphere. Even today, in the women around me I see strength, outspokenness, skill, and ability . . . but little in the way of a discernable feminist movement or an enculturated enthusiasm for higher education. I'm not at all surprised that the Madison women would have fought for and taken what they believed was their right; I am just surprised that what they wanted was college. And the fact that I am so surprised by that, by the existence of the Madison women at all, makes me deeply sad.

Small Stories, Part 4

Education, both formal and informal, influenced the choices that Madison's students (and by extension their descendants) made in their personal and professional lives.

Cordelia Downard

In her 1996 commencement address to Wellesley College, Nora Ephron explained that in her own graduating class of 1962, "We weren't meant to have futures, we were meant to marry them. . . . If you wanted to be an architect, you married an architect."[1] Given that Ephron, like the Madison women, was living in a time before the second wave of feminism hit its stride, the same would have been true for them. I wonder how much this affected their marital choices—did those who married professional men do so in the hopes of sharing in their careers, careers that were not open to them as women?

Cordelia Downard may have been such a woman. Born in 1831 to immigrant farmers Elizabeth and Daniel, she married fellow Madison alumnus Christopher Craig Smith in 1855. Together, Cordelia and Christopher, a physician, went west, raising a family in Iowa. That Cordelia appreciated the classical elements of the education she received at Madison, which would have included instruction in Latin and Greek, might be perceived in her children's names: Austia Valora, Ralph Xenophon, and Tryphena Smith. (Another daughter, Belle, born in 1862, was given the middle name Lincoln; given the timing, this seems like a political statement of support for President Abraham Lincoln.) Cordelia's children became teachers and, in the case of Ralph Xenophon, another doctor.

Cordelia is another example of a Madison woman choosing to marry a Madison man, and the Madison man in question was certainly proud of his educational roots. *The History of Mercer and Henderson Counties* outlines Christopher's educational history as including first the local common school, followed by a focus on mathematics and Latin at Madison College.[2] He learned medicine through apprenticeships with local doctors (a common means of medical training at the time), supplemented with medical lectures in Cleveland. While he began his practice in Antrim, he and Cordelia later moved to Illinois, and then to Iowa. The book notes that Christopher was such a successful doctor that he suffered from overwork. Despite this, he treated Civil War veterans at no charge.

How much involvement Cordelia had in Christopher's medical practice is unknown, but given that doctors often practiced in their own homes and that wives often served as helpmates for their husbands' professions at the time, it's very possible that Cordelia practiced some medicine herself. (There are cases of this happening among the Madison families, specifically the Brashears and the Gastons.) At the very least, she knew she was marrying a husband in the profession, and he knew he was marrying a woman whose college education rivaled his own.

Isabell "Bell" Coulter

Bell Coulter is one of the few Madison women who traveled from outside the county to attend the college, a fact that, coupled with other aspects of her family's educational history, emphasizes how valued education could be by women, men, and even families at this time.

Bell was born around 1836, the child of Jane and Robert, a cooper. Her family's most illustrious member was her brother, Thomas B. Coulter, who attended a neighboring Appalachian (and also now disappeared) school, Hopedale College, taught school for eight years, and was elected to local offices before capping his career with election to the Ohio Senate. Bell's educational choice of Madison College is a bit of a mystery. She lists her home address in the Madison catalogue as Hopedale, in Harrison County, where her brother was attending college. While Hopedale also became an early college to offer admission to women, it is unclear whether the school was coeducational at the time Bell would have sought to attend. If it wasn't, then her decision to travel to Antrim makes more sense, though even this emphasizes how much she must have wanted what a Madison education could provide. If Hopedale was already admitting women, the reason for her choice of Madison is murkier. Her choice is made even more mysterious by the fact that her family's main residence was in Jefferson County, where the 1850 and 1860 censuses show the family was based. Jefferson County was home to the Steubenville Ladies Seminary, which based on surviving catalogues offered a similar education to that at Madison. It also graduated ambitious women, counting among its alumni missionary Samantha Knox Condit, economist and social reformer Virginia Penny, and newspaper editor Eva Griffith Thompson. (The 1860 census has Bell's sisters Nancy and Margaret, ages 21 and 19 respectively, marked as attending school within the last year. Given their ages and the fact that they were living at home, it seems likely they were attending the Steubenville Female Seminary.) Perhaps her choice speaks to Madison's praiseworthy reputation—or maybe even more tantalizing, that she was for some reason not accepted at these other institutions.

Ultimately, however, we can see a family that valued education, with siblings spread out across three regional college institutions. There is very little surviving record of Bell, Nancy, or Margaret, except that Bell died young (in 1856) and that Nancy married and had children. We do know from Bell's gravestone that her loss mattered to her family. Her gravestone shows an epitaph (which many stones at that time did not have), that reads:

> *Thou hast left us,*
> *here thy loss we deeply feel.*
> *But tis God that hath bereft us,*
> *He can all our sorrows heal.*

This seems to have been a conventional epitaph (I've found it on multiple graves in different locations), but the sentiment conveyed is that of deep grief. As with Sarah McKittrick, her family didn't scorn her for her educational interests, interests shared by multiple siblings. In trying to gauge attitudes toward education at this time, especially for women, this is particularly useful and heartening to know.

However, as with many Madison students, I've found the paper trail that excludes them as individuals runs more distinctly through their male relatives. In this way, her brother Thomas Benton Coulter gives us a window on how education and its potential links to self-determination emerged in the generations that came after Bell's. *The History of Belmont and Jefferson Counties*, written in 1880 by J. A. Caldwell, includes a short biographical sketch of Thomas, including the description of his daughter (Bell's niece, Cora) as "an interesting girl"—a description that could serve as a euphemism for a bluestocking, or a so-called overly intelligent/educated woman. I don't know for certain whether this was the case here, but her daughter Sara's experience shows that it might well have been.

Sara, Bell Coulter's grand-niece, demonstrates that the family's social elevation—which began with Thomas's political career—continued after him. His grand-daughter was educated at Miss Bennett's School for Girls (also known as Bennett College) in Millbrook, New York, where many students hailed from upper-class families. She made an advantageous marriage to the wealthy Clifford Heinz (of the ketchup Heinzes). However, what interests me is not the social advantages her family's educational and political success gave her, but how it shaped how she valued education. In 1929, Sara sued for divorce, something that was rare for the time, especially when a woman brought the suit. More amazingly, in 1933 she sued for custody of their children (mothers were not necessarily favored in custody decisions, especially when the father was the source of money and influence between the two parents). Her reason for seeking full custody: her ex-husband, she asserted, was not being responsible about the children's education. According to a newspaper clipping posted on Ancestry.com, Clifford Heinz moved the children about from school to school, damaging their learning experiences. "It is unwise for them to change schools so frequently," Sara asserted in her petition.[3] Amazingly, she won.

Sadly, we cannot know exactly what Bell thought about her education, why she sought it and what it meant for her. Still, we can once again see an example of a family that began in Appalachia valuing higher education and putting it to use in their lives, beginning a ripple effect for their children.

Mollie and Elma Gaston

Sisters Mollie (Mary) and Elma Gaston are in the unique position of having not descendants but rather an ancestor whose documented history tell us something about what education meant and how it was gained in their community.

Mollie and Elma were born to Drusilla and Matthew Gaston, a lawyer. Both eventually married professional men—Mollie to banker Charles Randall, and Elma to real estate agent Andrew McLaughlin. Their futures diverged, taking Elma to Nebraska and Mollie to Connecticut. Both, however, were active in local events during their time in Guernsey County, organizing celebrations for returning Union soldiers as well as church bazaars.

However, perhaps more interesting than Mollie and Elma is their grandmother, Rachel Perry Gaston. Rachel was a practicing physician in neighboring

Belmont County forty years before the first woman became a licensed physician in the United States.

Born in 1773 in Maryland, Rachel Perry moved with her parents to Belmont County, where she married Dr. Alexander Gaston in 1801. She trained in medicine alongside her husband, eventually beginning to practice in her own name. She made house calls on horseback up to thirty miles from her home to physic the ill and injured in rural Appalachian Ohio.[4]

Rachel illustrates an interesting dynamic, one that I think deserves emphasis. She overcame the limits imposed on her gender by claiming her identity as a physician, not just the wife of one, even when that descriptor was not accepted in the medical establishment. She didn't have formal schooling—the first woman to graduate from a formal medical school was Elizabeth Blackwell in 1849, after a long fight for acceptance. Regardless, Rachel became a smart, skilled, capable woman whose life shows that learning doesn't start or stop at the classroom door. Those who did not have access to formal education were not necessarily lacking in intelligence or ability. I believe in the power of the classroom to strengthen our voices and communities, but formal education is not, and never has been, the *only* factor for achieving this in Appalachia. Rachel's descendants used their voices to claim a right to higher education, a right most women in the United States at that time did not have, just as their grandmother claimed a profession that much of the country wouldn't have deemed possible for a woman.

CHAPTER 5

Higher Ideals

*The Madison Women
and Social Action*

———

Appalachian Ohio may seem an unlikely place to have been a hub of higher education. It was, and still is, largely rural. Many of its residents made their living as farmers in the last decades before the national demise of the family farm or in trades such as blacksmithing that required training but not formal schooling. Despite the occupational profile of the region, many students, including women, took advantage of the access to higher education provided to them by colleges like Madison. Education and gender equality are two traits that are very rarely correlated with Appalachia in the wider U.S. imagination. I've formed two theories about what might have influenced these educational decisions, one related to the cultural politics of the local immigrant population and another to the gender politics that I still see in local culture. What intrigues me just as much, however, is the interrelated question of what Madison's students, especially the women, did with their learning. Once they had received their college education and literacy training, what did these women turn their attention to, and why? Given that few forms of employment required college, it's worth investigating how education affected their lives and outlooks.

It seems to me that the reasons why the colleges existed are inextricable from the question of why so many students in this region attended them and what they expected their education to do for them. Something must have been at play in their regional cultures that made these options seem useful or even possible. In one sense, the proliferation of higher educational institutions in this region is explainable when we consider the identities of the people who were living there at the time. While the Scotch-Irish were not the only local population ("Appalachian" and "Scotch-Irish" shouldn't be taken as the same thing), they were a sizeable one, as demonstrated by census records for the region throughout the nineteenth century. Presbyterianism was a large factor in how this population identified themselves and their values. Born as a form of Scottish Calvinism, the Presbyterian church came to see education and religion as deeply and explicitly linked. This does not necessarily make it unique among protestant faiths, but Presbyterianism championed the importance of higher education among the faithful, specifically for those considering careers in the church. In reference to the Scotch-Irish populations that migrated through Pennsylvania and into Ohio (eventually founding Franklin, Madison, and Muskingum Colleges), William Fisk describes: "Despite the privations of their origins, they so venerated an educated ministry that in Pennsylvania they founded colleges and academies with high priority for training ministers."[1] Veneration for education would indeed have been necessary to explain why a people who lacked affluence or social capital, living on the frontiers of their adopted country, would have put so much effort into founding the many schools that trailed in their wake.

However, it cannot only be prospective clergy who felt this veneration. Otherwise, how can we explain the many students who attended these colleges and seminaries who did *not* go into the ministry? This may be linked to the cultural context many of the Madison families had emigrated from. According to historian Andrew Holmes, the "the expansion of secular and denominational higher education was a prominent feature of Irish society" during the years preceding their emigrations.[2] Another more distant but possible cultural factor that could explain the region's high interest in education in the mid-nineteenth century may be rooted in even older ideologies imported by the Scotch-Irish. Histories of the United States have long been rooted in its historical connections with England, while histories of Britain have long focused on England's Anglo-Norman heritage. However, interest in Celtic history has been increasing in recent decades, giving us a better sense of the cultural forces in operation in Britain's "Celtic fringe," which includes Scotland and Ireland. Authors such as Katharine Scherman, Peter Berresford Ellis, and Thomas Cahill have shown that an interest in education and scholarship flourished in this region prior to English colonization. Cahill's popular book *How the Irish Saved Civilization* argues that this interest was essential in preserving the academic legacies of the Greco-Roman world, even as the rest of Europe largely neglected them. While there is a great deal of room to question the pervasive myth of the so-called Dark Ages as well as the positives and negatives of Greco-Roman cultural imperialism, the currently relevant point is that for a time the peoples of the Celtic fringe embraced and promulgated literacy and scholarship. As Cahill states of the medieval Irish, "Wherever they went the Irish brought with them their books. . . . Wherever they went they brought their love of learning."[3] Cahill notes that threads of this fascination with education, literacy, books, history, and writing continued to exist and intermingle in the Irish cultural milieu throughout the centuries.[4] Maybe the Scotch-Irish immigrants who settled in northern Appalachia possessed a cultural value for learning that was older than even they knew. If so, that would make the more recent barriers constructed between Appalachian cultures and formal education all the sadder.

However, gender is also at issue in the question of why education proliferated in Appalachia. This question is especially pointed when we ask why women specifically were seeking higher education, to the degree that many seminaries and institutions were founded in this region specifically to educate them. My suspicion is that regional gender politics intersected with wider cultural ideologies about women's roles in a particularly advantageous way. Women in Appalachian regions traditionally have taken part in the seemingly "masculine" world of physical labor, as multigender labor was necessary for the functioning of regional economies. Few farms would have survived without hard work on the part of both men and women. Even the coal industry has traditionally included women—although not always without controversy.[5] In my experience of the region, women's participation in activities such as hunting, sports, and farming are still not considered unfeminine—in fact, it's admirable. It isn't a great leap to suppose that local women could have benefited from this looser definition of feminine behavior by embracing academic interests, although such interests were gendered masculine in other places. Whether academia was ever fully gendered as a masculine activity here is debatable; it's certainly feminized today.[6] Combine a greater flexibility in defining "feminine" behavior/ interests with the increasing assertion, by figures such as Emma Willard and Lydia Sigourney, that higher education benefited women as future mothers, and it becomes easier to see why women found greater access to higher education locally than they might have had in other parts of the country, at least for a time.

The idea that women could use their education as better mothers assumes that these students sought a practical utility for their education, ways they could put the skills they gained to use. To a degree, they did this, not only via motherhood but also via teaching for some, religion for others, and even public participation in social issues such as temperance and benevolence. They also took active roles in maintaining Madison's alumni reunions through the rest of the century. However, there is another explanation of what the Madison women might have gained from higher education, or why they sought it in the first place: simply because they liked it.

Women embracing higher education in part or even purely for pleasure is to this day somewhat taboo, not only in Appalachia but much more widely. The specter of education as self-indulgent, divorced from reality, perhaps even ruinous for women whose energies are meant to be directed elsewhere is one that has haunted both U.S. and British society for centuries. I am, however, deeply struck by something Thomas Cahill noted about early Irish attitudes toward literacy: "The Irish received literacy in their own way, as something to play with."[7] It makes me wonder if an element of enjoyment was still present in how the Madison students encountered education. This idea could perhaps help explain the high numbers of students in attendance—since future employment alone can't have been the primary reason, especially for the women. (Nor could preparation for future motherhood, as not all of the women married—a prerequisite at the time for socially acceptable reproduction.) Even Ohio University's Maggie Boyd, whose encounters with college writing instruction made her feel so inadequate, was sorry to be nearing graduation: "I cannot help feeling sad to think this is my last year at college. Many a pleasant hour have I spent within [the college's] walls."[8] Pleasure in higher education was real for some, even if it was a motive that risked censure.

Women in both the United States and Britain were discouraged from formal education in a variety of ways, and those who acquired it felt pressure to defend their access in moral terms. Women's education could be accepted only if they had acquired it for utilitarian purposes, specifically for the benefit of others. There are examples of early British women, such as Bathsua Makin and Mary Astell, citing pleasure as a motive for women's access to education.[9] However, by the nineteenth century in the United States, defenses of women's education were focused almost entirely on the benefit it could bring to others. (Recall, for example, Emma Willard's argument that women should be educated because this benefited their sons and therefore the republic.) Piercing the otherwise masculine preserve of higher education simply for the fun of it wasn't good enough. It seems likely, though, that for women to have attended Madison in such high numbers without an overt economic benefit, at least some must have found learning enjoyable for its own sake, even if they felt compelled to claim it was all for the benefit of their future sons.[10]

My point is that the women attending Madison College and other regional colleges in the area must have benefited from it in multiple ways, including personally. It's inconceivable that so many women sought higher education without finding at least some pleasure in the process. As someone who also enjoyed my college experience, this seems entirely plausible. This is a point that I'd like to see more widely accepted locally, especially today: the process of higher education can, even should, be exciting. Learning, at its root, is about discovery of both the self and the wider world. An acceptance of (even an insistence on) this in the education we receive can do a lot to combat the general sense that college is something to suffer through if you must in order to get a good job.

However, many of these women did find a practical purpose for their education, albeit not in the ways we recognize today. Some became teachers, true—but most don't seem to have gained any professional advantage from higher education. Others saw to the education of their children, just as Emma Willard advised. Still others found an altruistic outlet for their energies through activism and community service.

What Do We Do with All This Learning?

Samuel Findley did not believe in student activism. In his "First Annual Report of the Philomathean Literary Institute" in 1838, he specified that

> the appropriate business of youth is the cultivation of their minds, and the acquisition of useful knowledge preparatory to the activities of subsequent life. That it does not become them in this stage of life to regard themselves, as in duty bound, to be the censors and enlighteners of public sentiment—that in attempting this, their minds will inevitably be diverted, and lose a relish for retired and tranquil study—that their interest in intellectual pursuits will thereby suffer injurious diminution—and that by a premature appearance in the ranks of reformers, they will impose upon their future influence a most embarrassing interdict.[11]

Findley seemed to recognize that something about college can make students want to become politically and socially active. However, in his perspective, they lacked the understanding and knowledge to do so wisely and successfully, at least while still students. This did not, however, stop his students from becoming activists later in life, as Findley argued they should. In fact, at least for some, social activism became an outlet for their talents that their limited professional opportunities could not provide.

Madison College thrived in a time before college education was required for many jobs. Several Madison graduates became teachers, doctors, or lawyers. However, these professions required examination or apprenticeship rather than, strictly speaking, a college degree. In fact, after graduation, many Madison students simply went back to work on the farms they'd been raised on. So why did they go to college at all? For the women, the question is even more distinct. They wouldn't have needed college to be teachers in the common schools at that time, and many married after leaving Madison, which meant that they wouldn't have been allowed to teach even if they had wanted to. So, if they didn't apply their education to professional work, in what ways did these students take their education beyond the classroom, into their communities and the wider world?

It is a step too far to say that formal education made these women what we might call feminists or that education alone opened them up to greater freedoms and gave them a better sense of their own voices. As has been shown, women in Guernsey County, and in Appalachia as a whole, had been insisting on their right to speak out and affect change long before Madison College existed. (I am reminded here again of the immigrant women who named Guernsey County after their home island, insisting that they would subject themselves and their children to no further wandering.) In fact, it is possible that in some ways the college education the Madison women received actually limited their sense of their rights and freedoms. While Emma Willard and Lydia Sigourney were strong proponents of higher education, they were also firm proponents of women's "proper" roles in the home, reinforcing the boundaries of acceptable behavior for women in society.

Propriety was a central preoccupation for Samuel Findley. For all the remembrances of his kindness, he also had a rigid sense of Christian behavior that strictly limited activities such as music and dancing. (Wolfe's Guernsey County history recounts how he opposed the introduction of organs into church services.) The 1854 Madison catalogue specified that women boarding at the college would be strictly supervised, including during their study and recreation, and that their "moral and religious instruction" would be given "special regard."[12] Findley drew a sharp line between the norms of moral, Christian behavior and the freedoms of recreation and self-expression. This division was one that not all local women recognized. In an interview published in the county newspaper in 1905, Susan Stage Masters, who was aged over one hundred, vividly recalled her years as a young woman in Antrim. She said, "I remember working all day many a time with my spinning wheel and then going five or ten miles to a neighbor's house where we would dance all night. . . . We had the most fun in the world in those days."[13] Susan, it appears, never attended college, which was probably a good thing from her perspective. I'm not sure Emma Willard, Lydia Sigourney, or Samuel Findley would have approve of their students dancing all night . . . or possibly dancing at all.[14]

I know plenty of women like Susan who wouldn't have cared about Willard, Sigourney, or Findley's thoughts on the matter. While it's likely that the women who chose to be educated at Findley's college were at least somewhat susceptible to his ideologies, the evidence does not show that these ideals of feminine propriety silenced them. The nature of what they learned at Madison College, especially in the realm of current affairs and argumentative rhetoric, made it more tempting than ever for Madison women to actively engage with community and national issues.

The correlation between higher education and public activism is fairly common, even in Appalachia. Educators such as Katherine Kelleher Sohn have shown that women can and do use their experiences in college to strengthen the power of their own voice and expand their sense of the possible ways of using it. However, without first-hand testimonies from the Madison women, I have had to look for other evidence about whether or how they used their voices in their post-college lives. The short answer is that many of them did, through contributions to their churches and communities and even to national debates—activities that required them to step, even just a little, beyond women's silent spheres.

A case in point: an 1863 article in a county newspaper describes the formation of the Antrim Women's Benevolent Association, whose goal was to collect and send clothing and educational materials to both Union soldiers and those recently freed from slavery. Many of the members were Madison students (including the corresponding secretary, Miss A. A. Lorimer) or relatives of Madison women (Mrs. Rebecca [Lindsay] Andrews, Executive Committee member and the older sister of student Martha Lindsay) who may have attended Madison but for whom records no longer exist.[15] This tells me that women attending Madison, as well as their families, were interested in progressive causes, in this case organizing donations of clothing, books, and paper that "may be of use to the freedmen." It also tells me that they were capable of a sophisticated degree of organization in order to make these aims possible. But what it tells me most of all is that local women were working together to act on a social issue that had implications far beyond the domestic sphere.

This was a time when many women were seeking for ways to have a more discernable impact on society outside the home, questioning the limitations of the "separate spheres" ideology. This questioning correlates with higher numbers of women receiving formal education in literacy and rhetoric. These subjects by their nature intersect with voice, in the sense that they encourage students to discover, hone, and practice writing and disseminating their ideas. Whether they were meant to or not, the Madison women felt this pull. In other words, they wanted their education to *do something*, even if that something did not always lead to a profession. And the more women began to push at the boundaries of their prescribed role, the more women followed them.[16]

Some of the Madison women did channel these energies into teaching, whether for a shorter time (like Sarah Owens) or as lifelong careers (like Violet Scott). Some, such as Mary Sleeth, also played a role in establishing an Antrim Teacher's Institute, which provided advanced training for public schoolteachers when Madison College was no longer available to do so. (They would likely have been familiar with the concept of teachers' institutes through the advocacy of Emma Willard.) Professional teaching, specifically in the burgeoning common schools, became an increasingly viable option for educated women as the profession came to be seen as increasingly feminine—a move that Emma Willard, among others, championed. However, women were forced to choose between this potential career and marriage, as they were expected to take on full-time homemaking when they married. This expectation was so entrenched that few schools would have allowed a married woman to continue teaching even if she wished to. However, one option was available to married women with a passion for education: voluntary Sunday school teaching.

Almost since its inception in the late 1700s, Sunday school teaching was more open to women and was possibly the first option many women had for playing a formal role in society outside the family circle. However, the effects of Sunday school ran deeper than offering an opportunity for teaching: it was often also students' first experience of being educated outside the home. Especially in the early 1800s before common schools proliferated, Sunday schools were a venue of literacy instruction for many who were excluded from formal schooling because of their gender or race.[17] By the latter half of the century, when secular schools were more widely available, the mission of most Sunday schools was less focused on secular literacy. However, as Anne Boylan points out, "education consists of more than learning to read; it encompasses all the means through which a culture transmits its standards and values."[18] In this sense, the influence of Sunday schools on the wider culture is hard to overestimate. As this form of schooling was primarily provided by women, this placed women's voices in a central position.

While Sunday school learning and teaching may have empowered women, it was still a fundamentally patriarchal institution. Boylan describes an anecdote used in the nineteenth century to advocate the benefits of Sunday school in which "an obstinately disobedient daughter" became "a useful and obedient child" through attending.[19] The society she was learning to be useful and obedient to was extremely patriarchal and misogynistic—one that, on the whole, would not have encouraged that formerly "obstinately disobedient" girl to seek out an education. It's debatable how positively many of us today might view stories like this. I worry for the girls who are taught to be entirely useful and obedient to a society that demeans them.

However, that does not necessarily negate the fact that Sunday schools provided a forum in which literate women could use their education meaningfully in society. Sunday school teachers also strengthened community ties and organized community resources such as small-scale libraries. More broadly, becoming Sunday school teachers allowed them to demonstrate expertise on religious matters while occupying positions of authority—albeit ones that were tightly controlled by the oversight of male church office holders.

Madison College's women students and their daughters and nieces became active members of their church communities. And some, such as Jennie Bell, became Sunday school teachers. They would have encountered the central dilemma: in order to play this expanded role in society, they had to accept what Boylan describes as the "evangelical ideal of womanhood [that] restricted the autonomy and independence of women teachers and limited their ability to challenge nineteenth-century gender-role prescriptions."[20] This is deeply reminiscent of the dichotomies Madison students encountered through Emma Willard and Lydia Sigourney, two women who became, through their writing, public authorities on women's right to education but with the provision that education should keep them out of the public eye and dedicated to the home. Ultimately though perhaps unintentionally, educational forums such as Sunday school teaching offered women critical stepping-stones into the public sphere.

Where those stepping-stones led for many was into the temperance movement. This is the arena more of the Madison women entered, an arena that would have provided an outlet for their skills and allowed them to champion women's rights in socially acceptable ways.

Temperance is one of the most underrated social movements in U.S. history. If thought of at all, it's likely perceived today as a group of uptight killjoys who wanted to take everyone's booze—and thereby their fun—away. Few people realize how temperance served as an early women's movement and a way for women to seize an opportunity to exercise their voice on public issues.

There are multiple factors that led to women's involvement in temperance being considered (mostly) socially acceptable, despite the ways in which it moved them into the public sphere. One was the increasing sense of women as the nation's moral arbiters. This premise had been utilized by women for some time in order to allow them to expand the domestic sphere. If women were to be the maternal angels of the house, then that mandate should also allow them to work toward the greater domestic comfort of others. That position required women to speak out about issues such as domestic violence, poverty, and access to education. This concept is perhaps most remembered through the work of Jane Addams and the settlement house movement, which essentially birthed the profession of social work among women in the late nineteenth century. Similarly, temperance allowed women to use the ideals of the domestic sphere to champion a public cause.

At its inception, temperance as a social movement was headed primarily by men and promoted abstention from alcohol and/or making alcohol illegal. Likewise, temperance was promoted at Madison College from a religious perspective by various school presidents, including both the Samuel Findleys and William Lorimer. However, several of Madison's women students entered the movement in a way that reflected a greater concern for the rights and protection of women in particular as members of the Woman's Christian Temperance Union (WCTU). This organization, as the name would suggest, focused on women's participation and voices, ultimately tying the temperance movement to a burgeoning call for women's rights.

What the Madison women's participation in the temperance movement might mean for our understanding of them requires a closer look at how temperance intersected with the issues facing women at that time. Whereas today the suffrage movement is seen as the root of American feminism, women in the temperance movement are more likely to be seen as conservative, perhaps even "complicit in their own oppression," a charge Carol Mattingly opposes in her book *Well-Tempered Women: Nineteenth Century Temperance Rhetoric*.[21] On the contrary, Mattingly sees these women as "strong, sensible . . . recogniz[ing] the real circumstances of their existence and str[iving], pragmatically, to improve life for themselves and for others."[22] The "circumstances of their existence," as women whose lives and livelihoods were controlled by men, lay at the heart of how temperance came to overlap with a call for increased women's rights.

In the nineteenth century, men were proportionally more likely to become alcoholics than women, and given the legal disadvantages married women faced, this could have catastrophic consequences. Women who married found that their personal property, incomes, physical persons, and children became the legal property of their husbands. They had few if any legal protections from abuse or theft by their husbands, and few if any ways to support their children should they attempt to leave a marriage—that is, if the husband didn't insist on keeping the children, as fathers were heavily favored in custody disputes. (These laws began to change in the later nineteenth century, largely due to women's activism.) Because men who drank heavily were more likely to be abusive and to spend their income on alcohol rather than on family needs, temperance took on the mantle of protecting women and their children. Activist women were able to use this opening to speak out about both the evils of alcohol and the dangers facing women at that time. And as women were supposed to focus their energies and attentions on the home and family, they were able to position their arguments as extensions of this role in a way that allowed them a wider social role than was available to women who fought for other issues, such as suffrage. They were speaking out to protect the domestic sphere.

This approach required women to break new rhetorical ground, using the private sphere to establish their authority while acting in the public sphere. Mattingly points out that they "presented arguments in comfortable, familiar language that made both women and men amenable to new ideas and evidence. . . . The great strength of temperance leaders was their ability to meld a progressive message with a rhetorical presentation and image comfortable to a large number of women and men."[23] An address at the Woman's Temperance Convention illustrated these ideas: "You who, clothed in the garb of womanhood, excuse yourselves from any participation in opposing the vice of drunkenness, under the plea of sacrifice of female delicacy, or of departure from your proper sphere, look for a moment at the condition of the drunkard's wife and children, and the nobler impulses of your nature will certainly prompt you to some effort to rescue and sustain female delicacy in the degraded home of the drunkard."[24] We can see from this excerpt that the speaker was using the idea of the domestic sphere as a prompt rather than a deterrent to public action. Likewise, this piece makes its argument against the dangers of drunkenness not by confronting the drunkard husband but rather by relating the pitiable state of his family to an audience of other women. In essence, the speaker is not engaging in a direct public denunciation of a man, which would certainly have been seen as threatening and dangerous from the mouth of a woman, but rather as a scolding of other women who had not yet stepped forward to take action. By doing this and by, at least on the surface, accepting the premise of separate spheres, it is easy to see how temperance women might be judged today as unprogressive. However, as Mattingly argues, it is too simplistic to divide women of the nineteenth century into the binary labels of conservative or progressive. Instead, they were complex, rhetorically skilled activists who opened the doors to greater rights for women than they had yet experienced in this country. Beyond their goal of making alcohol illegal, they also sought to raise the legal age of consent for girls and advance the cause of women's suffrage, whether or not this was an explicit goal. While not all members of the WCTU pushed for suffrage, some certainly did, and it is arguable that the sight of women taking public action through temperance prompted women to take organized action for suffrage. It showed, in essence, what was possible.

Many participants in the WCTU came to the organization without the benefit of rhetorical training or higher education. In fact, the WCTU served as something of a boot camp in training members in these skills. However, women with previous experience in effective rhetoric would have been especially welcomed in the organization. For example, a nineteenth-century WCTU pamphlet specifically encouraged the involvement of women with "a skillful pen."[25] The Madison women were undoubtedly useful in this respect.

In fact, their connections with the WCTU were regional as well as ideological. The WCTU was actually founded in Appalachian Ohio (in Highland County) in 1873 under the leadership of Annie Wittenmyer, a former female seminary student who developed a Sunday school specifically for low-income students. (I knew none of this prior to researching this chapter. Given the many years I've researched regional history, this is a sad statement about how much of that history has been forgotten.) The movement Annie Wittenmyer founded quickly took on national and international prominence.

Women from this region continued to take part, as I've learned in my investigations of the Madison women, including Jennie (Milligan) Moore, Eliza (McCulley) Ralston, and Violet Scott, who were active members of the local WCTU. Membership allowed them to utilize their abilities in ways they wouldn't necessarily have found elsewhere: Violet in teaching public speaking through the Demorest Contests and Jennie as a historian and writer. For example, Jennie is recorded in a newspaper article in 1903 as having written a resolution of respect to honor a member who had recently died, and in 1904 it was noted that she had written and presented a history of the Guernsey County WCTU at a meeting. (What I wouldn't give for this history to have turned up in an archive!) While I don't know precisely how Jennie, Eliza, or Violet translated their rhetorical education into expression with the WCTU, an article in the *Jeffersonian* regarding the group indicates that it transgressed Willard and Sigourney's prohibitions against women and public discourse: "True they cannot vote, but they cannot be cajoled, bullied into silence or brought to desert a cause when the crucial moment arrives."[26]

Viola Romans

Jennie is also recorded as leading the devotionals at a WCTU meeting in 1901, which was presided over by Viola Romans. I would like to digress here for a moment to discuss this brilliant, vibrant, and entirely too-forgotten woman in our Appalachian history. She was born Viola Doudna in Quaker City, another small hamlet in Guernsey County about ten miles away from Antrim, in 1863. She was approximately a generation younger than the Madison women, who were in their later years during their recorded participation with the WCTU. Because of this, attendance at Madison College was no longer an option when Viola came of age. However, she did what some of the daughters of the Madison women did and chose the next closest option: she attended Muskingum College, later becoming a professor of public speaking on their faculty at a time when women professors were very much a minority, especially those teaching public speaking.

Beyond her teaching, Viola became active in local chapters of the WCTU. However, her political work did not stop there. She was elected to the Ohio House of Representatives in 1924 as a representative of Franklin County, where she was living at the time, becoming the first woman in that county to do so (and one of the first women to serve in the Ohio House). Her biographical page on the Ohio Statehouse website points out: "Like many of the first woman legislators of her time, she was often asked about the significance of her views of women occupying a traditionally male occupation. In a 1925 speech, she stated, 'In speaking about newness of women in politics I have never understood a time when women were not active. . . . Women have blazed paths, and led the way toward higher ideals, and larger liberties, and great achievements.' She believed that women had long proven their worth in society and that more doors needed to be opened for women's full potential to be realized."[27] This tells me a great deal not only about her but about her experience growing up in Appalachian Ohio. In her experience, women were *already* active, *already* vocal, and *already* standing up for what they saw as their rights. Some of these women she described were Madison College's former students—women who would have been precisely the right age to influence her journey through the ranks of the WCTU. However, certainly not all the women Romans described would have attended college—many were simply reared and raised as fellow Appalachians. In her experience of gender in Appalachian Ohio, women were already speaking up. They just needed more opportunities to act on their potential—opportunities that the WCTU was providing.

I don't know to what degree Viola Romans would credit higher education with providing her the opportunities she found or what effect she would say it had on her voice as a politically active woman. However, given that a great deal of her career was spent in academia, my sense is that she certainly didn't feel *dis*empowered by her experience in higher education. Despite the ways that the rhetoric of Willard and Sigourney curtailed women's potential as public figures, the Madison women don't seem to have been silenced by their education—if anything, their participation in their churches, in schools, and in organizations such as the WCTU indicate the opposite. Romans is what I imagine the next generation of Madison women could have become if they had had the opportunity: educated, but also even more politically and socially active than those who had come before. However, in the absence of the easy proximity of Madison College and given the cultural changes that occurred around our concepts of formal education through the Industrial Revolution and the turn of the century, this potential didn't come to fruition. We forgot the Madison women, and we forgot Viola Romans.

Limitations and Possibilities

I've already noted several times in this book that higher education is not the only factor in whether people are vocal, empowered, or socially engaged. However, I do believe in the power of education to expand our understanding of other people's lives and experiences—their stories, in essence—and to help us understand and exercise our own voices. The first time I read Katherine Kelleher Sohn's exploration of how Appalachian women use their college literacies, I bristled at some of her suggestions. After conducting interviews with some of her former students, Sohn concluded that their college education helped them "become somebody," whereas in their home cultures they were "silenced by gender and class."[28] I am still quick to point out that the idea that Appalachian women in general are enculturated to be voiceless nobodies can be contradicted with evidence of the lives and experiences of vocal, empowered Appalachian women who didn't graduate from college. However, I think I understand better now what Sohn was trying to say. While college education allowed her students to think deeply about their voices and their roles in society, it didn't necessarily change their voices or identities. But it did help them become more confident about exercising those things publicly.

My concern has always been that we could easily go too far in crediting college for empowering Appalachian women and in doing so create another argument for why Appalachian students should be fundamentally "corrected" by formal education, even if we think it's for their own good. As Viola Romans pointed out, she grew up with an expectation of female strength that accords with my own sense of Appalachian cultural expectations, a view that isn't necessarily a product of formal schooling. The recent *Hunger Games* books and movies have led others to draw similar conclusions, pointing out that like Katniss Everdeen, Appalachian women are often socialized to be nurturing but also to be physically and mentally tough, unbending in their principles.[29] Emma Willard and Lydia Sigourney, on the other hand, encouraged an enculturated sense of feminine softness and submission known as "true womanhood." In this sense, they conceivably did as much to silence women as to make them more politically active. Viola Romans, I suspect, would not have seen many of these "true women" in our neck of the woods.

However, I still feel that higher education and the study of rhetoric can push us to exercise our voices in ways we might otherwise not, simply by showing us what is possible when we make our ideas and words open to wider audiences. The Madison women studied rhetoric and were encouraged to read about current affairs, and for them, the temptation to speak out on such issues was apparently overwhelming. That analysis would go some way toward explaining why Willard and Sigourney's push for female domesticity wasn't necessarily borne out in the lives of the Madison women. They used their skills in ways that had both local and national repercussions. There are, however, limits to how well college can serve as a venue for personal and community empowerment. Higher education does not guarantee that students will emerge more empathetic or socially aware, especially if they don't encounter diverse ideas or points of view.

Despite its potential to widen worlds and open eyes in powerful ways, higher education has also been complicit in racism, sexism, and slavery. In *Ebony and Ivy: Race, Slavery, and the Troubled History of America's Universities*, Craig Steven Wilder demonstrates the degree to which this country's most revered institutions of higher learning were built by and at the expense of enslaved people.[30] In New England in the late 1700s, slavery not only existed but was "thriving in the new college towns," a status that shows how little those colleges were doing to encourage critical thinking about identity and otherness among students. Most schools of that time would not have seen that as part of their mission.

Whether Madison was doing a better job is at least debatable. There is reason to believe that Madison encouraged more humanitarian social views, specifically on the issue of abolition, even if those views were not universally accepted. A better understanding of Madison's views on abolition can perhaps best be gleaned from the surviving records of its sister schools, Franklin College in neighboring Harrison County and Muskingum College in neighboring Muskingum County. Ohio's small independent colleges at the time tended to be hotbeds of abolitionist feeling, so much so that a comprehensive history of these institutions published in 2003 was titled *Cradles of Conscience*. Franklin College made no secret if its abolitionist fervor. So vocal were faculty and students about abolitionism that a minority of dissenters broke away from Franklin in order to start the short-lived Providence College, which failed within a year.[31]

Franklin and Madison shared many links, including students, faculty, and administrators, which could indicate that the social views of those groups were fairly in sync. Muskingum College was somewhat more ambiguous in its support, at least officially. Some early presidents, such as Benjamin Waddle and Samuel Willson, accepted slavery, while others who despised it nonetheless sought to keep the issue out of college life, fearing it would "consume the pathetically feeble college" during a time when it was financially unstable.[32] However, the student population tended to support abolition, having "imbibed the strong expectation of national progress and improvement" present in societal attitudes, attitudes that are also discernable in Samuel Findley's address to the Philomathean Institute.[33] It is difficult to know to what degree this support for abolition at any of the three colleges would have translated into rhetorical or physical action on the part of the students. There are few records that tell us how many students were actively speaking out (or writing) about their feelings toward slavery; given that physically aiding people who escaped enslavement was illegal, this could have made them even more secretive about their views. However, records show that several Madison students came from families associated with the Underground Railroad, including the Craigs, the Lindsays, and the McKittricks. And we know about the group of Madison students who organized to send clothes and books to people recently freed from slavery. Obviously, connections existed between Madison College and abolitionism.

However, that is not the whole story of Guernsey County's, or even the Madison alumni's, racial attitudes. The family of at least one student, Kate Harris, held enslaved people whom her grandfather had willed to her father. It is likely that this was the case for more than one student, especially given that some like the Harris family had ancestral ties to the South. Student Emma Campbell's family moved to Kansas and became close friends with proslavery terrorist William Quantrill. And county newspapers showed a perspective on slavery and racial relations in the nineteenth century that was far from progressive. During the Civil War, county newspapers published multiple articles against abolitionism and blamed it for the conflict using racist language that it is shocking to see in a newspaper. In the 1890s, one county newspaper published an article that openly invited all (ostensibly white) county citizens to a Ku Klux Klan parade in Cambridge, the county seat, on the Fourth of July.[34]

Madison College was gone by the time the KKK blatantly advertised its presence in the county newspaper. But even when it was present, it did not prevent ethnic hatred. That reality must have been frustrating for students who were Irish immigrants (or the children of immigrants); they would have known something of otherness in U.S. identity politics. The mistreatment of the incoming Irish has frequently been cited in recent years, too often disingenuously to assuage white guilt about the complicity of their ancestors in slavery.[35] Comparisons between the experiences of the Irish and the experiences of enslaved Africans are deeply problematic. However, the Irish were undeniably treated as a form of "other" in comparison to white, Anglo-Saxon people, both in the British Isles and in the United States. Prejudice increased as waves of Irish Catholics began to arrive in the later 1800s. The Madison families' status as Protestant Irish) rather than Catholic Irish could have allowed them to claim at least some exemption from, or even to justify participating in, persecution of Irish immigrants. One local history describes how the Know Nothing party "sprang up like 'Jonah's Gourd' in a night" in the Antrim community.[36] The Know Nothings aligned politically around xenophobia, presenting themselves explicitly as an anti-Catholic, anti-Irish, anti-immigrant movement—demonstrating how quickly at least some of the local population forgot its own roots when that forgetting was politically expedient.

Still, not all were willing to accept the prejudices encouraged by political factions such as the Know Nothings. Dr. Lorle Porter, a preeminent historian of the Scotch-Irish peoples in the United States, argues that many rejected the Know Nothing party specifically because of the hypocrisy of its anti-immigrant politics. She notes that literary societies at Muskingum College in the mid-1800s debated Know Nothing policy positions (including prohibitions against immigration and stripping voting rights from Catholics) and, in light of their own immigrant histories, soundly disagreed with them.[37]

Some students at Madison undoubtedly drew upon an awareness of their own families' backgrounds and identities as immigrants to nurture empathy with other "othered" groups, even those who had previously been positioned as their enemies (specifically, Catholics). Such self-awareness, sadly rare as it seems to be, is no more endemic to the Scotch-Irish or modern-day Appalachians as it is any other group of humans. In fact, strains of anti-immigrant prejudice appear to be particularly strong in many Appalachian communities today, proof that values don't necessarily transmit across generations. Likewise, prior to the mid-1800s when Madison students encountered such debates, the Scotch-Irish in general showed themselves to be unsympathetic toward the Native American peoples they encountered, despite themselves having experienced land clearances and witnessed the violence and devastation caused when one population attempts to colonize another, as was largely the case in northern Ireland.[38] In short, if the students Porter describes showed greater self-awareness, empathy, and tolerance toward other marginalized peoples, it isn't necessarily Scotch-Irish cultural values that created these traits. Perhaps the experience of college, a space where deliberation and reflection can thrive, influenced these understandings.

My point is that it isn't only our history with higher education that contradicts stereotypes of Appalachian backwardness, but also the fact that these communities had progressive views that aren't commonly associated with us today. It leads me to ask a question: If my region was a progressive and intellectually respected place two hundred years ago, why is it seen as the exact opposite now? Have we lost these traits . . . or have we only been told so often enough that we ourselves believe it?

Conclusion

Madison College did a great deal to empower its students, including the women, who went on to take part in progressive causes throughout the rest of the century. Education has the potential to foster empathy and social responsibility, qualities some of the Madison women demonstrated in their choice of activist causes. Higher education alone is not an automatic cure for xenophobia and racial prejudice. However, it can serve as a forum where ideas are shared and debated, as well as where unfamiliar perspectives are considered. College's potential for sponsoring ethical encounters with difference continues to be underestimated in discussions of the value (or lack thereof) of a college degree. Ironically, those who are most likely to recognize why college can be important to the creation of an active, thoughtful, compassionate citizenry are those for whom such a thing seems dangerous. Ultimately, very few today would describe modern Appalachians collectively as an active, thoughtful, compassionate citizenry, even if regional histories suggest something different.

My goal in this exploration has been to show that there are reasons why higher education proliferated here at one time and that those reasons drew women as well as men to seek it out, for purposes more personal than professional. The women who gained such an education made use of it, even when opportunities to do so were relatively rare. Yet even though students, faculty, and their families became involved in social issues such as abolition and women's rights, Madison did not eradicate sexism and racism in the community. However, the role higher education can play in fostering empowerment, tolerance, and empathy was and is very real—and that was no less true at tiny, rural Madison College. History has shown us that when Appalachian peoples band together to challenge injustice, the effects can be amazing. One need look no further than the push for labor rights in the early twentieth century. Today, we experience far-reaching inequalities in things like educational access, health care, and environmental safety. Acknowledging and using the power of higher education can do a great deal to help us fight these battles.

SMALL STORIES, PART 5

Interest is increasing in how education can translate into empowerment for Appalachian students. One of the most prominent studies, Katherine Kelleher Sohn's *Whistlin' and Crowin' Women of Appalachia*, demonstrates that a college education can help women strengthen their voice as members of regional, professional, and academic communities. The following stories indicate to me that this pattern was in place much longer than I'd realized.

Maggie E. Hyatt

Maggie was born in 1836 to Ellen (or possibly Bertha) and Noah Hyatt, who were merchants. Beyond her mention in the 1854 Madison catalogue, the next time she enters the historical record is when she married a carpenter named Robert Banford.

Banford, who was from Maryland, fought for the Union during the Civil War in the Maryland Volunteer Infantry. He had an impressive career; according to his 1902 obituary, he put his carpentry skills to use building bridges in Cuba (where Maggie may well have accompanied him), then later served as a legislator and a sheriff in Maryland. As other cases have shown, women at this time were expected to take an interest in their husbands' professions, serving as helpmates (if not, at times, doing the job themselves—see the story of Rachel Perry Gaston, grandmother of Mollie and Elma Gaston). If she did play any role in her husband's political life, a Madison education would have served her well.

However, in Maggie's case I once again see the best evidence of her educational interests coming through in the life of her daughter. Flora Banford (later

Zeigler) attended an institution of higher learning for women, graduating top of her class at the Kee Mar Seminary in Hagerstown, Maryland, which offered both bachelor's and master's degrees. Later she founded the Flora Zeigler Bible Class, an organization lauded again and again by Hagerstown newspapers that survived well after Flora's passing. Despite its name, the class was not merely a form of Sunday school—it was a large organization that incorporated literary activity (one meeting mentions the composition of limericks) and public service. (Flora herself is credited, in a 1954 newspaper story recounting the group's history, with securing their county's first public health nurse.[1]) Once again, there is no concrete evidence linking Flora's education, activism, and public voice with her mother. However, knowing the cultural importance of motherhood and maternal influence that Maggie would have grown up with, the link seems very likely.

Kate Green

Kate Green, born Mary Catherine Green, was the daughter of Susan Gomber Moore, whose recent ancestors were credited as the founders of Guernsey's county seat, Cambridge, and Dr. Milton Green, who is identified on his gravestone as the "First Secretary of Madison College." Kate became active in the Cambridge community after her time in Antrim. Among other things, she started the Founders Burial Ground endowment, which undertook the care and preservation of Cambridge's oldest cemetery. Both her interest in education and her community involvement also come through in her sons; one attended Princeton and another is credited in a *Jeffersonian* article from July 9, 1924, as having "great community spirit." Her son Charles's community spirit specifically involved education. While still a student himself, he wrote a history of Cambridge schools (which I would love to have, but alas), and throughout his life he made multiple donations to local schools.

While it doesn't specifically speak to her feelings about her own education, there is evidence that Kate had a strong personality—the kind that could easily have shaped her children's own priorities. In the 1920 census, when Kate would have been nearly 80, she was described as the head of her household, despite living in the home of her grown son. The authority of householder, at least on paper, lay with her rather than with her nearest male relative—and that recognition means something.

Lizzie Smith

Lizzie Smith intrigued me immediately, not for anything her family had done or went on to do but rather for her own occupation. The 1860 census, which followed her appearance in the college catalogue by six years, listed her occupation as a minister.

Female ministers were exceedingly rare in the 1860s. In fact, the Presbyterian church, which was most affiliated with Madison College, did not officially ordain a female preacher until 1889. Lizzie has been difficult to trace following the 1860 census, but one possibility would indicate an explanation for her occupation. An 1881 obituary for an Elizabeth Smith describes her not as a Presbyterian but as a Quaker.

If our Lizzie Smith was a member of the Society of Friends, that could explain both her occupation and her desire for an education. Quakerism was a popular faith in the area in the nineteenth century. My own ancestors were Quakers, early settlers of a nearby town dubbed, appropriately, Quaker City. The town of Barnesville, in neighboring Belmont County, is the location of the Olney Friends School, a highly regarded boarding school established in 1837 by Quakers. While the Quaker population has since dwindled, it makes sense that at least some of Madison's students at the time could have been Quakers.

The Quaker faith was, and is, exceptional for its gender egalitarianism. Women's authority, in both the community and the church, was seen as equal to men's. Quakers were also deeply invested in education. Some of the oldest and most prestigious colleges in the United States were founded by Quakers (including Haverford, Swarthmore, and Bryn Mawr—a women's college). Despite how little she left behind, Lizzie was an incredible woman, not just as someone who sought out education, but also as someone who insisted on recognition for her career. She didn't shrink from describing herself in the official U.S. census as something many in the United States would not have recognized: a woman who was also a minister.

Nancy Wallace

Of all the students I investigated, Nancy was the biggest surprise—once again, not necessarily as much for herself as for what her family indicates about her.

Nancy was born in 1834 to Irish immigrants Jane (McClenahan) and John Wallace, who operated a mill in Fairview. Fairview is, like many towns in Guernsey, a community that has faded greatly since its heyday. On the border between Guernsey and Belmont Counties, it was the site of a thoroughfare that has lost importance since the construction of the interstate. It is now roughly the size of Antrim; it consists of a few houses, a couple of churches, and its current claim to fame, the Pennyroyal Opry House, a modest building that hosts celebrated bluegrass acts.

Whatever it was in the 1850s, Fairview produced a remarkable family in the Wallace children. I almost missed it entirely—my initial research showed that Nancy Wallace had died by 1855, within a year of the catalogue's publication, which led me to suspect that I would find little information about her. A bit of digging proved me wrong. *The John McClenahan Folk*, a book of family records by John McClenahan Henderson, shows that she died of tuberculosis, the same condition that had recently killed the college headmistress, Adelphia Powers. However, prior to her death Nancy was more than just a student at Madison College; William Wolfe's *Stories of Guernsey County* describes her as also being an instructor of art and drawing. Nancy's need for employment makes sense in light of her family's financial problems. Her father died when Nancy and her siblings were young, leaving their mother Jane to make ends meet in a time when unmarried women had very few economic opportunities. Yet education was clearly prioritized in this family. I am impressed both that Nancy wanted to study so much that she was willing to work for the school to achieve it and that she was talented enough that the school hired her. While her grave is unmarked—another sign of her family's financial hardship—it is thought that she was buried in Fairview's cemetery.

I thought this was the extent of Nancy's story. It was not, however, the end of the story for her siblings. In fact, her brother David was the focus of a biography titled *A Busy Life: A Tribute to the Memory of the Rev. David A. Wallace*. David also attended Madison, but financial difficulty led him to leave early. He later attended other schools, including Miami University and Alleghany College, before graduating and taking on the presidency of Muskingum College. Though he was an ordained Presbyterian minister, it was the schoolroom rather than the pulpit that pulled David most strongly, as he went on to help found Monmouth College. This took me some time to process: a well-regarded college in Illinois owes its existence in part to a tiny village in rural Appalachian Ohio and the little-remembered scholar it produced. (I also came to discover that after leaving Madison but before continuing his education elsewhere, he taught at a one-room school called Greenwood near Fairview.

The land that housed the Greenwood school is now owned by my parents. My odd connections with Madison's students emerged throughout this research in the most random ways.)

The story of Nancy's younger sister grabs me even more. Eliza Wallace was too young to attend Madison in its heyday, but she attended her older brother's burgeoning Monmouth College, where she afterward became a math professor. This is pretty amazing even now, given the lack of women in the STEM fields. In the 1800s, it was even more so.

But Eliza wasn't done. In the late 1800s, she traveled to postwar Knoxville, Tennessee, where she took on a teaching and administrative role at the newly founded Knoxville College, a school for formerly enslaved and Black students. She was the first principal of female students, fighting alongside them against racist threats to the college's existence. Her work to improve health conditions in the Black community led to the establishment of the Eliza B. Wallace Hospital in 1907, a year after Eliza's death, which served as both a health-care facility and a training school.[2] This hospital saved many lives during the Spanish flu epidemic, and it educated the first African American Red Cross nurse in the United States, Frances Elliott Davis.

It's hard to overstate the feelings I have toward this family. Rural, poor, Appalachian, the children of immigrants, they went on to contribute each in their own way toward the education of their fellow citizens—in Eliza's case, regardless of race or gender. The biography of David Wallace attributes much of the children's development to the influence of their mother and grandmothers—who are described as "respected and loved by their children and grandchildren. Their influence over their children was great."[3] While this maternal influence doesn't surprise me, in other ways the Wallace children and their educational careers fly in the face of so many negative stereotypes about this region. Though they themselves have been largely forgotten, through them it can be said that tiny Fairview, Ohio, and Madison College made a mark on the nation. The effects of that mark echo into today.

Mary Lawrence

Born Mary Sleeth in 1833, she was the daughter of farmers Elizabeth and James Sleeth. She, too, became a farmer, alongside her husband, fellow Madison alumnus Alexander Lawrence. Mary became involved with the Antrim Teacher's Institute, an organization that tried to fill the educational void left by Madison's closure. An article in the *Jeffersonian* lists her and fellow Madison alumnus Jennie Moore as founding members. In fact, the Teacher's Institute was founded and run by Madison alumni and carried on for several decades, dedicated to teaching not only classroom management but also the "higher branches" of learning that students could no longer access in the county.[4] Later, she took part in annual alumni reunions, keeping connections between former students and the memory of the college strong. Mary is just one example of how Madison's former students, both men and women, clearly supported education in Antrim long after Madison College closed.

CHAPTER 6

The Future Is the Past

Formal Education and Appalachian History

———

Education and intelligence are not mutually exclusive—I've known that my whole life. Neither my parents nor my grandparents, nor anyone in my direct ancestry for as far back as family memory holds, ever attended college.[1] Yet they weren't stupid, or even what I'd consider uneducated. Some, I think, were purt-near genius. My grandfather, William Gallagher (or Pap, as he was known to his grandkids and great-grandkids), lost an arm and an eye in World War II, but that never stopped him. He was a hard worker all his life, but what awes me most are the ways he engineered his life to keep living around his disabilities. Honestly, it feels strange to think of him as disabled at all. One Christmas, when my mom was agonizing over a gift for him, I suggested a nice pair of gloves since he spent so much time outside. She looked at me with a level gaze and said, "Do you mean *glove*?" I had literally forgotten that he didn't have two hands. I say this because it didn't seem there was anything I could do with two arms that he couldn't do with one. He designed and built a motorized fishing pole for easier reeling (not that he used it much; he most often managed to wedge his regular pole under his arm and reel it in one-handed). He designed and built an extended metal pick that he strapped to his arm stump and used as a second hand to play the banjo (which he played damn good). When something didn't work for him, he found ways to engineer and build tools that made it work. After he had passed, I was doing genealogical work on that branch of the family tree and discovered that Pap's own maternal great-grandfather, William Groves, was described in a county historical source as "a natural mechanic and could make anything out of wood or iron that he wished to. He made the first spinning wheel that was used in the township and erected the first grist and sawmill on Stillwater creek."[2] In other words, although both lacked the kind of higher education we associate with college, both were self-motivated and self-taught engineers.

Pap is not the only person who illuminated for me the ways intelligence and ability could exist apart from formal schooling. One of my grandmothers never finished high school, but she could identify every flower and plant I asked about on our evening walks; the other could teach herself just about any crochet stitch (something I still struggle with after years of practice). My great-grandmother created quilts with the skills of a graphic designer. My point is that college education is not the final determinant in whether someone is intelligent, capable, creative, or self-confident. However (and it's a big how-ever), I don't want to underestimate the value college education can bring to someone's life. I speak as someone whose life benefited from it greatly.

I had seen the Ohio University Eastern campus from the outside many times when I was younger; any time we wanted to go to a mall or to the movies, St. Clairsville was our nearest option, about a 45-minute drive into the next county over. It was a grand building, one that for a long time shaped my expectations of what a college should look like. It didn't have any ivy growing that I could recall, but it certainly looked like it should have. I had been inside it once when I was in elementary school (my aunt was earning a master's degree in education and she shepherded me around one day), but any recollections of what I felt when I was there were forgotten by the time I became a student myself. That huge, classically structured building could also be intimidating, especially for those who weren't sure they belonged in college at all, which by then, I wasn't.

High school had been a harrowing experience for me. Despite the presence of some truly wonderful teachers, my time there was largely characterized by fear—fear of the other teachers who screamed and made me feel stupid at any opportunity. My college counseling had consisted of being shown a drawer full of brochures in the guidance counselor's office that I could make an appointment to look through on my own (not that I did—I wasn't even confident enough at the time to be that proactive). Besides, it had always been a given for me that college would equal Ohio University Eastern. It was a commuter campus close to home and I was in no way ready to live farther away and on my own. My brother was going there, giving it at least some sense of familiarity beyond my frequent, awestruck glimpses of it from the outside. But that didn't mean I thought it was something I would enjoy. If anything, it seemed like my high school tried to talk us out of college. (How many times did we have to hear, "If you think this is hard, you're in for a rough ride if you go to college"?) I was also offered a full scholarship on the strength of my academics, piss-poor math scores notwithstanding. To this day I'm a little horrified when I hear about incoming college students who turned down scholarships at cheaper schools to pay full price at ostensibly fancier ones. There is, it turns out, a whole genre on YouTube of college acceptance videos in which the ambitious young videographers let us see their reactions at being accepted or rejected from various colleges. It's not at all rare for them to receive hefty scholarships and financial assistance at "lower tier" colleges but to choose instead more costly Ivy League and equivalent schools. *How could they do that to their parents?!* I catch myself thinking, assuming that for them, as for me, paying for college is a family affair. That's an unfair assumption.[3] They might be planning to buy those pricier educations through student loans, in which case my question becomes, how can they do that to themselves?!

I don't remember what I thought of Ohio University Eastern the first time I entered the building for my own education, except that I was scared. It was a one-day group orientation event for prospective freshmen, which meant I'd be talking to people I didn't know (never an easy task) and displaying my ignorance in a series of placement tests. I'd taken AP English as a senior, the only advanced placement class offered by my school at the time, and had done well enough to test out of first-year composition. But math was never going to be an easy subject for me, despite having had one of the heretofore mentioned excellent teachers in high school. Mrs. Lucas even invented songs to try to teach me geometry, to very little avail—I honestly think she teared up at seeing my low ACT math score. I planned at the time to be a plant biology major, based solely on my interest in gardening, but I failed to grasp how much math would be required for such a degree. Nonetheless, that proposed major meant I was assigned to a science professor who would help with my scheduling that afternoon. She tried to make it easy, bless her—she had prepared a clear list of the math and science courses I should take my first semester, none of which sounded the least bit appealing to me. That dread of taking courses I didn't want to take in a place where I was already more than half convinced I didn't belong prompted me to speak up for myself. "I'd like to be a little more eclectic my first term," I said, after which she seemed to lose some interest. "Okay. Well, look through the course offerings," she said, and moved on to the next student in line. I did end up signing up for an entry-level math class, one that wouldn't even fulfill a requirement for my major, and eventually earned a C. But I also signed up for English and history courses—the stuff that did look interesting to me—and that, reader, made all the difference, as they say.

Ohio University Eastern's English and history faculty continue to be the model for my own teaching today. I learned from them just how much I could love learning. We talked about ideas in those classes; we weren't just presented with them and told to memorize. I could, and did, write what I thought about people and events and concepts that it would never have occurred to me to write about, or even think about, before. I can still conjure the feeling of walking through the doors of Ohio University Eastern, as I would come to do many times, and taking in the scent that to this day I associate with books and anticipation. I wanted to be there. I wanted to sit in the library between classes and lazily browse shelves for books that I checked out simply because they sounded interesting. (I kid you not, the librarian at my high school had such a fearsome reputation that I can count on one hand the number of times I entered it in four years, and I never once checked out a book. As an undergrad, I fell so hard for the campus library that I would visit it even on days I didn't have class, just for the joy of being there.)

I would change my major to English once it became obvious even to me that I wasn't progressing toward a bachelor of science degree but was getting nearer and nearer to a bachelor of arts. Eventually I would have to transfer to the main Ohio University campus in Athens to finish my degree, and I fell just as hard for its own special magic. But it was a different feeling, perhaps because I knew by then that I *could* love college. Love it so much, in fact, that while my campuses have changed, I've never truly left. I wonder, though, if I'd known about the Madison women earlier, would I have been more open to that magic when I first set foot inside Ohio University Eastern? Would those first steps have been less fearful if I had known that this school could become a part of my home and my identity? Because it has, in ways I'm not sure I could ever articulate. I wonder if the women at Madison College felt the same way.

And I wonder how many Appalachian kids will never get the chance to find this out for themselves.

Appalachia and Attitudes toward Education

Sharyn McCrumb prefaced her novel *The Rosewood Casket*, a story about place, family, and the loss of both in Appalachia, with a quote from playwright Arthur Wing Pinero: "I believe the future is simply the past, entered through another gate." I believe in this sentiment, especially today in a world that seems so unwilling to learn from its own history. However, there are times when that gate looks pretty different in significant ways. By that I mean that the present is not always identical to the past. Things do change; hopefully for the better, but not always. My region's access and interest in higher education have changed, I've discovered, in ways I hadn't expected.

As I've said, I was surprised to learn about Madison College. I was surprised that it existed, that it thrived, that it admitted women on mostly equal terms as men. That last point, on reflection, is not entirely accurate: it doesn't surprise me that the women stood up for themselves and fought for what they wanted. What surprises me is that what they wanted was to go to college. The fact of my surprise is significant because it tells me that I can't assume a perfect knowledge of the people in my own community two hundred years ago. The cultural messages that have formed my modern assumptions about college education and its worth are necessarily at least somewhat different from what the Madison women encountered.

Let me explain this a bit. From my perspective, the cultural message about college in my community is that it's something you do, if you must, to get a decent job. It's not something you're expected to love and make a career of. It's a means to an end, not the end in itself. Most of my high school classmates went to local community colleges if they went to college at all. I don't say this to knock community colleges; my own experience at Ohio University Eastern had the deepest impact on my love of learning. Also, given the increasing cost of attending college, seeking the cheapest and quickest way to earn a degree makes a lot of sense. The high cost of college and the distances many of us must travel to reach one are circumstances that probably have a lot to do with why my region thinks of higher education as something that is often unattainable. Maybe if it were more accessible and affordable it would be more acceptable to seek out learning for its own sake. But right now, college is a very utilitarian endeavor in my region. I experienced some backlash over my continued schooling; multiple people asked if I expected to "have any common sense left" once I'd finished graduate school. While my parents were incredibly supportive of my educational interests, even if they didn't share them,[4] my grandfather began to complain once it became clear I needed to move to Athens, Ohio, to finish my English degree.[5] As far as he was concerned, I could have studied education at the regional campus instead and been teaching high school by now. It's a complaint that I know was based in fear: fear for me being away from the family on my own and fear for my future prospects.

This isn't a unique story. In *The Rhetoric of Appalachian Identity*, Todd Snyder investigated attitudes about college education in his West Virginia community that mirror my own experiences. What he heard was that college can be the way to a good job, but that, and only that, is why you'd put yourself through it. At the root of this attitude seems to be a fundamental sense that college and Appalachia don't mix well together.

Snyder surveyed the parents of high school students in Webster County, West Virginia, to ascertain their thoughts about their children's college aspirations. The results showed that the participating parents, none of whom had attended college themselves, were far from enthusiastic about the prospect. In addition to believing college was too expensive and their children too poorly prepared academically to succeed by their high schools, they also associated college with danger. In some cases, this was physical danger. As one mother said, "The shape of the world these days. It's wicked out there. There are so many things that can happen. You just want to protect your kids from it all."[6] In other ways, the danger was moral. Parents feared the "party" atmosphere of college, concerned it would lead their children to trouble.[7] Some also wished high schools would focus more on vocational training than college preparation, with the view that vocationally trained students could make careers locally without ever needing higher education. While these parents associated their rural county with physical and moral safety, they associated "college" with the opposite.

In her study of Appalachian students at a small college in Kentucky, Katherine Kelleher Sohn drew similar conclusions, while learning that public schools played a role in alienating Appalachian students. She noted that the local attitudes she witnessed toward education were complicated by negative experiences. For example, one of her students, Lucy, faced neglect or outright hostility from her public school teachers, who, though themselves from the region, treated Lucy as an inferior. Lucy commented, "Our teachers were from 'generational' families, ones whose mothers and aunts and uncles were teachers as well. They had to teach me, and that's basically the only relationship I had with them. . . . Our family with seven kids has always been poor, and the teachers had no use for me or my family."[8] The idea that formal education runs in families, as with the teachers Lucy noted, is something I'm seeing with at least some of the Madison students, who both taught and had children who became teachers. However, the idea that formal education makes regional students disdainful of their cultural background and of those, like Lucy, who remain attached to it is also a deep concern among Appalachian families.

It's not an entirely unfounded concern. Memoirist Linda Scott DeRosier described going away to college and learning that what her new peers consider "normal" was not the same as what she grew up with: ideas and an accent that were dubbed "hillbilly." She became obsessed with excising any aspects of herself that could mark her as Appalachian—a process that scholar Erica Abrams Locklear calls "passing for 'normal.'"[9] While DeRosier later became troubled by the powerful social pressure that drove her desire for "normalization," it can't be denied that academia has a history of presenting Appalachian identity as a negative, a deficit. Kim Donehower sees the anti-Appalachian attitudes of educators exemplified in James Moffett's book *Storm in the Mountains: A Case Study of Censorship, Conflict, and Consciousness*. The book describes Moffett's experiences in West Virginia, where he came into conflict with a rural school district. The community in question banned a set of high school textbooks that Moffett had edited, leading Moffett to interview and analyze, from his academic, Socratic point of view, the motivations behind the ban. While Moffett's grievance against the community promoting the censorship was valid, Donehower points out that Moffett failed to examine or understand the viewpoints he received during his interviews. Instead, Moffett declared that the reasoning behind the ban boiled down to a region suffering from "'agnosis'—a term he coined to mean, essentially, the desire to be ignorant."[10] In other words, Moffett and his popular book presented a clear dichotomy: to be formally educated is to be clear headed and reasonable; to be Appalachian is to be reactionary and willfully ignorant. If these are our two choices, and too often that is how they are presented, I can easily see why someone would be tempted to choose the former and disdain the latter. I can also see how, feeling rejected or attacked, a person might—consciously or not—dig their heels into the latter and reject the identity Moffett presents of the educated, enlightened academic.

Closer to home, similar research has uncovered these dynamics in Appalachian Ohio. Nathan Shepley's interviews with his first-year writing student, Matt, are deeply reminiscent of similar experiences I and my students have had. Matt notes that he feels that he is rarely allowed to write about his home and family experiences in the classroom, even though he feels much more engaged when he does. He also presents his grandfather as a major influence on his own sense of what intelligence means: "Intelligence was in things that applied to him, you know, gardening or farming or something like that. That was where it applied to him. It wasn't, you know—he didn't know about Shakespeare of Virginia Woolf or things like that. It didn't appeal to him. It wasn't useful in his world."[11] Matt actively resists the idea that intelligence and formal education are inextricable; his grandfather could be smart without Shakespeare. But he also indicates his own sense of alienation in the classroom, a space where he doesn't feel his own identity or interests have a place.

This lack of place can have repercussions for Appalachian students' sense of themselves and their ability to succeed in college. In 2004, Ohio University conducted a series of studies to better understand students' and faculty's perspectives on Appalachia. A survey specifically on issues of regional education found that Appalachian students saw themselves as being stereotyped as stupid, poor, and backward by faculty and students from outside the region.[12] The local respondents also felt that the university failed to understand their difficulties in attending college. For example, attendance can be compromised by issues such as commuting (most regional students either live at home or attend one of the nonresidential branch campuses), work responsibilities, and family obligations that non-Appalachian students might not have. As one respondent noted, "Our families are very important. In the Appalachian region we were raised to believe that family is #1."[13] However, a sudden family need is not always accepted as a valid reason to miss class.

In her article "Student Resistance to Schooling: Disconnections with Education in Rural Appalachia," Katie Hendrickson found that three fundamental issues arise in creating the sense of alienation students can feel from local school systems: family values and expectations, the relevance of education, and misunderstandings between teachers and students. Families that value vocational learning over traditional formal education pass those values on to their children, who often make educational choices with the goal of pleasing parents. Also, given that the jobs more highly educated students qualify for are often located outside the region, families fear that college will lure children away more permanently. Likewise, "the incompatibility of academic content and community life" makes formal education seem not only irrelevant but at times potentially hostile to local cultures.[14] While Hendrickson was not specifically looking at attitudes toward college education, these dynamics no doubt influence the ways Appalachian students feel about higher education as a prospect.

Dichotomies, however, are never as clear cut as people might pretend they are. It is far too simplistic, and inaccurate, to say that all Appalachians have negative feelings about formal, especially higher, education, just as not all educators regard the cultures of their Appalachian students as unacceptable in the classroom. There is evidence that proves that these are not all-encompassing phenomena. For example, Sohn found multiple cases in her research where parents, especially mothers, served as strong literacy sponsors and academic role models for their children. Even mothers who hadn't experienced college themselves showed great encouragement for their daughters' literacy journeys—as mine did. This experience of maternal influence over literacy learning is echoed by other authors, including Amy Clark, Linda Scott DeRosier, and Linda Spatig. The evidence also attests, though, that the tensions between formal education and Appalachian cultures are real and are felt by many. I find it particularly intriguing that Antrim and the Madison students didn't seem to feel them in the early to mid-1800s, at least not to the same degree as today. It's worth considering where these tensions might have come from.

An answer to this question requires some historicizing about the role and expectations of higher education in Appalachia. There is very little definitive data about attitudes toward formal education before the twentieth century, but what exists goes some way toward explaining the cultural apprehensions that might have appeared later.

Building the Wall

In her study of the role newspapers have played in Appalachian community literacy, Samantha NeCamp takes to task the idea that we are or have been an anti-literacy region. The stereotypical story that we are, however, does great damage to both what others think of us and what we think of ourselves: "Recovering this history of eastern Kentucky and Appalachia more generally can help rewrite both the past and the future of Appalachia. . . . If the region has always been illiterate, poor, and backward, it is impossible to imagine how the future can be different. . . . If, instead, we recognize that the educational inequalities that now characterize Appalachia are of relatively short duration and that the region has in fact never been illiterate, poor, and backward, we can 'shake ourselves free, and envision alternative futures.'"[15] I didn't truly understand NeCamp's point that the alienation between Appalachia and formal education is actually relatively new until I discovered Madison College. If, as I've come to agree, we were once an educationally strong region, what is it that changed?

For one thing, the location of our education as well as the decisions made about it have altered in more recent years. Prior to the turn of the twentieth century, education in Appalachia tended to be a local occurrence, in that small schools were built and operated by communities. Such a model was not without drawbacks; attendance was not compulsory until the 1900s, and the quality of the education given could vary widely between communities. However, the schools and communities tended to be tightly bound, each benefiting the other, in ways that were lost as educational and curricular decisions became dominated by outside forces. Education in Appalachia came to be seen as a missionary project, figuratively if not always literally. Many parts of the Appalachians came under the auspices of schools founded in the early twentieth century by the American Missionary Association, whose evangelical curriculums also worked to "save the mountain child from the errors of his background" by correcting "his ignorance, his accent, and his values."[16]

However, even schools that were not conspicuously missionary in their outlook came to take on a similar philosophy, in the sense that Appalachian discourses, identities, and values were things to be standardized and "corrected" through education. As control over schools became more centralized through the state, consolidation caused many communities to lose their local schools, moves that often coincided with the withering of the communities themselves. This is a story that Antrim learned intimately as it slowly lost its schools, beginning with Madison College and then eventually a high school, a middle school, then an elementary school, until the district finally abandoned Antrim altogether in the late twentieth century.

It isn't my intent to discuss the benefits and drawbacks of either school consolidation or the community control of education, although both of these topics continue to play out not only here but in many regions throughout the nation. Rather, I want to show these dynamics as part of a pattern that led to an alienation between my region, as part of Appalachia, and the systems of formal education available to us. Both Snyder and Sohn have shown that one of the greatest concerns that parents and students have about higher education is the fear that it will disrespect students' families and roots or even distance students from them. History shows that this concern is a valid one, as education throughout the twentieth and into the twenty-first century has often consciously tried to do just that.

The question of why educational systems might feel it is in students' best interest to abandon their communities and/or identities is a haunting one. The roots seem lodged in the issues of Appalachian economics. Major change occurred in many regional economies throughout Appalachia in the late nineteenth and early twentieth centuries. Extractive industries that were almost exclusively owned by outside operators overtook family farms as the dominant form of employment. Logging, coal mining, and factory work (particularly, in the northern edges of Appalachia, in steel mills) became the expected occupations of most Appalachian peoples. Regional census data demonstrates the shift from agriculture to mine work. While it is arguable that we simply exchanged one form of manual labor for another, the most significant alteration is that people no longer employed themselves: they were subject to the rules and dictates of bosses who could exert extreme influence over the lifestyles, safety, and even identity of workers. Todd Snyder demonstrates how industrial forces changed how Appalachian peoples came to see themselves and the value of their labor; they were encouraged to see and value themselves as what Ira Shor calls "the laboring hands of society."[17] Snyder explains that this process has had deep effects on the livelihoods and possibilities open to both men and women:

> First, companies bought up the land, legally claiming ownership over vast portions of the region. Because of the region's isolation, these businesses became the only way to sustain a modern way of life—a lifestyle influenced by consumer capitalist identity. Due to a clear lack of employment opportunities, Appalachian women, like many American women during the early days of the industrial revolution, were relegated to the household. Deep mines, saw mills, and railroad tracks called for traditionally masculine work. There were, of course, few, if any, dual-income families in Appalachia's early days. It was the father's duty to provide for his family. The mother was to bear children; the extract industries needed her to do so because their enterprise called for new generations of hardworking Appalachians. . . . Even today, Appalachia continues to lag behind the rest of the nation in regard to education, health care, and economic opportunity.[18]

In other words, we've been cajoled into seeing physical rather than academic labor as worthy, brave, even natural, despite the effects it has had on our region's health and opportunities. As Snyder put it, "We have been conditioned to believe our fates are unchangeable. When high school is over it is time to pick up your dinner bucket. This socially constructed Appalachian truth becomes engrained into our consciousness at a very young age."[19] If physical labor is valorized, then intellectual work—which the industrial dichotomy positions as the opposite of physical labor—is presented as weak and strange, an unnatural or even self-indulgent choice. To this day, sitting down and writing this chapter rather than being up and *doing something* seems guilt-inducingly lazy to me, even knowing as I do the amount of mental energy it takes.

While coal mining has died down in the region as an economic activity (although it has not by any means disappeared, nor has it in Snyder's part of West Virginia), the imposed separation between physical and mental work still exists in a way that it likely didn't for the students at Madison College. Many of them came from farms and returned to them after their college education, indicating that college wasn't perceived as a separate or antagonistic entity. This also opens up the question of why students were flocking to Madison College even if, as is especially the case for the women, their economic futures were not dependent on it. This was discussed in a previous chapter, but it deserves some mention here for what it tells us about how our ideas in this region have changed. Certainly college helped some students achieve their career goals. Some (male) Madison students became ministers, and others became lawyers or doctors. They obviously saw something of value for these future professions in gaining the kind of classical education Madison offered. But that fails to explain the many students who carried on farming after college or, if they were women, married and became homemakers. The fact that they were going to college without an expectation that it was necessary for a sustainable career says to me that they were getting something from their education that was more personal. They were choosing to go to college because they wanted to, and they believed that wanting to do mental rather than physical work was an acceptable thing.

Of course, our shifting sense of what acceptable work is and is not can't be seen as the only barrier between Appalachian students and higher education. Physical barriers such as distance and costs have changed in the years since Madison. Without the plethora of educational options that existed in Appalachia's higher education heyday, students today are faced with the options of commuting to the nearest college or moving to a campus, both of which entail costs in terms of both money and energy. Many students struggle with the financial burden of upkeep on vehicles and with balancing travel time, study, work, and family obligations. I've had students who literally cannot come to class because they can't afford gas for their car that week. Add to this the rising cost of tuition and the general increase in cost of living (but not in wages in most local jobs) and the choice to attend college can start to seem self-indulgent indeed.

But beyond the logistical barriers modern Appalachian college hopefuls face is another factor that has been built over the years since Madison College disappeared: the declining respect for Appalachian literacies and cultures in wider American society. Appalachian students too often encounter a sense that the literacy they learn in academic classrooms is either irrelevant to their daily lives or dismissive of their home discourses, a prejudice rooted in economic and social factors.

The sense of Appalachia as a region of "otherness" had already begun in the Madison era, but it had become more concrete by the turn of the century. The popular imagination had begun to see Appalachian people as ignorant, lazy, violent, and in need of civilizing. These stereotypes benefited the extractive industries that profited from Appalachian labor. As Elizabeth Catte notes, "Coal companies often justified their expansion and the recruitment of local populations into their workforce as benevolent actions that would bring backward mountaineers into their own as equal participants in America's expanding spirit of industry."[20] Exploitative forms of capitalism, in short, could save Appalachian peoples from themselves. They could be "tamed and put to industrial purpose . . . then they might be spared the bloodshed, vice, and moral degeneracy natural to their primitive existence."[21] This view ignores the fact that bloodshed, vice, and moral degeneracy are pretty far from the picture Madison College presented of the region.

However, these stereotypes did have educational repercussions; the sense that Appalachian people were somehow more savage than people from other parts of the country made civilizing and standardizing them a moral imperative that schools could and should accomplish. Even today, teachers who recognize the deep economic distress of many Appalachian regions see standardizing students' languages, literacies, and ideals as a means of saving them, of giving them the tools to escape the region and succeed in mainstream, middle-class U.S. culture.[22]

However, this viewpoint overlooks a great deal and risks devaluing the literacies that students bring with them into their classrooms. As Shepley's student Matt noted, the knowledge of local food production he learned from his grandfather was not welcomed in most of his classes. Amy Clark has examined the varied literacies prevalent among Appalachian women, such as knowledge of family stories, quilts, and recipe books. These forms of literacy run counter to the myth prevalent in schools that there is only one correct definition of "literacy" that "results in benefits (such as cognitive development and upward mobility) that cannot be attained in other ways."[23] This is an issue that even affects Appalachians who become faculty members in academia, as Linda Scott DeRosier discovered. Her book *Creeker*, about the kind of historical family literacy many Appalachian peoples value, was deemed unscholarly by her colleagues and not worthy to count toward her tenure.[24]

Not all Appalachian students recognize the ways academia can devalue their home literacies. In fact, some who have bought into the stereotypes of Appalachian inferiority would say they *want* to be standardized by their education. However, it can't be denied that the perception of academic literacy as superior or at least incompatible with Appalachian cultures—a perception both educators and students are liable to feel—can make school, particularly higher education, feel intimidating, unwelcoming, or even dangerous to potential students. In the case of Madison College, these feelings may have been less distinct for multiple reasons. For one, Appalachian otherness had not yet become concrete in the ways we experience it today. Also, these students were largely being taught by educators who were integrally tied to their communities: the community support for the school and the local origins of many of the teachers could have made attending college seem like less of a culture shock than it can be now. However, there are hints that Madison College's educational philosophy also included some regional prejudices of its own regarding what higher education was meant to achieve for the student population.

Madison College and the Dynamics of Education

In short, Appalachia as a whole has long been seen as antithetical to education. Of course, this stereotype includes a narrow definition of education as only what occurs in schools—something that for lack of a better term I call formal education. It overlooks the many ways that Appalachian peoples can and do learn to interpret and express their realities—the ways culture teaches us to survive and make sense of our worlds.

However, even the assumption that Appalachian peoples by and large have little interest in formal education is called into question by the existence of these regional colleges. If anti-education attitudes exist, then they exist in contrast to our own history. Even if the existence of Madison College and its sister schools indicates that fewer tensions once existed, that doesn't mean that students and faculty would have been completely unaware of or unaffected by the complicated cultural dynamics surrounding their rural identities and formal education.

There is, in fact, some indication that the college was aware of and was even actively wrestling with these issues during its existence. In his 1838 address to the Philomathean Literary Institute (which would soon be renamed Madison College), founder Samuel Findley discussed the ideology that underpinned his founding of the school, a founding that from his perspective walked a fine line between the "civilizing" function of education and respecting the strengths of the community he served. He presented his vision of the relationship between educator and student as "chiefly if not wholly paternal," a stance that could be seen as either comfortingly in step with the familism prevalent in regional culture or as patronizing, even threatening. He expanded on this thought, adding:

> It certainly ought to be so, as nearly as the assumed relation between the teachers and students can be made to assimilate to the natural relation existing between parents and children; and this assimilation, between faithful teachers and obedient students, is more perfect than can be ascertained except on trial. The ties are intimate, tender, and strong, and last through life. But while the government is paternal and gentle, it must also be steady, firm, and when necessary, decisive; so that no one may be permitted to remain in the literary family, whose presence and conduct will be injurious to the members.[25]

The familial strain of these statements seems regionally relevant to me, in the sense that family ties are traditionally valued in Appalachian cultures. By positioning the teacher-student relationship as familial, Findley was echoing an ideology that most students would have understood. However, these comments also expose anxieties about control and regulation that are common to the education of marginalized student populations. The students in Findley's statements are, like too many Appalachian students today, positioned as potentially dangerous disruptors of the educational norm. The tension between respect for students' backgrounds and the desire to control and shape them into a standardized mold plays out throughout Findley's address.

There are striking ways in which Findley conveyed his respect for his students' local origins. For example, he noted that while there had been struggles in the process of bringing the college to life, community support had not been one of them: "The popular interest taken in [the college's] prosperity, has been laudable in no ordinary degree. And it is with peculiar pleasure, I have to state, that its present footing is much more encouraging than ever before."[26] In *Stories of Guernsey County*, William Wolfe echoed this degree of community support for the college; he noted that some local people had donated funds and labor beyond their means in order to build and sustain it. Findley also saw great potential for local students to become future teachers, an idea that indicates that he saw no reason why these regional students shouldn't themselves enter the field of education.[27]

Findley also recognized that the costs associated with college could be prohibitive for local students, and therefore he promised to keep tuition affordable for students in the surrounding communities. He rejected the idea that making Madison more financially accessible would make it less educationally respectable. Although he was intent on keeping tuition low, he emphasized that a low cost should not be taken to mean low quality: "Too frequently [low tuition] creates a suspicion of inferior services; which by a noble minded community, is more repulsive than a high price. We are willing, however, to submit our labours in this Institute to any test."[28] Interestingly, he not only defended the school's educational value, he also presented the local community as "noble minded"—able to recognize academic quality and unwilling to pay for a shoddy education.

Findley's pedagogy was also prescient in certain ways, in that he preferred that students learn "habits of thinking" rather than simply memorizing information: "It is to this evolution, this drawing forth of the powers of the mind, this systematic enlargement of [students] by their own activities that we apply the term education. The object of schools, academies and colleges is to give a start to this endless series of operations. This, rather than the present attainment of a large stock of second handed knowledge, is the main design of intellectual education."[29] Many teachers today would agree that encouraging a habit of critical thinking is their educational goal in the classroom. However, Findley was also indicating that he saw his students as capable of independent thought instead of individuals who needed to be shaped to fit a more mainstream mold. The classrooms where this learning happened were to be places where power was decentralized and shared, at least to a degree, and where students and teachers engaged in "familiar and easy conversations" on the subjects under discussion.[30]

As we've established, however, Findley was not entirely forward thinking in his teaching goals and methods. While he may have welcomed "familiar and easy conversations," he also espoused a controlling, paternalistic style of teaching. Students should be allowed the freedom to question their professors, albeit "proper[ly] and respect[fully]."[31] Given Findley's strict sense of acceptable behavior, this might not have left much room to debate what was "proper and respectful." He also specified that recitation would be a main form of student learning. The value of recitation as a learning method fell out of favor in the ensuing decades, particularly as a method of attaining the type of critical thinking Findley claimed to pursue for his students. He also specified that students would be "carefully and correctly taught the principles and practices of good speaking."[32] The idea that Appalachian dialects are inherently inferior and incorrect continues to be perpetuated in too many classrooms today. Ultimately, the tension between respecting and controlling the regional student population isn't resolved in Findley's essay, and I don't have enough evidence to show how these ideas played out in the day-to-day operation of Madison's classrooms. Something, however, kept local students attending, indicating to me that the college was able to incorporate itself into the community in ways that avoided student alienation.

Evidence for this is shown in the way that Findley solidly positioned the college in service to, rather than distinct from, the surrounding community and its people. In his view, education should benefit not only students but also their families and neighbors in a way that anticipated modern rhetorical theory. Findley wrote that when education engages people in relevant ideas and topics, even someone who has never been to school will feel "the influence of public sentiment, and hence is led to reject many superstitions and injurious errors, and to adopt more elevated views, even without understanding their origin."[33] This is potentially problematic in the sense that Findley left blank what constituted "superstitions and injurious errors" (especially at a time when the accusation of error and superstition was often used to support religious intolerance). However, Findley's view also recognized the power of ideas to spread through populations, ideas that could ultimately shape our democracy. This concept has been echoed recently by both scholars of rhetoric and public intellectuals.[34] Findley seems to have argued for the validity of small, rural communities contributing to the national discourse. He didn't encourage his students to leave their communities; he envisioned an educated populace who could better serve those communities in ways that would potentially benefit the entire nation.

Conclusion

In 1996, the last physical remnant of Madison College was torn down. It was a former boarding house, a type of unofficial dorm for students who traveled from far enough away to need lodgings. The owners were sorry to see the house go but felt that it was too far gone to repair by the time it came into their hands, and they were worried that it would be a hazard to local children who might be tempted to play in it. Their views, however, were not what struck me about this commemorative article in the *Jeffersonian*. Rather, I was struck by what the journalist described as the verdict from local historian Dave Meredith: "He said even though he has heard a lot of great stories about the college and its heydays in the 1860s, he thinks it's time for some history to be left in the past."[35]

Reader, this horrified me. But in retrospect, it doesn't exactly surprise me.

Meredith's decision that Madison needed to be left in the past, its stories forgotten, fits with the wider change in attitude I've witnessed about the value of higher education. It's no secret that Appalachian high school graduates are less likely to attend college than the U.S. average.[36] I receive newsletters from local school districts that provide brief interviews with their graduating students each year. Even without the benefit of statistics, I notice that, in relaying their future plans, many local graduates don't list college. The reasons for this are no doubt varied, but it does not help that we too often lack the sense that attending college is a natural or valid choice. However, the reasons it isn't as actively encouraged as it is in other parts of the country—reasons that include economic and social perceptions about residents of Appalachia—did not originate with us.

Appalachia is not an inherently anti-intellectual region. And although our relationships with formal education may be complicated today, they weren't always this way, at least not to the degree they have become.

There are still distressingly many voices, even in the field of education, who feel that Appalachian students are not suited to college, at least not as they are when they arrive. I remember during my master's program at Ohio University (a school in Appalachian Ohio but where students from the region are a minority) overhearing the non-Appalachian teaching assistants with whom I shared an office discuss "local kids." One said, "I don't even know why they're here," adding that "*maybe* a community college" would work for them, but not a university. In fairness, I don't know if this view was based on their students' educational preparedness or some other aspect of their classroom performance, and I deeply regret now that I didn't try to join in the conversation to find out. However, the basic message that these "local kids" weren't cut out for higher education (or that a community college would be less challenging, something I can attest is not true) was clear.

Others argue that the problem isn't that Appalachian students aren't suited to college, but rather that colleges, and educational systems in general, are unwilling to adapt themselves to the needs of these students and their communities. There are examples of what can happen when educators make these needs and students' home literacies central in the classroom, including the Arthurdale project in the 1930s, the Foxfire initiative in the 1960s, and recently author Adriana Trigiani's Origin Project.[37] Each is similar in that each actively brought/ brings students' stories, families, and knowledges into the classroom to help students grow as writers and thinkers. However, these forms of place-centered learning have not yet become prevalent in classrooms in the region, especially at the K–12 levels. Learning requirements in these classrooms are set by state and national mandates that local schools do not control, for both good and ill. The role of communities in forming classroom curricula is still a contentious topic that resonates throughout the region. However, most college classrooms have at least some greater freedom in deciding if or how to invite students' literacies in. Madison College, it seems, did so, at least to a degree; it was highly supported by the community and saw itself as responsible for addressing community needs. However, even it perceived part of its role as "improving" society by means of civilizing—or standardizing—the student body in ways that are still well known to us today.

SMALL STORIES, PART 6

———

One of the stereotypes about higher education in Appalachia is that it will alienate us from our roots—something that did not happen to Sarah Morrison. It is also stereotyped, far beyond Appalachia, as a form of liberal indoctrination, which was not the experience that played out in Emma Campbell's family.

Sarah Morrison

I found little about Sarah (McBride) Morrison's early life or parentage before she married George Morrison, who is described in census records as a saddler—a profession that is mostly a lost art today. Sarah became a community midwife, a profession that she likely learned little about in school. My own ancestor Elizabeth "Granny" Stevens likewise served as midwife and root doctor, skills she certainly learned outside of any academic classroom. A "granny woman," I learned later, was actually an Appalachian term for a healer. I had just assumed people called her Granny Stevens because she was old. I don't know if Sarah was likewise called a granny woman, but she was one, and in so being, was a living example of how local women embodied both academic and regional knowledge.

Two photographs of Sarah have been preserved by family members on Ancestry.com, both from later in her life when photography would have been somewhat more common. In one image she appears to be in her fifties, wearing a formal, high-necked dress, facing the camera with a clear-eyed gaze and the start of a gentle smile on her face. (I've seen photos of my own ancestors from approximately the same time, so I can say definitively that not all sitters chose to smile in their pictures, probably because they had to hold their expressions longer than we do for photos today. In fact, these family images scared me when I was little, because the people in them looked so *mean*. Sarah's photo, on the other hand, wouldn't have seemed so frightening.) I tend to think of this photo as showing the academic Sarah, while the other, taken when she was even older, is Sarah as the granny woman. She stands outside amid a slew of growing plants almost taller than she is, hand on a walking stick she might well have just picked up from the forest floor. It's easy to imagine her collecting herbs for teas and tisanes, as my own ancestor would have. Both are images of a woman I take great pride in.

Her daughters perhaps give us more insight into Sarah's educational life and views. One daughter, Elizabeth, attended the Antrim Normal School, established and run largely by former Madison College students, prior to beginning a career as a teacher. She also worked with the Child Conservation League, an organization founded in the early 1900s to promote "worthy and effective relationships between parents and children in the home and the community . . . [and] to provide an avenue for systematized efforts pertaining to childhood and its needs through education, philanthropy, and legislation."[1] Sarah's desire for education, it seems, found a healthy fruition in her daughter's career.

While Elizabeth worked to provide educational opportunities, her sister is interesting for a different reason. Sarah's daughter Bertha Morrison (later Steffy) is described in census records as "in school" at the age of 19. It is possible that this means she was attending college, perhaps at Muskingum (as a daughter of Sarah's sister-in-law and fellow Madison alum Elizabeth Stockdale did), or it could mean she was also attending the Antrim Normal School.

Bertha demonstrates a sense of self-determination that, at least today, is admirable. In the 1910 census, she and her young son are living with her parents, despite the fact that she was married. She divorced her husband in 1916 on the grounds of willful absence, a divorce that was only granted on the judge's insistence that she never remarry. When she decided to remarry anyway, the judge threatened to annul the divorce decree, effectively attempting to hold her hostage to her absentee ex-husband. While I haven't been able to find more information on the legal outcome, she *did* remarry. Somehow, her stubbornness and defiance carried the day.[2]

It's not outside the realm of possibility, I would argue even the probability, that Bertha's determination to live her life on her own terms despite her gender is something she learned from a mother who became a college-educated woman in a time when many women in the nation were barely educated at all.

Emma R. Campbell

Of all the students I've researched, Emma's story is perhaps the most out-wardly troubling from my modern standpoint. Her family history intersects with the nation's enduring history of racial violence, illustrating the limits of education as an antidote to prejudice.

On the surface, Emma's story bears similarity to others I've found; she married and had a child who went on to be well educated like her mother. At some point after leaving Madison, Emma married Albert Wagstaff, a Guernsey County man with a family connection to some of her Madison classmates (Albert's brother, W. R. Wagstaff, practiced law with Matthew Gaston, the father of Madison students Mollie and Elma Gaston). Traveling to Kansas with Emma and his brother, Albert started the first newspaper in Paola, Kansas, before leaving Emma a widow in 1863 with a two-year old daughter named Myrtle. At some point, Emma remarried a man named John Brady (a fellow Ohioan), with whom she and Myrtle moved to Washington state. There, Myrtle "received a liberal education at one of the first schools at Portland, Oregon," becoming "a young lady of rare beauty and culture."[3]

However, it's Emma's niece rather than her daughter who complicates this narrative. Emma's brother-in-law William Ross Wagstaff was a graduate of Muskingum College who became a lawyer in Cambridge, Ohio, and whose law partner Matthew Gaston had daughters who attended Madison. William moved to Paola, Kansas, with Emma and Albert, where he married a widow named Mary Jane Torrey and adopted her daughter, Flora Torrey. (Flora then took on the surname Wagstaff.) W. R. Wagstaff, who would later become a prominent Kansas judge, saw to Flora's education, teaching her law and lan-guage. Flora entered law school in St. Louis in 1879 (as the only woman), becoming the second woman licensed to practice law in Kansas in 1881 (she missed being first by one week). She went on to support another woman in a traditionally male field as an attorney for Hetty Green, a female financier known as the "Witch of Wall Street."[4]

On the surface, this is an amazing story, one that exemplifies the power these small colleges in Appalachia had to affect women's lives and worlds: Madison College educated Emma, who then saw that her own daughter received a comparable education. Her brother-in-law, educated at neighboring Muskingum College, prepared his adopted daughter to become a prominent and early female lawyer, whose professional career intersected with other prominent women. However, Flora's background was not entirely rosy. While she might have had somewhat proto-feminist career aims in that she saw herself as a woman who was capable of and had a right to operate in male-dominated fields, her story also touches on some of the ugliest race-related violence the country has ever seen.

Flora's birth father, Henry Torrey, was something of a neighbor of Emma, Albert, and W. R. Wagstaff in both Ohio and later in Kansas. He moved to Paola, Kansas, from Dover, Ohio, located in Tuscarawas County—the county that shares Guernsey's northern border. They may even have traveled to Kansas in the same party, as they all went west the same year (1857). However, Henry Torrey also brought along his friend, a fellow Dover native named William Quantrill.

For anyone who knows this history, the name Quantrill is enough to turn the stomach. Seeing it in connection with any of my Madison research was a shock—especially seeing how closely it intersects. There's every chance that Emma Campbell would have known Quantrill; her niece Flora Torrey certainly did. While I don't have any evidence for Emma's feelings about Quantrill or his views, Flora apparently thought well of him.

William Quantrill, despite hailing from a Union state, became a devoted Confederate sympathizer, largely on the basis of racism. He formed a group of bandits dedicated to capturing escaped slaves (or free persons of color whom he then sold as slaves) in Kansas and Missouri—and this is only the tip of a large, violent iceberg. He continued a reign of terror against both Blacks and Union-sympathizing whites across several states. He is most well known for the Lawrence Massacre of 1863. Lawrence, Kansas, was a town known for its Union sympathies and abolitionist, anti-slavery sentiments. Quantrill led upward of 450 guerilla terrorists into the town in the early morning of August 21st. They burned the town and massacred over 150 men and children deemed old enough to bear arms.

Flora's birth father maintained a close friendship with Quantrill, despite the fact that Quantrill was known to steal from him. One witness remembers Quantrill, fresh from a brush with the law, coming to the Kansas hotel run by Henry Torrey, where Torrey's wife and daughter (who must have been Mary Jane and Flora) cheerfully chatted and packed sandwiches for Quantrill to take with him.[5]

It can't be proven that the family's friendship indicates an ideological agreement, but at the very least, it shows that the Torreys weren't bothered by Quantrill's terrorist activities. This story reminds me that formal education doesn't automatically lead to tolerance, empathy, or open-mindedness. Quantrill himself was a well-educated man, a schoolteacher. This was an era before curriculums, specifically higher education ones, incorporated discussions of difference as an ethical imperative for preparing citizens to participate in a democracy. We can't say for certain that Flora Torrey Wagstaff, whose life was certainly influenced by an Appalachian Ohio college via her stepfather, shared Quantrill's racial views. But I find it hard to escape the image of her as a young girl, smiling as she prepares a picnic lunch for a man with that much blood on his hands.

CHAPTER 7

What Was Lost,
What Remains

Madison College's
Sister Schools

———

That this book has focused on Madison College was something of an accident of location. I chose it because it was closest to home, literally. Learning about its existence was the prompt to do further research, to learn about the many other regional colleges that existed in the nineteenth century in Appalachia. In some ways, Madison wasn't the most logical choice for a focus—it wasn't as long lived as some of the other schools and it didn't produce the greatest number of or most famous graduates. But really, that wasn't what I was looking for; I wanted to see the ways that a college such as Madison mattered regionally, not just nationally (although through some former students such as Monmouth College president David Wallace, I can see that it did matter far beyond our county). Even in its short life, Madison meant something to this region, and those effects carried on for at least the next one or two generations and possibly further.

But as I've said, Madison was not unique. Similar schools existed throughout the region I'm examining, almost certainly more than I've yet discovered. For example, this book could just as easily have been written about West Virginia's Wheeling Female College, which was unique in the fact that most of the teachers and principals were women and which also graduated many unsung educators and activists. Likewise, I could have focused on the Chillicothe Female Seminary, presided over at one point by Samuel Findley, Jr., prior to his presidentship of Madison College. At its inception in 1834, the board of trustees were in communication with Mary Lyon, founder of Mount

Holyoke College and one of the most prominent women in higher education at that time, who agreed to hand select among her own students a teacher and headmistress for this new school. There was also Hopedale College, founded in 1849 by abolitionists Cyrus and Jane McNeely, which also became an early adopter of coeducation and likely served as a station on the Underground Railroad (despite also having the dubious distinction of graduating George Armstrong Custer, thereby proving that education is not an automatic antidote to racism). I could have written about Pennsylvania's own Madison College, the alma mater of Bishop Matthew Simpson, who gave Abraham Lincoln's funeral oration, or about Washington Female Seminary, which graduated author and activist Rebecca Harding Davis.

I could have chosen any of these or many more from a still-growing list of former schools now coming to my attention because they all have important elements in common. They were institutes of higher education that emerged in a place that modern stereotypes tell us they shouldn't have been: rural Appalachia. Not all their locations are rural today; for example, Wheeling, West Virginia, and Washington, Pennsylvania, are cities. Others, such as Antrim, have remained distinctly rural or small town. Nonetheless, the prevalence of institutions of higher education, most of which either admitted women or were solely focused on women's education, force a requestioning of what the nation thinks it knows about Appalachia as a region.

While my selection of Madison College was focused largely on its geographical closeness to my own family's homeland, it wasn't the most prominent or longest lasting of the Appalachian colleges I've looked into. In fact, Madison had two "sister schools" across a three-county expanse: Franklin College in Harrison County (to the east) and Muskingum College in Muskingum County (to the west). Both outlasted Madison, although only one, Muskingum, still functions today. This chapter will take a closer look at these schools in order to better understand what we as a region have lost in the closure of so many colleges and what Madison itself might have looked like had it survived.

Franklin College: 1818–1919

Franklin College was begun by people who believed that education and morality were inextricable and that there was no greater moral imperative than the ending of slavery. I discovered Franklin College not long after beginning my research on Madison; I sought out the book *Cradles of Conscience: Ohio's Independent Colleges and Universities* hoping for some mention of Madison (it's there, but only briefly), only to find a somewhat more detailed discussion of Franklin College in Harrison County, Ohio. Antrim is near Guernsey

County's border with Harrison; as a child, I went to Sunday school at a church in Harrison County where my cousin was a volunteer teacher. I had never heard of Franklin College, although I had heard of—but never visited—the town it was in. (I mostly recalled that because of its pronunciation: if you live there, you know that New Athens, Ohio, is called New Aaay-thens, with a long *a*, not New Aaa-thens, with a short *a*.) A quick Google search told me three things: one, that the college building was still standing; two, that it was now a museum I could visit; and three, that the building looked a lot like the surviving drawing of Madison College.

As heart stopping as seeing the picture of Franklin College was, I now know that its resemblance to Madison is likely coincidental. The surviving Franklin building wasn't the same one that stood in the 1800s but was instead constructed after Madison's demise. However, the Franklin Museum remains a treasure to me; I felt, upon visiting it for the first time not long after, the way I imagine most people feel stepping foot inside Notre Dame or Windsor Castle—a mixture of reverence for the age, awe of the purpose, and respect for the deep love people have had for a place that makes it feel sacred. Franklin's memory is kept alive by a small but dedicated group of people who see the value this remembrance can have for its community. My love for Franklin is tinged with sadness that I'd never known about it or even thought to look for it before.

It isn't just geographical proximity that makes me call Franklin, Muskingum, and Madison Colleges sister schools. In addition to a loose Presbyterian affiliation, all three had a history of sharing students and personnel across campuses. Franklin College, begun in 1818 under the name Alma College, may well have been the model Samuel Findley followed in his founding of Madison. He would have been familiar with it because it was the college his son Samuel Findley Jr. attended prior to Madison's founding. In 1838, Madison conferred a doctorate of medicine on Franklin's founder, John Walker, and the schools had at least one president, Andrew Clark, in common.[1]

These schools may have shared faculty, administrators, students, and curriculums, but one area in which Franklin outshines Madison is in social activism, specifically on the topic of abolition. There is reason to believe that Madison College had abolitionist leanings, given the number of families affiliated with Antrim or Madison who were known to have ties with the Underground Railroad. Franklin, however, was far more vocal in its progressive stance. In *Cradles of Conscience*, Erving Beauregard described Franklin College as "a bastion of antislavery advocacy, with the administration, faculty, and students demanding the immediate and uncompromising abolition of slavery."[2]

In his book on the history of Franklin College, titled *Old Franklin: The Eternal Touch*, Beauregard emphasizes that abolitionism permeated multiple levels of education at Franklin; even the student literary societies sponsored abolitionist speakers and published abolitionist addresses.[3] In addition to talking the talk, Franklin College walked the walk—it retained its moral stance even when some in the community split off to form a short-lived rival school, Providence College. In 1837, Titus Basfield earned his degree from Franklin, becoming one of the first African Americans and formerly enslaved people to graduate from an Ohio college. He went on to become an educator and a minister to formerly enslaved people in Ontario, Canada.[4]

Franklin's educational record among women is also impressive. While it began admitting women students later than Madison did (1857 is the first year Franklin officially recorded women students), the caliber of students it attracted and the education it provided them deserves recognition. Women graduates of Franklin College became teachers, professors, authors, and doctors (according to the Ohio Historical Society, three of Ohio's first licensed female physicians graduated from Franklin).[5] Even those who, like many of the Madison women, didn't go on to use their education professionally treasured it long beyond their school days, forming alumni clubs and other social groups. Also like the Madison women, the Franklin women's stories illustrate the important ways that education affected their families and communities. For example, Charity Vincent became a licensed physician who studied alcoholism and later worked with the United Presbyterian Orphanage in Pittsburgh (her gravestone reads "The Beloved Physician").[6]

We can also read through their stories the ways that an interest in education created connections across communities and institutions. Jennie Wilkin became one of the first female professors at Franklin College, bringing with her a familial tie to another rural Appalachian college, Bethany College in West Virginia. Jennie was the granddaughter of Jane Campbell McKeever, an Irish immigrant and prominent educator. After Jane's family arrived in the United States, they moved between western Pennsylvania, eastern Ohio, and Kentucky, where Jane opened her first school. Despite the school's popularity, Jane and her family couldn't stomach living in a proslavery state and they returned to western Pennsylvania. There she began a new school for boys and girls. By 1830, her school was well established and was operating under the name Pleasant Hill.

While the Pleasant Hill school seems to have focused more on primary education, Jane's brother Alexander Campbell founded Bethany College in Bethany, West Virginia, about twenty miles away from Jane's home in West Middleton, Pennsylvania. Jane followed suit, shifting Pleasant Hill's focus to the higher education of women (changing the name to the Pleasant Hill Female Seminary). The curriculum largely matched that of Bethany. Jane continued as the principal until retiring in 1868. However, her influence as both an educator and activist (for women's education and abolition) is hard to quantify, stretching as it surely did across the many students her school educated. Her daughter Lora went on to become an author and educator, followed by her daughter Jennie, Franklin College's professor of music. Jane's story links three educational institutions in Appalachia—Franklin, Pleasant Hill, and Bethany College, which still survives—across a community of higher learning that I only recently learned existed at all. Her legacy also shows that all traditions have a beginning. If the value placed on education carried on for multiple generations of the Campbell-McKeever women, it is because it began with Jane, a woman who had little opportunity for formal schooling and no opportunity for any kind of accreditation or degree but who found ways to gain for herself the learning she wanted and pass it on to others. Her example also reminds me of how little I know about the mothers of the Madison women. Their daughters had an opportunity to obtain formal schooling that their mothers lacked—but that doesn't mean the mothers didn't want it or possibly even had it, perhaps through less formal means.

While Franklin College likely provided the model for Madison, Madison had a profound effect on Franklin, not only as an example of coeducation. Specifically, the fall of Madison College frightened the educators at Franklin. Former Madison student Robert Campbell became president of Franklin in 1867 and fought hard to keep the college thriving with a strong faculty, which, under his watch, welcomed women.[7] That fear did not diminish over the following decades. In 1876, Franklin alumnus John Welch published an address delivered at Franklin College titled *A Plea for Small Colleges*.[8] This address was delivered at a time when the state legislature was making it hard for private colleges to survive; among the more daunting requirements was that a college had to have an endowment of at least $10,000 in order to confer degrees. In addition, taxation of private colleges was increasing.[9] This was around the same time that public and land-grant colleges and universities such as Ohio State in Columbus were beginning to thrive, making competition for students stiffer. Nearly all the small Appalachian colleges I've examined were private; as costs for running these schools increased and rural economies decreased, the fears for these small schools were well-founded.

Although Franklin outlasted Madison by roughly sixty years, it too succumbed to its own perfect storm of administrative failure and changing social and economic conditions in the region. In 1916, the Franklin board of trustees fired its president, E. M. Baxter, who was found to have embezzled $75,000, taking both college funds and borrowing heavily on the college's behalf. The situation was dire enough by 1921 that the trustees voted for closure. While Baxter's theft undoubtedly broke the camel's back, it wasn't the only straw that precipitated this loss. As Beauregard points out:

> New Athens' isolation due to being on no railroad line had eliminated once thriving recruiting grounds. . . . The area in and around New Athens itself was being depleted by the insatiable takeover of land by the mining companies. The farmers, whose dairy and sheep operations had enabled them to send their sons and daughters to Old Franklin as well as contribute to her fund drives, were selling out to the mining companies whose absentee owners had no sentimental attachment to the venerable college. Furthermore, the auto age had reached the market village of New Athens, undermining the once thriving services—livery stables, feed stores, blacksmith-ferriers—whose owners had been loyal patrons of Franklin.[10]

The change from localized economies to those driven by extractive mining operations meant that even those with deep attachments to the college could no longer afford to support it. Community interest in the college didn't disappear; as with Madison, "occasionally rumors appeared about reviving Franklin" long after its demise.[11] The funds, however, were simply not there—an economic change reflected throughout the Appalachian region.

Officially, Franklin merged with Muskingum College in 1926. In practical terms, this had little effect. Muskingum administrators agreed to absorb and undertake the "rights and duties" of Franklin's charter, in spirit if nothing else—they couldn't physically take possession of the charter, which had been stolen by Franklin's embezzling president Baxter.[12] It also took possession of Franklin's archive, which was unfortunately meager for reasons that are still unknown. Erving Beauregard posits that the majority of Franklin's records were either stolen by Baxter, destroyed in an 1899 college fire, or misplaced in the transfer between institutions. The loss to New Athens, a community that had once served as an epicenter of intellectual inquiry and social activism in the Appalachian hills, was immeasurable.

Muskingum College (University): 1837–?
The first time I visited Muskingum University (then called Muskingum College), it was for a college visit. My high school didn't do many of these—in fact, the trip to Muskingum is the only one I remember us having, probably

because it was the closest college to us, at about forty-five minutes down Interstate 70. I didn't feel any connection to it then. I knew I would be going to Ohio University Eastern, a branch of a public university where my GPA would guarantee me free tuition for the first year. I don't regret that choice, but I wish now that I'd been more open to Muskingum College as a place, to seeing if I could feel about it the way I would later feel about Ohio University Eastern. Because when I visited it again recently, after learning everything I've learned about Madison and Franklin, I realized that I could. Muskingum isn't just a college (and now a university), it is a survivor; it is everything Madison College would have been had it been the one to last.

I also have a familial connection to Muskingum; my grandfather's two sisters attended there. Significantly, none of their brothers followed their sisters' examples.[13] I'm sure I was aware of this fact when I visited campus that time in high school, but I don't recall the knowledge meaning much to me at the time. I had low expectations for college to begin with and didn't enjoy high school, and I barely knew these particular great-aunts; one had predeceased my birth, and the other had moved far enough away that I'd only met her once, and even that was when I was very young. Now I find myself thinking about them a great deal. Why did they seek out college? What did they take from the experience? Was Muskingum chosen simply because of geographic proximity or was there something about it that drew them in?[14] My second visit to the Muskingum campus, embroidered by all that I've learned about Madison, regional education, even my own family, was very different from the one I'd made long before.

Muskingum College was the last of the three sister schools to open its doors; its official founding date is 1837. As with Madison and Franklin, there was no hesitation in the belief that the surrounding community would welcome and nurture a college. The Friends of Education committee that formed to petition for a college noted that New Concord was a community of people "friendly to literary pursuits"—not a description we're likely to hear about many parts of Appalachia today.[15] Judge David Findley, a relation of Samuel Findley, donated the land that housed the first campus building. For several decades after its founding, Muskingum hobbled along as "a poor relation of Franklin" but managed to survive in no small part due to strong community support—another historical fact that flies in the face of stereotypes of modern Appalachia as anti-education.[16] However, Muskingum has outlasted both Franklin and Madison (which is said to have also officially transferred its charter to Muskingum upon closing, although no documentation of this survives in the Muskingum archives). In large part, this survival seems due to location: New Concord's access to a train station as well as its location alongside the national road (and later

Interstate 70), made travel to and from campus a simpler affair than it would have been for either Madison or Franklin.[17] And thankfully, Muskingum didn't have to contend with financial dishonesty at its time of greatest vulnerability, the nail in Franklin's coffin.

Yet Muskingum's existence has often been and remains perilous. Muskingum graduate William Fisk concluded his brief history of Muskingum College in the book *Cradles of Conscience* with the question: "How will Muskingum cope with the disadvantage of its location in one of the less prosperous regions of Ohio?"[18] Gone are the days when Madison's founders perceived its rural location as *more* fitting for an institute of learning; gone are the days when a Franklin student described the region as "the literary land of promise . . . the intellectual Canaan, the land flowing with the milk and honey of mathematical, scientific, and classical lore."[19] Where we are is now a detriment to academic survival.

Still, it's a question worth asking. Community support has not abandoned Muskingum College, just as it didn't abandon Madison or Franklin. On my recent campus visit, I discovered a building named Cambridge Hall—Cambridge is the name of the county seat in Guernsey County, where Madison was located. A dedication plaque just inside the doors explains that when a new science building was proposed in 1920, "money poured in from Cambridge residents, businesses, and civic organizations" for its construction. This, for a college not even in their own county and from a people in a region I am told is every bit as anti-science as it is anti-education.

Guernsey's support of Muskingum College after Madison's closure has deep roots, as class lists and flyers demonstrate. Multiple Madison students began attending Muskingum once their home college was no longer an option, even though the travel required would have undoubtedly been more difficult. Some of Madison's women students, such as Margaret Stormant, Harriet Haney, and Nannie McClenahan, appear to have resumed their studies at Muskingum, and others, such as Elizabeth Stockdale, Nancy Wallace, and Mary Sleeth, had daughters, sisters, or nieces who attended there. Mary Sleeth's great-niece, Libbia Sleeth Giffen, both supported and benefitted from Muskingum College in particular ways. After she was widowed in 1918, she opened her New Concord home (dubbed "Fort Giffen") to student boarders. Homes like hers offered students affordable accommodations, easy access to campus, and a more familial atmosphere—something I'm guessing many students from the region, who likely were away from their own homes for the first time, appreciated. By doing this, she was able to earn the tuition funds that not only saw all five of her own children through Muskingum College but that also allowed her to earn her own college degree. She graduated the same year as her youngest son. Libbia's story and photograph are recorded in *Muskingum College*, part of Arcadia Publishing's Campus History Series. The black-and-white photo shows Libbia and her sister Mabel surrounded by a sea of smiling young faces—both men and women students.

As the last one standing of the three interconnected schools, Muskingum College has inherited a legacy deeper than I had realized prior to my search for Madison's past. It carries the ghosts of many such regional schools that didn't make it through the twentieth century. Muskingum today is arguably a university run by women: as of 2022, the president, the provost, and the chair of the board of trustees are all women, making it very much a rarity among colleges in the United States. This is particularly interesting given what I now know about this region's history of women's interest in higher education. It no longer surprises me that a woman-led college would exist here. Instead, it now makes a poetic sort of sense to me.

I very much hope to see Muskingum carry on into the future, much like I want to see all the surviving Appalachian colleges thrive. However, it doesn't help that many of these colleges are private and have been since their inception—before most public universities were even a thing. Private colleges tend to be more expensive because they don't receive state funding. This isn't to say that Muskingum and other schools like it don't offer generous aid packages, but student debt is no joke. It can ruin lives. Is it any wonder that potential students from working-class families might get sticker shock and decide that college isn't for them? Or that, fearing the potential costs, they might not even try to find out what kinds of financial aid are available?

I hate that there are students who will never give college a try, either because of its cost or because they don't feel they would belong there. How many doctors, engineers, historians, and writers has our society lost because of it? When it comes to tuition costs, at least, I am beyond grateful for the community colleges and regional campuses that also exist in many of our communities; I am both the product of such a school and a current teacher at one. Despite what some might think, these less costly options offer much the same education that students receive at larger, more prestigious colleges and universities. Yet they are not reflections of our histories and our communities in quite the same ways that colleges such as Muskingum are.

Appalachians have an intellectual history that has been largely forgotten or distorted over time. The consequences of this loss have been profound for communities such as Antrim and New Athens. Even I, a nervous and reluctant first-generation college student, didn't grow up feeling like higher education could be part of my identity. We lose a great deal more than a college with every closure. But can any of it be regained?

Looking Back to Look Forward

Today, New Athens and Antrim continue to have a great deal in common besides the fact that they both lost their colleges. Both are tiny communities, smaller than what they once were in their heyday, and both are off the beaten path of interstate travel. New Athens, however, has kept the college building, which became a public school after Franklin College closed. This school closed in 1987, and the community transitioned the building into the Franklin Museum in 1990. The museum examines the history of Franklin College but also a great deal more: it uses Franklin's history as a springboard into understanding both state and national history through the college's experiences with abolition, education, and political thought. Visitors can view photographs of former students as well as displays about the Civil War and early versions of typewriters. In a sense, the town continues to revolve around Franklin, which, while no longer a college, is still the village's most striking feature.[20]

Antrim has continued to be an important place for a small but loyal contingent of people in the surrounding hills and valleys. The yearly Fireman's Fair brings families to eat barbecued chicken and homemade pies, to watch the county's high school band parade down the main street, and to win dishes at the fund-raising nickel toss. (My cousin Emily is currently a saxophone player in that marching band, and my cousin Dale may just be the nickel-toss champion of all time.) However, there has been a development over the past year that is bringing something else back to the village. The building that once housed Cole's store (the purveyor of chewing gum and dusty canned goods when I was a child), mere steps away from where Madison College once stood, has recently been revitalized. It is now The Station on 22, an ice cream and sandwich shop that is already popular with kids and their parents. However, it's also taking steps that have me deeply intrigued. It hosts a weekly meeting space for a local creativity club: people can come together to socialize and chat while working on projects such as painting, writing, or sewing. They have also established themselves as a visiting location for the county library's bookmobile and, significantly, they offer a lovely collection of used books for sale. This, to my knowledge, makes them the first booksellers to operate in Antrim since the time of Madison College, more than 150 years ago. If tiny rural Antrim, Ohio, can once again sustain a bookshop, then anything may just be possible. Even if Madison College itself never again rises from its ashes, then perhaps the pride in and value placed on education that it symbolized in our region can.

SMALL STORIES, PART 7

The following are stories that encapsulate for me the contradictions the Madison women faced as educated and engaged members of their communities. In some ways, their literacies helped them act on the issues they cared about. However, their societies still encouraged codes of feminine behavior—and silence—that they had to continually negotiate. What can be certain is that these women found ways to push boundaries—a battle that began with their decision to seek out higher education and continued as they used their voices in public venues.

Jennie Moore and Eliza Ralston

I'm combining the stories of these two women because they intersect in an important way: both, in addition to having studied at Madison College, were involved in the Woman's Christian Temperance Union (WCTU). The WCTU has deep intersections with both the early women's rights and suffrage movements. While of course not all members would have held the same views, Jennie and Eliza evinced a greater belief in women's rights than many would have held by the sheer fact of their attendance at Madison College. In a country where women in higher education were still very much the exception rather than the rule, they pushed the boundaries of what women should and could do.

Jennie and Eliza's work with the WCTU brought them into close contact with Viola Romans, a remarkable woman who deserves far more remembrance than she has received. In addition to her work as a professor of public speaking at Muskingum College and as a WCTU leader, she also became one of the first women elected to the Ohio State House of Representatives. As noted in chapter five, in 1925 she delivered a speech proclaiming: "In speaking about newness of women in politics I have never understood a time when women were not active. . . . Women have blazed paths, and led the way toward higher ideals, and larger liberties, and great achievements." It is important to remember that the women she was talking about would have been the women she grew up around in Appalachian Ohio—among them Jennie and Eliza.

That these three interacted is shown in surviving newspaper articles discussing their WCTU work. In 1901, Jennie led the devotionals at a chapter meeting headed by Viola Romans. Jennie also undertook literary work with the union; in 1903, she wrote a resolution of respect for a deceased member, and during a 1904 meeting read a history she had composed of the Guernsey County WCTU. Obviously, she was putting her literacy skills to work. Eliza, who died in 1905, was the focus of a WCTU memorial, which means that she too must have contributed a great deal of time, energy, and ability to her chosen cause. Beyond her temperance union work, there are other indicators that Eliza saw herself a woman of active and high ideals. In 1898, she went to court to defend against a challenge to her inheritance from her late husband . . . and won.

Sarah Owens Longsworth

I feel a special love for Sarah Owens Longsworth for a few reasons, one of which is completely unrelated to anything she did in life. When I began this project, my mother and I made a point of seeking out the local graves of Madison women. Most were easy to find because they were in cemeteries that I was already familiar with—some because I had relatives buried in them, some because they were cemeteries where my grandfather and I had set out veterans' flags every May. Sarah was the one we couldn't find. She was buried in a graveyard that, while still in Guernsey County, was farther north than any we'd ever visited. We tried not once, not twice, but three times to find it, using maps and GPS, only to get turned around by the changes that gas and oil companies had made to the already twisty and turny gravel roads that should have led us there. On a final try, we were fortunate to encounter a road work crew. The woman directing what traffic there was (which was mostly us and oil-company employees) was able to put us on the right path. It didn't escape me that we were being led to Sarah by a woman in a male-dominated field, something I suspect Sarah understood.

A year later, after I'd moved to New Philadelphia to begin my new job at Kent State Tuscarawas, I was making my way back to my parents' house for the weekend. Although my destination was only a little over an hour away, I wanted to avoid the interstate to take a more scenic route. Using my GPS, I went from hardtop roads to dirt ones, driving for so long and making so many turns I'd completely lost my sense of direction and started to seriously doubt the accuracy of satellite technology. When I had been driving for almost two hours, I was contemplating calling my mom to see if she recognized any of the road names I'd encountered when I saw it: I was going past Sarah's cemetery. I knew where I was, and I knew which roads would bring me out behind Antrim. I felt like Sarah had found me this time, and she showed me the way home.

There are other, more concrete reasons to admire Sarah. For one, she exhibits a strong sense of self-identity through her gravestone. Although she was married, she has her own stone—one that, though not the largest I've ever seen, is also far from the most modest. The stone also shows her maiden name; she isn't obscured as only the "wife of" her husband. While it isn't unknown for women's maiden names to be included on their stones, it's far from common. Most nineteenth- and early twentieth-century women in our local cemeteries only get their first names, usually beneath that of their husband. Something about Sarah gave her a sense of her own identity outside that of her husband. This wouldn't become widespread until the late 1960s and the 1970s. Even today, my married friends who have chosen to either hyphenate their surname or even keep their maiden names after marriage have faced public backlash for doing so.

However, what makes Sarah the most unique of the Madison women that I've found is her obituary. I've discovered obituaries for roughly half of the Madison women I've researched, but they tend to be perfunctory. They date before the heyday of the detailed obituary, and they often only state things like name, age, names of spouse and/or children, and the name of the church the deceased attended. Any additional details are highly important in allowing me to read between the lines; they might indicate something about the woman's personality, interests, and—what I'm particularly seeking—views on education and community participation. For example, a woman whose obituary tells me she was "well-known and regarded in the community" indicates to me that she had—and used—a voice in community affairs; a description of a woman's "keen mind" tells me she probably cared about education and ideas. This kind of critical guesswork isn't needed in Sarah's case.

Sarah's obituary is one of only two I've found that explicitly describes her as a graduate of Madison College. Not only was Sarah proud of her education, her family (or whoever wrote the obituary) was as well. While I've found that the obituaries of several male graduates refer to their status as Madison alumni, the women's obituaries don't—a fairly pointed indicator that gender expectations surrounding education were still unequal. While Madison might have educated women at a time when many were barred from such studies, being a college-educated woman was still apparently not something to crow about in the late nineteenth and early twentieth centuries (although men could do so). Sarah broke this rule. She was proud enough of both her education and her career that both warranted mention in her obituary: "Mrs. Sarah A. Owens Longsworth . . . was a graduate of Madison College at Antrim and was an excellent schoolteacher until 1860 when she was married to William Longsworth, who with one stepson, Ex-Mayor John C. Longsworth, survives her."[1] There's a lot of potential to unpack in this statement. Does the pointed reminder that she gave up her teaching career for marriage (as married women were not socially sanctioned to have careers outside the home at this time), a career she was "excellent" at, indicate dissatisfaction? Does this relate to the fact that her husband doesn't share her stone? We can only be sure that she valued her own education as well as the education of others. She likely also brought these values to the raising of her stepson, who was seven when Sarah married his father and who went on to become a successful lawyer and mayor of Cambridge, the county seat. Again, the amount of influence Sarah had on this is unknowable, but we can say for certain that Sarah was proud enough of her education that the author of her obituary made a point of it. She is also noted in newspaper clippings as both attending and speaking at Madison alumni reunions up until her death. Given the struggles academic women even today are having to gain recognition and respect for their educational achievements (consider the flack that historian Dr. Fern Riddell and First Lady Dr. Jill Biden have received for wanting to be called *doctor*—such immodest women!), Sarah was ahead of her own time, and sadly, also a bit ahead of ours.

It is worth noting, however, that one of Sarah's step-granddaughters, Edna Longsworth, born in 1880, attended the College of Wooster. She became a teacher and later a principal in the Cambridge school system, a career she chose to maintain until she retired, despite being married. Sarah, I'm betting, would have been proud.

Lizzie Moss

For every Sarah Owens Longsworth, who proudly proclaimed her educational, professional, and familial identities, there are far more Lizzie Mosses, whose lives were shadowed by the circumstances of their gender in the world they lived in. Lizzie in particular stands in the shadows of her father and her husband, a reality enforced on women for centuries. She was the daughter of Mary and James Moss, the latter of whom was a close friend of Samuel Findley and the purveyor of the Antrim bookshop that supplied Madison's students with their textbooks. He was also the college trustee whose political disagreements with the Stockdale family are recorded as causing a rift in the Antrim community. Even more well known was the man who became Lizzie's husband, John McBurney. Also a Madison College alumnus, McBurney had a distinguished career as a teacher, as the superintendent of Cambridge schools, as a teacher examiner in Guernsey County, as a founder of the Eastern Ohio Teachers Association, and as a professor of natural sciences at Muskingum College (now Muskingum University). He also founded a professional journal called *The Guernsey Teacher* which quickly grew to become *The Ohio Teacher*. An influential publication, it continued to run for decades, even after McBurney's passing.

Where was Lizzie in all this? She is recorded, often along with her husband, as attending several Madison College reunions under the name "Mrs. John McBurney." Most other women alumni in attendance at least used their first names rather than their husband's name. My first inclination is to see this as a silencing, a buy-in to patriarchal norms that completely subsumed Lizzie's identity into that of her husband. If Lizzie chose to relinquish her own name (or whether it was her choice at all), the image of Lizzie as accepting her own inequality doesn't quite mesh with one piece of surviving evidence from her student days. A flyer for an 1855 exhibition of Madison's Sigourney Literary Society shows that Lizzie took part in a public debate in which she argued *against* the idea that women's mental abilities were inferior to those of men. If Lizzie believed in the argument she was making, that women were the intellectual equals of their male counterparts, then it is unlikely that she saw herself as the inferior of her husband. Perhaps, given John's status in the community, she felt empowered rather than disempowered by using his name rather than her own. Regardless, it took some time and digging before I was even able to put together the identity of Mrs. John McBurney with that of the Lizzie Moss listed on the flyer and in the 1854 college catalogue. Whatever her intentions, she had effectively become obscured in the historical record.

However, like the other Madison women I've uncovered, Lizzie found ways to push back against society's boundaries. The July 1900 edition of *The Ohio Teacher* published an obituary of her that starts out not with the details of the deceased but instead, once again, with a mention of her husband, noting that

Dr. John McBurney's "pleasant home" had been "darkened" by a recent death. The obituary does, however, go on to note her given and maiden names, referring to her as "Mrs. Elizabeth Moss McBurney," who was "modest and retiring in her manner." The latter description is juxtaposed with the fact that she had, secretly, been a "valued contributor" to the journal: "In the nineteen years in which Dr. McBurney ably conducted this paper, his gifted wife quietly assisted both in the writing and the selecting for its well filled columns." The obituary also identified her as "one of the brightest students in Madison College." As was the case with Sarah Longsworth, the obituary does not place her in the Antrim Female Seminary.[2] The obituary concludes, however, not with a further elucidation of Lizzie's life and works but by returning to praise of her husband John.

I can't help but wonder once again how many of the Madison women may have left far more to the textual record of history than is recognized, simply because those contributions have been either misattributed or not attributed at all. I can say with certainty that Lizzie Moss's writing survives in the form of archival issues of a professional journal to which she was a contributor—something that is powerful in its rarity for women at this time. However, I can point to none of it specifically because it was all done anonymously.

I have to pull myself back from assuming too much, from seeing Lizzie as someone who felt trapped by the confines of acceptable feminine behavior, once again because of what I *don't* know about her. Just as she might have felt empowered by replacing her own name with that of her husband in those reunion notices, perhaps her noted "modest and retiring" manner meant that she felt more free when she wrote for the journal namelessly. I also wonder to what degree this reticence about recognition was an enculturated trait. Author Loyal Jones has noted that humility is an Appalachian cultural value, and I've noticed it myself in many, but certainly not all, of the people around me. An article from a county newspaper that I found early in my research but foolishly didn't save—and now can't find again—caught my attention because it spoke to this idea. It had a quote from an unnamed member of the nineteenth-century Antrim Women's Benevolent Association who took issue with the paper assuming the group had disbanded. They had continued their work, this member stated, but simply not bragged about it. Still, it must be said that if Lizzie was too modest to take credit for her writing, her husband didn't share the same problem. Regardless, as an author in this statewide journal, Lizzie Moss—rural woman from a small Appalachian college—had a voice in the developing field of education science, a voice few women within this profession would have had. The tradeoff was that she had to do so in the shadows.

Conclusion

Why Does It Matter?

———

I've wrestled over and over during the writing of this book with the question of why it matters. Is it even worth trying to write a book about people for whom so little in the way of definitive records remain? I'm sure that some readers will find the "might have been" and "seems likely" repetitions frustrating. Trust me, so do I—I would love having primary sources, written descriptions of their experiences and ideas that I could share and use in forming my own thoughts. However, the fact that we don't have these is part of the point. It says something that the writing these students, especially these women, did in their lives is gone and that their experiences as college-educated people has been forgotten. This absence, more than their shadowy remaining presence, is the point of this book. It matters because in forgetting them, we as a region and we as a nation have forgotten a vibrant and important part of our story.

Ask any random person to describe the characteristics of Appalachian peoples, and I guarantee that "educated" or even interested in education will not be among them. (In fact, asking someone to describe Appalachians might be a stretch. You might have to say "hillbilly.") In the present moment, we are haunted by the specter raised by J. D. Vance's *Hillbilly Elegy*, which not only lays out a blanket definition of the Appalachian hillbilly as poor, lazy, violent, and drug-addled, but presents himself and his own desire for education as something extraordinary. Seeking higher education, he seems to say, made him a special case of what we all could be if we'd just decide to be less hillbilly, to straighten up and fly right. In other words, what Vance repeats is the "tellable" narrative, the one that has played over and over again so often in the past century that it is taken for granted as the truth, the whole truth, and nothing but the truth.

Except that it's not. The Madison women, I suspect, would beg to differ with Vance's sense of his own exceptionalism.

Re-Seeing the Story

I never felt like loving college or getting graduate degrees made me better than the people I came from, although I often hear the fear that it will in the literature about Appalachian students and the college experience. Fear that it will "get you above your raising" is a complex idea, one that says something about not only our college experiences but also our sense of ourselves. I will say, however, that I did feel like I was strange for my particular educational choices, choices that I would try to play down when asked what I was doing these days. (Even now I have trouble telling people that I'm an English professor; it seems easier to simply say, "I teach.") It's this same feeling, that college is somehow not a part of "who we are" in my particular neck of the woods, that made me so surprised to learn about Madison College and its regional compatriots. Like Vance, I hadn't believed higher education to be a natural part of our story.

This is in itself a problem I want to see rectified. The stories we tell ourselves about our identities shape what we think and value, even what seems possible. In *The Lies That Bind: Rethinking Identity*, Kwame Anthony Appiah discussed the troubling ways identities limit us:

> People who give reasons like these—"because I'm this, I should do that"—are not just accepting the fact that the label applies to them; they are giving what a philosopher would call "normative significance" to their membership in that group. They're saying that the identity matters for practical life: for their emotions and their deeds. And one of the commonest ways in which it matters is that they feel some sort of solidarity with other members of the group. Their common identity gives them reason, they think, to care about and help one another. It creates what you could call norms of identification: rules about how you should behave, given your identity.[1]

Of course, Appiah points out, this is a problem, because the sense of identity that people within groups are acting (and feel acted) upon are always incomplete and contestable. It's a lot harder, though, to see the cracks when you're inside the group, when the identity and its limits are not discussed, simply lived.

If Appalachian peoples live the story that higher education is something distinct from their identities, it does more than make college attendance less likely or desirable. It adds to a suspicion of the expertise of college-educated professionals, even when that expertise is essential. Witness the troubling backlashes against the medical advice given by doctors and public health officials during the COVID pandemic. I am currently writing this in one of the least-vaccinated counties in my state. (Early in the pandemic, I read a speech written in 1845 by Madison College graduate Thomas Merrill, where he stated, "Never was there a period in the history of our beloved country, when more wisdom, prudence, and moral firmness were requisite in the management of the political concerns of the nation."[2] In the margin next to it, I've written: hold my beer.)

If failing to see higher education as part of our regional identity is harmful, as I think it is, I also don't believe it's an issue that is our fault. The plethora of nineteenth-century colleges that existed and the level of community support for them prove that we were not an anti-educational region. However, expanding corporations and the extractive industries found themselves with a need for a large pool of (one could argue easily dispensable) laborers in their mills, mines, and factories. Todd Snyder has examined the ways that mine owners explicitly worked to create a sense of identity among miners that divided physical and intellectual work, an identity in which the miners were to pride themselves on being physical, not mental, laborers. It's a phenomenon that isn't limited to the coal mines; we can see it happening across working-class communities throughout the country up to the present. No longer were we hearing the stories of farmers propping up their books on the plow. A recent, and egregious, example occurred in 2017, when the director of the White House Office of Budget and Management argued that it was unfair that coal miners should pay taxes to support PBS . . . the implication being that of course the educational programing on PBS would have no relevance to a coal miner.[3]

My question is how does the story change when we factor in Madison College? In other words, how does it change when we look at the very real interest that both my county and other parts of Appalachia had in formal education? (As Samantha NeCamp's *Literacy in the Mountains: Community, Newspapers, and Writing in Appalachia* points out, this interest wasn't just present in the northern part of Appalachia.) For one thing, it smashes the wall that others, and that we ourselves, have put up between our identities as rural people, as working-class people, as Appalachians, as hill folk, as whatever we want to call ourselves, and higher education. Scholarship is our history, too, and it can also be our future. If we are to find a future in which the rural/urban divide in this country doesn't rip us apart, in which we learn how to share and listen to each other's ideas, it has to be.

This latter point intersects with what I want our intellectual future to be, but getting there will take willingness and cooperation not only on the part of Appalachian peoples but also on the part of the institutions that are meant to educate us. If I am asking for more Appalachian peoples to give college a chance, I am also asking those colleges to give more Appalachian students a chance. This will include practical measures like providing scholarships and childcare while seeking out and valuing students' home literacies. I am recalling here the works of scholars like Amy Clark, Katherine Kelleher Sohn, Linda Scott DeRosier, Kim Donehower, Todd Snyder, Nathan Shepley, and Sara Webb-Sunderhaus, who all echo a similar refrain: Appalachian students' home knowledges are not, as a rule, welcomed in academia. There has to be a way of welcoming Appalachian students into the classroom that opens doors for them to learn about new identities, ideas, and ways of thinking—which is what ultimately education is supposed to do—without telling them that those new concepts are by nature better, or that the identities and ideas they bring with them are inferior. Some are already working toward a vision in which students' stories and regional knowledges are worked into curriculums rather than excluded. But there is much, much more work to be done.

What College Can Do

My college experience, especially in my writing and English classes, introduced me to voices and realities in the world I might never have encountered otherwise. More than this, it asked me to think deeply about other people's lives, to think about how their stories compared with my own and what the similarities and differences I found might mean. It made me feel more wholly and interconnectedly human, a feeling I still get every time I open a new book. I say this knowing that everybody is different. Not everyone enjoys reading or writing, for example, no matter what it is they're asked to read or write about—and that's okay. Not everyone wants to go to college—something that likely won't change no matter how much or little it's considered part of their identity. My point, however, is that there are things students can get from college that they don't necessarily get elsewhere, especially when they are asked to think carefully and critically about their own and others' ideas.

At times in the past when I've pointed this out, I've been accused of elitism—oddly enough, often by other people in academia. I think I get where they're coming from: their concern is more for the potential debt that students could incur, especially students who, because of their cultural, economic, and/or academic histories, are at a high risk of not finishing. (This is a criticism I especially get from various audiences when I'm perceived as encouraging liberal arts/humanities majors—such a waste of money!) It's a fear I understand. The hurdles between Appalachian peoples and higher education are not solely ideological, they are also matters of funds and resources, and these issues deserve their own discussions. All I'm saying is that the motivation for education can't be entirely extrinsic, based solely on the job we expect to get for "putting in time" at school, not if that time is going to amount to more than simply accumulating technical skills. Technical skills are essential, of course, and are fully worthy of respect. But education can also be more. That the Madison women couldn't expect to gain self-sustaining careers from their education tells me that they too found something more in their learning. How can I tell that writing and rhetoric mattered to my foremothers even if none of their writing survives? Because they sought out a college education that was grounded in those subjects.

I reject, then, the idea that telling the Madison women's, and my own, story—that higher education can and should be part of our regional identity—is somehow potentially harmful. That it either "gets us above our raising" or will mire us in more debt with "useless" degrees. On the contrary, I see it as illuminating, at least for me, the ways that colleges can positively promote growth and connection within our communities.[4]

Madison's alumni certainly didn't doubt that their experiences had been worthwhile. They argued for the ways that schools such as Madison could be important for others. At one alumni reunion, graduate C. J. Hunter said, "The small college possessed an advantage to the pupil in the fact that at such institutions the young and inexperienced students were pushed to the front in literary and other college efforts and were not suffered to hide behind the many as in larger institutions. The influences of such colleges never die. The pupils come in closer touch with their instructors in the small schools."[5] While the benefit of pushing shy and/or unprepared students to the front is debatable today, in other ways Hunter raises an educational issue that is still deeply relevant: that smaller classrooms and more in-person attention from instructors creates better learning conditions. At the same reunion, John McBurney raised similar concerns: "He too spoke of the usefulness of the small college and its benefit to the student. He mentioned the legislative effort of last winter to wipe out the small colleges and enumerated some of the instructors that the larger institutions had found in the smaller schools. Muskingum had given a president to both Chicago and Miami universities."[6]

This is still an exceedingly relevant point. Small liberal arts colleges are at a particularly precarious juncture, despite the very great benefits such schools can have on people and their wider communities. A declining emphasis on the importance of liberal arts in our society has already put pressure on many smaller colleges throughout the country. Likewise, a U.S. population that is growing at a slower rate and whose proportion of young people is shrinking means that there will be fewer and fewer students to go around. The financial losses of the COVID pandemic are predicted to cost us more small colleges. Because most small liberal arts colleges are private, their comparatively higher tuition rates means that it is harder to sustain them in regions that tend to lack economic affluence, such as rural Appalachia. Muskingum, the surviving institution of the original Franklin-Madison-Muskingum tri-county college trifecta, will have an even harder row to hoe for the perceivable future.

This is not to say that schools such as Muskingum, Madison, and Franklin don't have something to teach us today about the value of small colleges and a liberal arts education. For me, they say a great deal about what colleges can and should be for their communities, especially here. Trends indicate that "regional colleges will be under pressure to cut liberal arts courses and expand professional programs"—exactly what happened to Wheeling Jesuit University, just across the border in West Virginia, in 2017.[7] This potential outcome, that we will see even fewer colleges in Appalachia and at the ones that survive, fewer opportunities for the liberal arts, is the specter of Madison that haunts me the most.

Madison's students valued their liberal arts education. The evidence of this shines through the long life of the alumni reunions and the glowing descriptions in speeches former students gave at them. Over and over, speakers returned to an enduring theme: Madison's influence on them would never die. They, however, would eventually die—and unfortunately, so did the memory of the college and its influence on the community.

The positive influence of a liberal arts education was likewise described by decades of students at neighboring Franklin College, a school that outlasted Madison by sixty years. Dr. Erving Beauregard, the author of the college's official history, describes how "Franklinites stressed their everlasting debt to the tiny institution tucked away among the rolling hills" and sums up its students' feelings in the book's subtitle: *The Eternal Touch*.[8] In the book, he describes how "the classical tradition spread its tentacles to nearby communities" via the college's alumni, including how "through the years a Cadiz women's group [had] been meeting for lunch and then a discussion of Latin."[9]

This image, of a group of former college women in a small Ohio town surrounded by woods, hills, farms, and coal mines, getting together to retain their Latin is evocative. My point is not that the specific subjects of their classical education ought to be retained or reinvigorated today—I'm rather thankful to have avoided Latin myself—but that even the subjects that were not seen as economically beneficial were valued by the students learning them.

The questions Madison College's disappearance raises for me, questions connected with how we as a region and even as a larger nation will value higher education, are also inextricably linked to the ethical questions of humanity. I want to broach an argument that appeared in the *Chronicle of Higher Education* in 2016 titled "How Humanities Can Help Fix the World." Although the title might be a touch exaggerated, author John McCumber makes a very valid point. When the humanities are written out of our curriculums, we risk losing the classes that teach a wider understanding of the human condition and, most important, how to empathize in ways that can prevent the dehumanizing impulses that lead to mass violence. McCumber challenges readers with the reality that even if many—especially white—young people learn that racism is wrong, they may never learn *why* it is wrong or even what racism looks like. As McCumber asks, "Is it possible to have a society full of young people who are creative, energetic, entrepreneurial, technologically informed—and wholly comfortable with mass slaughter? I know the answer. I'm in a German department." While I don't mean to indicate that Appalachia is somehow more prone to racism, violence, or otherwise Nazi-like behavior than other places—although we are burdened with this stereotype—we as much as anyone need and deserve the chance to learn about the realities of human experience within and beyond our own communities. The liberal arts can, as McCumber notes, help us "open ourselves up to what is different," something he argues will be essential to creating a future humans can actually live in well. Likewise, the liberal arts prompt us to ask questions about what we as communities want and need in order to thrive. In other words, it's not enough to teach a student how to run a business if they aren't also learning about the morality of business practices, the pitfalls of implicit biases in hiring, or the ability of local businesses to revive decimated regional economies. Why should we bother trying to improve communities like ours, where industries and policies have wrecked our climate, poisoned our land, and tanked our economies? It is these very questions that a liberal arts education asks us to ask.

Yet, we are at a crossroads when the very courses that would ask such questions are being removed from college curriculums. Why we should care about Madison College and her students is a question that relies on the humanities for an answer.

There is hope that Madison's spirit can indeed live on forever, as its alumni proposed, and that Samuel and Margaret Findley's works can continue to follow them in life, not disappear with them in death.[10] Community colleges in Appalachia, as well as regional campuses for larger universities, can play the same roles that Findley envisioned for Madison. They can provide professional training, as Madison was keen to do for future clergymen and engineers, without asking us to sacrifice the humanities, our communities, or even our own identities.[11] In the article "Becoming to Remain: Community College Students and Post-Secondary Pursuits in Central Appalachia," Christina Wright quotes the president of Southeast Community and Technical College in Kentucky: "You know, we're fond of saying that if you're doing your job right, you don't know where the college ends and the community begins, and I think there's some truth to that. Community colleges, of course, were founded, and I'm sure you know all this, to be community centered institutions . . . helping communities to accentuate some of the positive things that they had going on, the culture and place. . . . So those that are engaged with their community are doing their job properly."[12] In order for this belief to become more widespread in Appalachia, we need more recognition of the positives that our community cultures can bring to the table (or even the recognition that positives *do exist* in Appalachian communities), as well as how education can add to more than just our technical skills. Whether or not this wider recognition will happen remains to be seen.

What Madison College teaches us—perhaps me most of all—is to question our own mythologies. Appalachia was not, as Samantha NeCamp emphasizes, an educational backwater from its beginning. Madison's students saw higher education as much their right as it was for anyone for reasons that went beyond the job market. Some former students did leave the area, but many also stayed, putting their education to use in public services and actions. Women graduates took active part in debates in both college and in their communities; they read about and spoke publicly on issues of the day. And they encouraged these practices in their children, even after Madison's closure put college education out of the reach of many.

Madison College and the women who attended it demand that we expand the "tellable narrative" of what it can mean to be Appalachian. The narrative that Appalachia doesn't value formal education is one with many causes and many repercussions, including a cycle of mutual disinterest or even alienation between students and schools. However, even if there is a lot we can't know for certain about these women, what we do know brings new possibilities to what their stories were and what our story can be in the future. Appalachian people can seek and have sought out education, even seemingly for its own sake. They took an active part in receiving and providing education in their communities, education that worked for those communities. Yet these are the stories that didn't get told, and without them, our communities and our worlds changed.

Stories are powerful, but only the stories we value get told—and what we value can change over time. When formal education ceased to be a prominent social value locally, for myriad reasons, the stories faded. Let me give an example, in the form of one last small story.

SMALL STORIES, PART 8

_____

Maud Clouse Gallagher

I know a good deal about my grandfather's mother, Maud, even though she died before I was born. She lived in the Old House, the small, dilapidated dwelling where my grandfather and his father had been raised, falling to wrack and ruin next to the trailer I grew up in. I knew that in addition to her own kids, she took in children from a neighboring family. Two of her daughters went to Muskingum College (though at least one of these great-aunts of mine "put on airs" at college and moved out of state—this being the common danger narrative of higher education throughout Appalachia). But what I never heard before starting this project was that my great-grandma Maud had herself been a teacher.

This was a discovery made during one of my many census searches. My grandfather has passed on, so I don't know if he even knew; she seems to have only taught one or two years before marrying my great-grandfather. If she never told her children about her previous profession, it says a lot about how devalued that profession had become. If she had and Pap never thought to mention it to me, even as I started teaching too, it says just as much. (In fact, Pap was never thrilled with my decision to teach at the college level, fearing that it would require me to move a long distance from home, which, thankfully, it hasn't. However, during one of his attempts to sway me toward public school teaching—a more locally feasible option—he would have scored major points for his argument by telling me about these familial connections.)

I don't know if Maud had a college education, which wasn't strictly required to teach in her time, or if she did, where she got it. Unless more documentation turns up, I probably never will. But I know this: two of her daughters, my great-aunts Wilma and Xerxa, went to college. Xerxa, too, became a teacher in the local community. And Maud's valuation of literacy extended beyond her professional career. My mother recalls her helping neighbor children practice their reading. I never knew Maud, Wilma, or Xerxa, but something of their interests must have stuck down the generations, even for my mother, who, despite not attending college herself, made damn sure her children did. Maud's interest in teaching, in education, is something I want to reclaim, loudly and overtly. I want to reclaim every local woman who cared about learning and made it happen—for others, even if not for themselves. I especially want us all to remember that once upon a time, men and women in Appalachia founded and attended colleges because they wanted to, because they saw value in the act of learning. The women who attended college used what they learned to work within their communities and to step outside social restrictions in ways I'd never considered before. The Madison women, alongside the students at largely vanished colleges throughout the region, still have things to teach us, even if the paper trails they left behind are often silent. We just need to learn how to listen—and to *want* to listen in the first place.

Notes

Introduction

1. Adams, "Maternal Ambivalence," 557.
2. Derreth and Guthrie, "Presbyterians and Higher Education," 569. Technically, the term should be Scots-Irish, but I'm going with the local terminology I was raised with.
3. Nelson, "Public Education in the Old Northwest," 224.
4. Rousculp, *Rhetoric of Respect*, xiv.

Chapter 1

1. For a fuller history of the ways education has traditionally worked to standardize student languages, identities, and values, see Spring, *Deculturalization and the Struggle for Equality*. The conflict between standardization and diversity among marginalized student populations continues today. See, for example, Lisa Delpit and Joanne Kilgour Dowdy's edited collection *The Skin That We Speak* and Vershawn Ashanti Young and Aja Martinez's *Code-Meshing as World English*.
2. Royster, *Traces of a Stream*, 83.
3. Royster and Kirsch, *Feminist Rhetorical Practices*, 71.
4. Royster, *Traces of a Stream*, 13.
5. Sohn, *Whistlin' and Crowin' Women of Appalachia*, 19–20, 126.
6. One example is Clark, "Letters from Home: The Literate Lives of Appalachian Women."
7. McCrumb, *Sharyn McCrumb's Appalachia*, 7.
8. Royster, *Traces of a Stream*, 84.
9. Blankenship, *Changing the Subject*, 11.
10. Shuman, *Storytelling Rights*, 54.
11. Webb-Sunderhaus, "'Keep the Appalachian, Drop the Redneck,'" 12.
12. Lerner, "Archival Research as a Social Process," 204.
13. Harney, "A Strange Land and a Peculiar People," 430–438.
14. Ferrence, *Appalachia North*, 134.
15. I have used the noun "women" and the pronouns "she/her" to describe the Madison students under discussion. I do, however, recognize that then, as now, some would have had complicated relationships with their own gender identities that they would likely have lacked the freedom to express publicly.

Small Stories, Part 1

1. Loyal Jones's book *Appalachian Values* has been critiqued for oversimplifying and essentializing Appalachian culture, but his argument about the power of families echoes my own experience as well as those shown in multiple studies of Appalachian identity.
2. Despite his enduring image as an educator, McGuffey also enslaved at least three people after moving to Virginia, something that would have put him at odds with his McKittrick cousins.
3. Even if it is meant to be the Bible, this choice indicates the value given to literacy on the part of the deceased or their family, who may have chosen the stone carving. I've also noted local gravestones that are topped with two or three stacked books. Even if one is meant to represent the Bible, this would indicate an interest in the symbolism of literacy.
4. Clark, Johnson, and Mathews, "The Gendered Language of Gravestones," 1849–1850.

Chapter 2

1. I have tried to interest archeology departments at Ohio universities in studying Track Rock, as weathering is quickly eroding away any trace of its majesty. None have shown an interest, because, I've been told, rock carvings are too difficult to date.
2. Some Native populations remain in Ohio today, such as the United Remnant Band of the Shawnee Nation. Native groups fought to remain in other parts of Appalachia. Author Marilou Awiakta, who identifies as Cherokee-Appalachian, has written about the correlations and contrasts between these peoples, including in terms of education, in her book *Selu: Seeking the Corn-Mother's Wisdom*.
3. O'Snodaigh, *Hidden Ulster*, 29–33.
4. Sharyn McCrumb has pointed out that this geographical similarity can be linked to geology because the hills of Appalachia and those of Ireland and Scotland were once connected before continental drift. See McCrumb, *Sharyn McCrumb's Appalachia: A Collection of Essays on the Mountain South*, 28.
5. Donehower, "Rhetorics and Realities," 49.
6. In fact, the pepperoni roll, which has become something of a culinary hallmark in West Virginia and southeastern Ohio, owes its existence to Italian coal miners.
7. Col. C. P. B. Sarchet, "Paper # 15: The Campaign of 1840," *Guernsey Times*, May 11, 1893.
8. Even though as Presbyterians their brand of Protestantism at times put them at odds with the English Anglican church.
9. Hanna, *History of Greene County, Pa.*, 177.
10. Wolfe, *Stories of Guernsey County*, 897. For more on William Findley, see Eicholz, "A Closer Look at 'Modernity:' The Case of William Findley and Trans-Appalachian Political Thought."
11. Wolfe, *Stories of Guernsey County*, 897.
12. He did, however, continue to preach in Old Washington and another village, Fairview, as well as publishing the *Religious Examiner* and farming, before the bulk of his time became invested in Antrim and Madison College.
13. This report lays out school rules that are both hilarious and heartbreaking. On the side of hilarity, it specifies that "no Student shall exhibit or put off fire works, fire-balls, balloons, or other combustible matter on the premise of the Institute" (Findley, "First Annual Report of the Philomathean Literary Institute," 5), which makes me wonder what they were teaching in those chemistry classes. On the side of heartbreaking, it points out that each student "shall subscribe his name with date and address, in a matriculation book" (4). This is heartbreaking because from what I can tell, this rich source of information no longer survives.
14. Wolfe, *Stories of Guernsey County*, 438.

15. Many of these trustees had children who attended Madison College, including daughters once the school began to admit them.
16. Findley, "First Annual Report of the Philomathean Literary Institute, 1838," 6.
17. Findley, "First Annual Report of the Philomathean Literary Institute, 1838," 8.
18. Findley, "First Annual Report of the Philomathean Literary Institute, 1838," 9–10.
19. Findley, "First Annual Report of the Philomathean Literary Institute, 1838," 11; italics in original.
20. Findley, "First Annual Report of the Philomathean Literary Institute, 1838," 11–12.
21. Donahue and Falbo, "(The Teaching of) Reading and Writing at Lafayette," 40. Nineteenth-century college catalogues differ from more modern versions in that they were much more detailed, containing "educational policies and pedagogical specifics" (40). This makes them useful as sources about what education looked like at these institutions.
22. *Catalogue of the Officers, Course of Studies, Etc., of Madison College and Antrim Female Seminary for the Year Ending Sept. 27, 1854*, 15.
23. *Catalogue of the Officers, Course of Studies, Etc., of Madison College and Antrim Female Seminary for the Year Ending Sept. 27, 1854*, 15.
24. Samuel Findley Notebooks, 1813–1862, Western Reserve Historical Society Library, Cleveland, Ohio. Based on the surrounding entries this piece was written in 1813, but there is no month listed.
25. According to the catalogue, women also had access to a seminary reading room, "provided with about 40 of the choicest religious, literary, and secular journals, thus affording young ladies the only proper appliances for keeping up with the progress of the age, in all the departments of human thought and enterprise." It is unclear if this reading room was distinct from the one offered to the male students or whether the journals the women had access to were different from those offered to the men. However, it's interesting to note the emphasis on keeping women knowledgeable about the events and issues taking place in the wider world. This attention to national issues would bear fruit for several of the women who went on to take part in activist groups. The desire of women to understand current issues was so definite that the women students were given "one hour . . . daily appropriated to the perusal of current events and to general reading." *Catalogue of the Officers, Course of Studies, Etc., of Madison College and Antrim Female Seminary for the Year Ending Sept. 27, 1854*, 16.
26. *Catalogue of the Officers, Course of Studies, Etc., of Madison College and Antrim Female Seminary for the Year Ending Sept. 27, 1854*, 10.
27. *Catalogue of the Officers, Course of Studies, Etc., of Madison College and Antrim Female Seminary for the Year Ending Sept. 27, 1854*, 9.
28. *Catalogue of the Officers, Course of Studies, Etc., of Madison College and Antrim Female Seminary for the Year Ending Sept. 27, 1854*, 10.
29. *Catalogue of the Officers, Course of Studies, Etc., of Madison College and Antrim Female Seminary for the Year Ending Sept. 27, 1854*, 10.
30. However, if traveling proved necessary, the catalog noted that area was blessed with "abundant thoroughfares," although this would not be among the best descriptors for sleepy Antrim today; *Catalogue of the Officers, Course of Studies, Etc., of Madison College and Antrim Female Seminary for the Year Ending Sept. 27, 1854*, 10.
31. Literary societies at Madison will be discussed further in a later chapter. These societies, which were common at most colleges in the United States in the nineteenth century, provided practice in argumentation, speaking, and writing for students outside the classroom, although the expectations for these societies could differ based on gender.
32. Program, "Closing Exercises of Madison College, 1867," John McBurney Collection, Marietta College Special Collections, Marietta, Ohio.
33. "Old Madison College: Grand Reunion and Picnic at Antrim," *Guernsey Times*, August 13, 1896.
34. Sarchet, "Paper #15: The Campaign of 1840."

35. R. W. McFarland, "The Antrim Almanac for 1854," John McBurney Collection, Marietta College Special Collections, Marietta, Ohio, 11.
36. Sarchet, "Paper #15: The Campaign of 1840."
37. "Assignee's Sale," *Jeffersonian*, April 15, 1864.
38. While I have no knowledge of where Madison College's possessions, including books, globes, blackboards, lab equipment, and furnishings ended up, I have not given up hope that at least some of these still exist somewhere. It seems plausible that at least some of these things, such as blackboards, would have been recycled into other schools, and books or globes from Madison College may well exist in corners of local attics or basements.
39. "Old Madison College."
40. "Old Madison College."
41. "Antrim," *Cambridge Herald*, December 7, 1882.
42. "Winchester," *Jeffersonian*, February 12, 1891.
43. "Antrim Schools Closing Day," *Guernsey Times*, April 25, 1913.
44. "Antrim," *Cambridge Herald*, December 23, 1886. The Chautauqua movement was a national push for adult education and social engagement. Speakers could include teachers, ministers, and musicians whose goal was to educate, entertain, and raise public awareness of social issues.
45. "Antrim," *Cambridge Herald*, January 16, 1890.
46. "The Teachers' Institute," *Jeffersonian*, January 10, 1867.
47. "The Normal School," *Jeffersonian*, July 31, 1884.
48. "Antrim Farmers' Institute," *Jeffersonian*, March 3, 1904.
49. "Antrim Farmers' Institute Program," *Jeffersonian*, February 13, 1902.
50. "The Farmers' Institute," *Jeffersonian*, February 27, 1902. While I cannot definitively tie C. F. McBride to Madison College, many McBrides did attend. C. F. is potentially a former student or a child of former students.
51. Quoted in Col. C. P. B. Sarchet, "Paper No. 16: The Campaign of 1840: That Old Central Committee and Some General Political History," *Guernsey Times*, May 18, 1893.
52. Samuel Findley Jr. went on to become a distinguished professor of rhetoric at the University of Pittsburgh in 1861. In 1878, he published a book of entomological studies and stories called *Rambles among the Insects*.
53. At least some, however, did make the change to Muskingum, as demonstrated in class lists and flyers. Likewise, some Madison students, such as Elizabeth Stockdale, had children who attended Muskingum.
54. Wallace, *A Busy Life: A Tribute to the Memory of the Rev. David A. Wallace*, 24.

Small Stories, Part 2

1. *Catalogue of the Officers, Teachers, and Students of the Moravian Young Ladies' Seminary*, 12, italics in original.
2. "Imogen Oakley, Civic Leader, Dies," *Philadelphia Inquirer*, September 15, 1933, 3.
3. Robin Toner, "The Nation: Pulling Strings; Invoking the Moral Authority of Moms," *New York Times*, May 7, 2000, 1.
4. Ruggles, "Marriage, Family Systems, and Economic Opportunity in the United States since 1850," 8–9.
5. Porter, *A People Set Apart*, 491.

Chapter 3

1. Colombo, Lisle, and Mano, *Frame Work: Culture, Storytelling, and College Writing*, viii.
2. Rhetoric as a term is a bit complex. It has traditionally been defined as the art of persuasive argumentation. My take on rhetoric defines it even more widely: as the use of

language to create meaning as well as how language, culture, and ideology influence each other to create our sense of identity. I doubt, however, that most teachers in the 1850s would have defined it so broadly. Regardless, written argument essays were part of most approaches to rhetorical instruction at this time.

3. Ricks, "'In An Atmosphere of Peril,'" 73.
4. Connors, *Composition-Rhetoric*, 53.
5. Cabaugh, "A History of Male Attitudes toward Educating Women," 167.
6. Cabaugh, "A History of Male Attitudes toward Educating Women," 173, 175.
7. Connors, *Composition-Rhetoric*, 54.
8. Donawerth points out that even though the intention was to limit women students to a "safe," domesticated form of communication, this form of rhetoric could be powerfully influential. It also played a role in the eventual opening of education as a field for women. By the turn of the twentieth century, most composition teachers in the United States were women. (Donawerth, *Conversational Rhetoric*, 128).
9. Connors, *Composition-Rhetoric*, 53.
10. Golden and Corbett, *The Rhetoric of Blair, Campbell, and Whately*, 24.
11. In fact, there was quite a bit about the Scottish university system that Samuel Findley would have found familiar. The Scottish system saw its mission as civilizing a rustic population, a mission that Findley arguably alluded to in an early address regarding the purpose of Madison College. However, the Scottish universities were also open-admission institutions, which meant they made college preparatory work part of the curriculum they offered, which Madison also did. The University of Aberdeen, for example, actively sought to open higher education to students who would have been considered too poor and rural to be likely candidates in England. Findley believed that this kind of outreach was important. See Horner, *Nineteenth Century Scottish Rhetoric: The American Connection*, 24, 45, 139.
12. Horner, *Nineteenth Century Scottish Rhetoric: The American Connection*, 33.
13. Golden and Corbett, *The Rhetoric of Blair, Campbell, and Whately*, 14.
14. Whately, *Elements of Rhetoric*, 5, italics in original.
15. I'm not sure I've ever sat down to write knowing exactly what I wanted to say, but then again, I've never lacked pen and paper.
16. Whately, *Elements of Rhetoric*, 17.
17. Welsch, "Thinking Like *That*: The Ideal Nineteenth-Century Student Writer," 20.
18. Quoted in Golden and Corbett, *The Rhetoric of Blair, Campbell, and Whately*, 37.
19. Quoted in Golden and Corbett, *The Rhetoric of Blair, Campbell, and Whately*, 41.
20. Horner, *Nineteenth Century Scottish Rhetoric: The American Connection*, 181.
21. Golden and Corbett, *The Rhetoric of Blair, Campbell, and Whately*, 15; Kitzhaber, *Rhetoric in American Colleges*, 54.
22. Whately, *Elements of Rhetoric*, 13–14.
23. Whately, *Elements of Rhetoric*, 20–21.
24. This is a topic that is very much at the forefront of rhetorical and writing studies today. Linguists have long shown that nonstandard dialects are no less logical or communicatively valid than standardized varieties. Likewise, the enforcement of standardized English in the United States has a long correlation with white supremacy and the forced colonization of native and marginalized peoples. This is no less true for Appalachia. Appalachian dialects continue to be perceived as less valid and their speakers as less intelligent.
25. Whately, *Elements of Rhetoric*, 22.
26. Hayes, *The Politics of Appalachian Rhetoric*.
27. Whately, *Elements of Rhetoric*, 23–24.
28. Hayes, *The Politics of Appalachian Rhetoric*, 111–117.
29. If so, Whately wouldn't have been the only pedagogue to overlook regional varieties of argumentation. I'm reminded of Kim Donehower's analysis of James Moffett's book

Storm in the Mountains. When a West Virginia school district in the 1970s banned a set of textbooks Moffett had edited, he traveled there to change their minds, armed with an academic, Socratic style of argument. He was baffled when his adversaries responded with what, to him, were irrelevant anecdotes and analogies. As Donehower notes, Moffett completely failed to see that they too were engaging in a form of rhetorical argument. Donehower, "Rhetorics and Realities," 51.

30. Whately, *Elements of Rhetoric*, 96.

31. Whately, *Elements of Rhetoric*, 29.

32. This, in fact, echoes more modern (and equally problematic) approaches to what has been dubbed the discourse of poverty culture. In *A Framework for Understanding Poverty*, popular pedagogue Ruby Payne equates the type of standardized, sequential writing that students learn in school with their ability to think clearly, an ability that will determine their opportunities and social class. Specifically, the casual register of communication utilized by students raised in poverty culture is characterized by meandering disorganization, as opposed to the straightforward and sequential formal register the middle class uses. While casual register is potentially entertaining, Payne argues that only formal register uses the "skills necessary for problem-solving [and] inference." Payne, *A Framework for Understanding Poverty*, 49.

33. These authors include but are not limited to Kim Donehower, Katherine Kelleher Sohn, Sara Webb-Sunderhaus, Nathan Shepley, and Amy Clark.

34. Officers and Students of the Ohio University, *Annual Catalogue of the Officers and Students of the Ohio University, Athens, Ohio, for 1871–72*, 16.

35. Margaret Boyd Diary, 1873, 21, Ohio University Libraries Digital Archival Collections, https://media.library.ohio.edu/digital/collection/archives/id/40940.

36. Wright and Halloran, "From Rhetoric to Composition," 231.

37. Rothermel, "'Our Life's Work,'" 144.

Small Stories, Part 3

1. Guernsey County Genealogical Society, Guernsey County Community & Family History Book, 231.

2. Scott, *Hugh Scott: An Immigrant of 1670, and His Descendants*, 136.

3. "The Demorest Contest at Milnersville," *Jeffersonian*, April 21, 1892. (The original article is much more verbose. I've tried to streamline the quote to the points relevant to this discussion.)

4. "William H. Craig," Find A Grave, accessed July 21, 2021, https://www.findagrave.com/memorial/169858136/william-h-craig.

5. "Mrs. Margaret Casner, Avid Gardener, Dies at 84," *Courier-News* (Bridgewater, NJ), May 17, 1956, 11.

6. *Catalogue of the Officers, Teachers and Students of Madison College for the Session Ending September 15, 1858*, The John McBurney Collection, Marietta College.

Chapter 4

1. Snyder, *120 Years of American Education*, 76.

2. Lutz, *Emma Willard*, 27.

3. For example, in 1857 Cincinnati's Ohio Female College explained that it had altered its curriculum "in view of her sphere of duty in actual (not imaginary) life, her relative social position as society truly is (not to say as it should be)" (14). It also specified that as students, the women would experience "only a proper amount of intellectual effort" (30) because too much thinking was thought by some to be dangerous to women's health. *Catalogue and Prospects of the Ohio Female College*.

4. Mary Lyon, the founder of Mount Holyoke and a particularly influential advocate for women's higher education, specifically opposed the "ornamental" educations that women's seminaries are fallaciously thought to have focused on. Some did, undoubtedly, care primarily about producing women who could charm and entertain as wives and society women, but as other catalogues show, this was far from the priority at many schools. Turpin, *A New Moral Vision*, 45.
5. Parker, "The Historical Role of Women in Higher Education," 6.
6. *Catalogue of the Officers, Course of Studies, Etc., of Madison College and Antrim Female Seminary for the Year Ending Sept. 27, 1854*, 15.
7. Ricks, "In an Atmosphere of Peril," 69.
8. Spring, *The American School*, 144–145.
9. Sicherman, "College and Careers," 148–149.
10. Connors, *Composition-Rhetoric*, 55.
11. This does not mean they were admitted on an equal footing. Not all classes were integrated, and women students at Oberlin were made to serve their male counterparts by performing tasks such as cleaning and laundry. See Eschbach, *The Higher Education of Women*, 44. While women could attend Oberlin's rhetoric courses with men, they were not permitted to speak during them; Mattingly, *Well-Tempered Women*, 59.
12. "The Demorest Contest at Milnersville," *Jeffersonian*, April 21, 1892. Demorest Contests were speaking competitions in which the participants, young men or women, delivered speeches by well-known figures in the temperance movement. Thus, the new speakers "signal boosted" temperance rhetoric to new audiences. In effect, the Demorest Contests were an early form of re-tweeting.
13. Quoted in Connors, *Composition-Rhetoric*, 53–54.
14. "Literary and Musical Entertainment of the Sigourney Literary Society of Antrim Female Seminary, 1856," Program, John McBurney Collection, Marietta College Special Collections, Marietta, Ohio.
15. "The Reunion of the Old Madison College Students," *Guernsey Times*, August 20, 1896, 3.
16. "Old Madison College: Grand Reunion and Picnic at Antrim," *Guernsey Times*, August 13, 1896, 7, my italics.
17. This, however, is ultimately unknowable, as is much about Lizzie's life. She participated in Madison College reunion events, but she is listed only as Mrs. John McBurney. This form of identification was not used for all women participating in these events, with some, such as Sarah Owens Longsworth, including their maiden name alongside their married one. It was only through census records that I was able to deduce Mrs. John McBurney's identity as Lizzie Moss at all.
18. Harding, "College Literary Societies," 1.
19. Harmon, "'The Voice, Pen and Influence of Our Women,'" 90.
20. Hobbs, "Introduction," 18.
21. Literary societies could be coeducational, as they were at least briefly at Muskingum College. Women were admitted at Muskingum in 1851, and in addition to their participation in the women's Erodelphian Society, they were at one point allowed into the initially male Philomathean Society. However, college president F. M. Spencer evicted them from the Philomathean in the 1880s, requiring the founding of another women's literary society, the Aretean. Giffen, Kerrigan, and Worbs, *Muskingum College*, 17.
22. None of these essays seem to have survived, at least not in local archives. Also, it is worth noting that even what we call "personal essays" or stories can, especially in Appalachian rhetoric, be utilized to make specific arguments.
23. "Literary Entertainment of the Emma Willard Society of Madison College, 1856," John McBurney Collection, Marietta College Special Collections, Marietta, Ohio.
24. Quoted in Lutz, *Emma Willard*, 11.

25. One man reportedly responded to Willard's calls for women's education with, "They'll be educating the cows next." Lutz, *Emma Willard*, 33.
26. Willard, *An Address to the Public*, 34.
27. Willard, *An Address to the Public*, 6.
28. Willard, *An Address to the Public*, 16.
29. Wolfe, *Stories of Guernsey County*, 315. John Hunt Morgan, a Confederate general, raided multiple towns in Ohio, including Antrim, during the Civil War. A fuller picture of what came to be known as Morgan's Raid appears in Wolfe's *Stories of Guernsey County*, 303–333.
30. She also notes that after we started school, neither my brother nor I were willing to listen to academic instruction from her. I can't remember ever making a conscious decision not to accept her help, but she is right. I can recall her trying to teach me a different way to do times tables, something I struggled with, but I was afraid to go against my teacher. The idea that formal education tells Appalachian students, not always overtly but at least tacitly, to distrust knowledge imparted by their parents and families is an issue that is beginning to be discussed throughout the region.
31. Sohn, *Whistlin' and Crowin' Women of Appalachia*, 43.
32. Willard, *An Address to the Public*, 28.
33. Willard, *An Address to the Public*, 28.
34. As Summer Conley explained in a recent article, women in Appalachian cultures have found empowerment in motherhood. She writes, "Throughout our history, Appalachian women have been leading the efforts to provide better lives for their families. . . . The truth is Appalachia is a matriarchy." Conley, "Commentary: What My Mamaw Has Taught Me about Women's Labor and the Appalachian Matriarchy."
35. Much of Sigourney's poetry, which heavily emphasized melodrama and feminine virtue, doesn't translate well today. Gail Collins describes it succinctly as "pretty dreadful." Collins, *America's Women*, 95.
36. In the article "A Woman's Place Is in the School," scholar Jessica Enoch credits Sigourney's rhetoric with opening the teaching profession to women by linguistically changing schools from a masculine to a feminine space. In doing so, she helped solidify the idea that a woman could have charge of the classroom.
37. Sigourney, *Letters to Young Ladies*, 51.
38. This correlates with Samuel Findley's statements in his commonplace book, that the influence of educated women could better society (through their moral and high-minded influence on men). If we take away the element of gender, it also tracks with current theories about the ecological nature of rhetoric. Jenny Edbauer describes the influence of rhetorical acts this way: "The rhetorical situation is part of what we might call . . . an ongoing social flux. Situation bleeds into the concatenation of public interaction. Public interactions bleed into wider social processes. The elements of the rhetorical situation simply bleed." Edbauer, "Unframing Models of Public Distribution," 8–9. In other words, the ideas we espouse intersect and grow around us in both remarkable and mundane ways, and every interaction can shape, alter, or reinforce our identities and ideals. Both Sigourney and Findley sought some control over the ideas that would flourish in this rhetorical ecosystem via the education of women.
39. Sigourney, *Letters to Young Ladies*, 59–60.
40. Sigourney, *Letters to Young Ladies*, 91.
41. Sigourney, *Letters to Young Ladies*, 75.
42. Sigourney, *Letters to My Pupils*, 41.
43. Several had granddaughters or great-nieces who supported suffrage, however.
44. Sigourney, *Letters to My Pupils*, 1.
45. Sigourney, *Letters to Young Ladies*, 3.
46. Sigourney, *Letters to Young Ladies*, 55.

47. Sigourney, *Letters to Young Ladies*, 147–148.
48. "Program of the Literary and Musical Entertainment of the Sigourney Literary Society of Antrim Female Seminary, 1855," John McBurney Collection, Marietta College Special Collections, Marietta, Ohio.

Small Stories, Part 4

1. Quoted in Traister, *All the Single Ladies*, 65.
2. Mercer County Historical Society and Henderson County Historical Society, *History of Mercer and Henderson Counties*, 468.
3. "Mother Seeks Custody of Three Heinz Children," *Los Angeles Times*, February 9, 1933, 22.
4. Gaston, *Portland, Oregon*. The author, Joseph Gaston, is a grandchild of Rachel and Alexander.

Chapter 5

1. Fisk, "Muskingum College," 324.
2. Holmes, *The Irish Presbyterian Mind*, 32.
3. Cahill, *How the Irish Saved Civilization*, 196.
4. Cahill, *How the Irish Saved Civilization*, 216.
5. For more, see Moore, *Women in the Mines*.
6. Todd Snyder discusses the ideologies of gendering education in *The Rhetoric of Appalachian Identity*. This gendering of academia as a feminine rather than masculine space seems to be having practical repercussions: a recent institutional study showed that the student body at my regional college campus is only about 35 percent male.
7. Cahill, *How the Irish Saved Civilization*, 164.
8. Margaret Boyd Diary, 1873, 10, Ohio University Libraries Digital Archival Collections, Athens, Ohio, https://media.library.ohio.edu/digital/collection/archives/id/40940/rec/3.
9. Hall, "Intellectual Pleasure and the Woman Translator in Seventeenth- and Eighteenth-Century England," 103–131.
10. As Edith Hall notes in her essay "Intellectual Pleasure and the Woman Translator in Seventeenth- and Eighteenth-Century England," the necessity of couching education in altruistic terms makes it difficult to know how women truly felt about learning: "The requirement for women who were educated to cite altruistic reasons to defend their privilege obscures evidence of such love of literature even in the documentation which we do have available" (109).
11. Findley, "First Annual Report of the Philomathean Literary Institute, 1838," 16, Ohio Historical Society Archives, Columbus, Ohio.
12. *Catalogue of the Officers, Course of Studies, Etc., of Madison College and Antrim Female Seminary for the Year Ending Sept. 27, 1854*, 15.
13. "In Perfect Health Despite Her Age," *Jeffersonian*, April 20, 1905.
14. Religion as well as gender could play a role in one's view of acceptable behavior. Even today it's not uncommon to hear stories of people who "got religion" and underwent dramatic changes in behavior, for better and for worse, depending on your point of view. It's a well-known story in my own family that my great-grandma got religion at some point and disallowed the playing of cards in her house. My great-grandfather wasn't best pleased, but he chose to say nothing because he was just relieved she still let him in the bed.
15. "The First Meeting of the Female Benevolent Association," *Jeffersonian*, October 9, 1863.
16. For an exceptional exploration of one educated woman's struggle to have a public voice and fulfill her roles as a wife and mother, see Brakebill, *Circumstances Are Destiny*.
17. Boylan, *Sunday School*, 23
18. Boylan, *Sunday School*, 33.

19. Boylan, *Sunday School*, 37.
20. Boylan, *Sunday School*, 122.
21. Mattingly, *Well-Tempered Women*, 1.
22. Mattingly, *Well-Tempered Women*, 1.
23. Mattingly, *Well-Tempered Women*, 1–2.
24. Mattingly, *Well-Tempered Women*, 13.
25. Quoted in Mattingly, *Well-Tempered Women*, 60.
26. "The State W.C.T.U. Convention," *Jeffersonian*, March 30, 1905.
27. "Viola Doudna Romans," 2022.
28. Sohn, *Whistlin' and Crowin' Women of Appalachia*, 38, 158.
29. In the article "A Look at Appalachian Culture and History in *The Hunger Games*," Jim Poe quotes Rachel Parson's point that "Katniss Everdeen is everything a girl from Appalachia hopes and has to be. . . . Katniss had my attention because I knew her—I was her, and am her." He also quotes Elizabeth Baird Hardy on Katniss: "[Appalachian women] just connect so much to her, because they know her; and if they're not Katniss, then their mamas, their grandmamas or their aunties are." Jim Poe, "A Look at Appalachian Culture and History in *The Hunger Games*," *Times West Virginian*, November 15, 2015.
30. Wilder, *Ebony and Ivy*, 114.
31. Beauregard, *Old Franklin*, 41–44.
32. Fisk, "Muskingum College," 326.
33. Fisk, "Muskingum College," 328.
34. "Fourth in Cambridge," *Jeffersonian*, July 2, 1891.
35. "Claims that Irish people were enslaved in British North America are a longstanding myth and online meme sometimes associated with neo-Confederates and white nationalists. The claim, which experts say is also often politically motivated, is untrue." Matthew Brown, "Fact Check: The Irish Were Indentured Servants, Not Slaves," *USA Today*, June 18, 2020, https://www.usatoday.com/story/news/factcheck/2020/06/18/fact-check-irish -were-indentured-servants-not-slaves/3198590001/.
36. Col. C. P. B. Sarchet, "Paper #15: The Campaign of 1840," *Guernsey Times*, May 11, 1893.
37. Porter, *A People Set Apart*, 205–206.
38. Porter, *A People Set Apart*, 205–206, 130.

Small Stories, Part 5

1. "Flora B. Zeigler Class Observes 50th Anniversary Thursday Night," *Daily Mail* (Hagerstown, MD), February 23, 1954, 8.
2. Fleming, "Knoxville College," 89–111.
3. Wallace, *A Busy Life*, 5.
4. "Special Notices to Teachers," *Jeffersonian*, April 13, 1876, 3.

Chapter 6

1. Members of my extended family attended college: two great-aunts and three aunts. Interestingly, all of the college connections in my family were women.
2. Caldwell, *History of Belmont and Jefferson Counties*, 367.
3. It is an assumption with cultural roots, however. When reading a historical source titled *The John McLenahan Folk* about the family of some of Madison's students, I saw dynamics I recognized. One was the reluctance of some students or their family members to take part in public exhibitions because an "averseness to parade" made them wary of anything that smacked of showing off. (Even now, my school has a very tough time getting high-achieving students to take part in public research colloquiums.) Additionally, the author describes what he calls a "dread of dependence" among locals. His mother's reaction, when

asked about her sons receiving outside aid to pay for college, was succinct: "Never. I'll wear my fingernails off first." This sounds a lot like my own mother's feelings about student loans. I was lucky: I went to college during a brief window when my grades in high school earned me free tuition at a regional campus, so I never had to struggle with the cultural implications of loans. Most today don't get that luxury. Henderson, *The John McLenahan Folk*, 56.

4. I firmly believe my mother could have loved college if given the chance. She's a natural problem solver who loves to debate ideas. However, as she puts it, she was so happy to be done with high school that she never even thought of college—which says a lot about the problems regional kids can encounter in the educational system.

5. Athens is still part of Appalachian Ohio, meaning that I stayed in the hills I love. However, the geographical similarity notwithstanding, it takes at least two hours of some fairly twisty roadways to get there from where we lived.

6. Snyder, *The Rhetoric of Appalachian Identity*, 107.

7. Snyder, *The Rhetoric of Appalachian Identity*, 108–109.

8. Quoted in Sohn, *Whistlin' and Crowin' Women of Appalachia*, 68–69.

9. Quoted in Locklear, *Negotiating a Perilous Empowerment*, 97.

10. Donehower, "Rhetorics and Realities," 51.

11. Quoted in Shepley, "Places of Composition," 83.

12. "Appalachian Perspectives at Ohio University: Findings of the Spring 2004 Survey," 6, Appalachian Faculty Learning Community, 2005. In author's possession.

13. Appalachian Perspectives at Ohio University: Findings of the Spring 2004 Survey, 7.

14. Hendrickson, "Student Resistance to Schooling," 47.

15. NeCamp, *Literacy in the Mountains*, 93.

16. Quoted in Teets, "Education in Appalachia," 123.

17. In Snyder, The Rhetoric of Appalachian Identity, 61.

18. Snyder, *The Rhetoric of Appalachian Identity*, 29–30.

19. Snyder, *The Rhetoric of Appalachian Identity*, 71.

20. Catte, *What You Are Getting Wrong about Appalachia*, 37.

21. Catte, *What You Are Getting Wrong about Appalachia*, 42.

22. This pattern is not exclusive to Appalachian populations. The idea that students who are economic, cultural, and/or ethnic minorities can and should conform to academic/ mainstream language and culture is also prevalent on a wider scale through the influential works of educational consultants such as Ruby Payne. Payne argues in *A Framework for Understanding Poverty* that the key to economic and social prosperity lies in this conformity and that it is the school's duty to promote assimilation.

23. Clark, "Letters from Home," 55.

24. Locklear, *Negotiating a Perilous Empowerment*, 93.

25. Samuel Findley, "First Annual Report of the Philomathean Literary Institute, 1838," 12, Ohio Historical Society Archives, Columbus, Ohio.

26. Findley, "First Annual Report of the Philomathean Literary Institute, 1838," 11.

27. Findley, "First Annual Report of the Philomathean Literary Institute, 1838," 12.

28. Findley, "First Annual Report of the Philomathean Literary Institute, 1838," 13.

29. Findley, "First Annual Report of the Philomathean Literary Institute, 1838," 8.

30. Findley, "First Annual Report of the Philomathean Literary Institute, 1838," 14.

31. Findley, "First Annual Report of the Philomathean Literary Institute, 1838," 14.

32. Findley, "First Annual Report of the Philomathean Literary Institute, 1838," 15.

33. Findley, "First Annual Report of the Philomathean Literary Institute, 1838," 10.

34. For examples of rhetorical analysis, see Nathaniel Rivers and Ryan Weber's article "Ecological, Pedagogical, Public Rhetoric," or Marilyn Cooper's "Rhetorical Agency as Emergent and Enacted." For a popular book by a public intellectual, see Appiah, *The Honor Code*.

35. Mark Claffey, "Over a Century of History in Boarding House: Remnant of Madison College in Antrim Will Be Razed Soon," *Jeffersonian*, March 30–31, 1996, 1.
36. Haaga, "Educational Attainment in Appalachia," 4.
37. For more information on these projects, see Clapp, *Community Schools in Action*; Wigginton, *Sometimes a Shining Moment*; and Trigiani, "The Origin Project."

Small Stories, Part 6

1. Collection description, Ohio Child Conservation League, High Hopes League, Rutherford B. Hayes Presidential Library & Museums, accessed September 21, 2023, https://www.rbhayes.org/collection-items/local-history-collections/ohio-child -conservation-league-high-hopes-league/.
2. "Judge May Annul Divorce Decree," *Tribune* (Coshocton, OH), July 19, 1916, 8.
3. "Marriage Notice," *Miami Republican* (Paola, KS), October 29, 1880, 1.
4. Miami County Kansas History, "Miss Flora."
5. Miami County Kansas History, "Miss Flora."

Chapter 7

1. Beauregard, *Old Franklin*, 32–33.
2. Beauregard, "Defunct Colleges and Universities," 559.
3. Beauregard, *Old Franklin*, 69.
4. Beauregard, *Old Franklin*, 27.
5. "Franklin College (New Athens)."
6. "Dr. Charity Jane Vincent," Find A Grave, accessed July 21, 2001.
7. He also enticed Franklin's most famous graduate, John Bingham, to return to the school as a professor of political science and international law. Bingham was an assistant judge advocate general in the trial of the Lincoln assassins and the principal framer of the Fourteenth Amendment, which granted citizenship rights to formerly enslaved people. Beauregard, *Old Franklin*, 27–28.
8. Welch, *A Plea for Small Colleges*.
9. Beauregard, "Defunct Colleges and Universities," 561. The timing of these legislative changes makes it likely they were intended to promote public, land-grant universities, luring away students and thereby thinning the herd of small, private regional colleges.
10. Beauregard, *Old Franklin*, 196–197.
11. Beauregard, *Old Franklin*, 197.
12. Beauregard, *Old Franklin*, 197–198.
13. That women in Appalachia have come to be more likely than men to attend college says interesting things about gender—that formal education has become culturally "feminized,"—while also troubling the definition of Appalachian cultures as hyperpatriarchal.
14. If proximity to home was important, which I'm sure it was for two unmarried girls in the early 1900s, then Muskingum was their only option. There were no public university regional campuses, and Franklin, the other local option, had already closed. It is worth noting that even for a private college, tuition was not as prohibitive then as it would become over the course of the century. My great-aunts Wilma and Xerxa put themselves through school by making and selling baked goods.
15. Giffen, Kerrigan, and Worbs, *Muskingum College*, 9.
16. Fisk, "Muskingum College," 329.
17. In fact, Muskingum County once had two small colleges. However, the rival school, McCorkle College, foundered after only a couple decades, largely because it was harder for travelers to access.

18. Fisk, "Muskingum College," 337.
19. Quoted in Beauregard, *Old Franklin*, 64.
20. This, unfortunately, hasn't translated to as much renown as it deserves. Even I, having grown up in the next county and with a deep interest in higher education history, discovered its existence almost accidentally while researching Madison. When I visited the museum, a volunteer told me that attendance grows smaller and smaller every year—and that was before the COVID pandemic.

Small Stories, Part 7

1. "Mrs. William Longsworth," *Guernsey Times*, August 4, 1898.
2. "Death of Mrs. John McBurney," *Ohio Teacher*, July 1900, 280, John McBurney Collection, Marietta College Special Collections, Marietta, Ohio.

Conclusion

1. Appiah, *The Lies that Bind*, 10.
2. Thomas Merrill, "Address Delivered to the Members of The Franklin Literary Society of Madison College," in *Catalogue of the Officers and Students of Madison College for the Year 1845*, 9, Western Reserve Historical Society Library, Cleveland, Ohio.
3. Alana Horowitz Satlin and Sam Levine, "White House Budget Director Says Single Moms Shouldn't Have to Pay for PBS," *Huffington Post*, March 16, 2017, https://www.huffpost .com/entry/white-house-budget-sesame-street-pbs_n_58ca8cade4b0be71dcf1d3eb.
4. Madison College is still connecting me with my community in unexpected ways. When I started looking at Find A Grave for some of the Madison women's burials, I discovered that several local cemetery documentations had been done by a woman who was once my 4-H group leader, whom I hadn't seen in years. While visiting one of the cemeteries, my mother and I were invited to "stop for a spell" on the porch of a nearby house. The couple who owned the house didn't know us prior to the invitation, but we learned from the ensuing conversation that they had once had my great-aunt Xerxa as an elementary school teacher.
5. Quoted in "Old Madison College," *Guernsey Times*, 1896.
6. "Old Madison College."
7. Jill Barshay, "College Students Predicted to Fall by More Than 15% by 2025," *The Hechinger Report*, September 10, 2018, https://hechingerreport.org/college-students-predicted-to -fall-by-more-than-15-after-the-year-2025/.
8. Beauregard, *Old Franklin*, 208.
9. Beauregard, *Old Franklin*, 202. Cadiz is the seat of Harrison County, where Franklin College was located.
10. As noted earlier in the book, I consider Madison's existence to be attributable to Margaret as well as Samuel. Whether or not she had an academic role, her labor provided her husband with the time and opportunity to build the college.
11. In my mind, Findley's original curriculum could have offered even more in terms of the humanities. True, students at Madison studied languages and history, but not, at least to any great extent, literature, which I see as the greatest means of promoting human understanding. Findley's curriculum, however, was in keeping with his times.
12. Quoted in Wright, "Becoming to Remain," 9.

Bibliography

Adams, Sarah LaChance. "Maternal Ambivalence." In *Maternal Theory: Essential Readings*. 2nd ed., edited by Andrea O'Reilly, 555–566. Ontario: Demeter Press, 2021.

Adichie, Chimamanda Ngozi. "The Danger of a Single Story." TEDGlobal 2009 video. https://www.ted.com/talks/chimamanda_ngozi_adichie_the_danger_of_a_single_story.

Appiah, Kwame Anthony. *The Honor Code: How Moral Revolutions Happen*. New York: Norton, 2010.

———. *The Lies That Bind: Rethinking Identity*. New York: Liveright Publishing, 2018.

Awiakta, Marilou. *Selu: Seeking the Corn Mother's Wisdom*. Golden, CO: Fulcrum Publishing, 1993.

Beauregard, Erving. "Defunct Colleges and Universities." In *Cradles of Conscience: Ohio's Independent Colleges and Universities*, edited by John William Oliver Jr., James Hodges, and James O'Donnell, 558–573. Kent, OH: Kent State University Press, 2003.

———. *Old Franklin: The Eternal Touch*. Lanham, MD: University Press of America, 1983.

Blankenship, Lisa. *Changing the Subject: A Theory of Rhetorical Empathy*. Logan: Utah State University Press, 2019.

Boylan, Anne. *Sunday School: The Formation of an American Institution, 1790–1880*. New Haven, CT: Yale University Press, 1988.

Brakebill, Tina Stewart. *Circumstances Are Destiny: An Antebellum Woman's Struggle to Define Sphere*. Kent, OH: Kent State University Press, 2006.

Cabaugh, Gary. "A History of Male Attitudes toward Educating Women." *Educational Horizons* 88, no. 3 (Spring 2010): 164–178.

Cahill, Thomas. *How the Irish Saved Civilization*. New York: Nan A. Talese, 1995.

Caldwell, J. A. *History of Belmont and Jefferson Counties, Ohio, and Incidentally Historical Collections Pertaining to Border Warfare and the Early Settlement of the Adjacent Portion of the Ohio Valley*. Wheeling, WV: Historical Pub. Co., 1880. https://archive.org/details/oh-belmont-jefferson-1880-caldwell/mode/2up.

Catalogue and Prospectus of the Ohio Female College. Cincinnati, OH: Ben Franklin Print, 1857.

Catalogue of the Officers, Course of Studies, Etc., of Madison College and Antrim Female Seminary. Columbus: Ohio State Journal Company, 1854.

Catalogue of the Officers, Teachers, and Students of the Moravian Young Ladies' Seminary at Bethlehem, Ohio. Bethlehem, OH: 1863.

Catte, Elizabeth. *What You Are Getting Wrong about Appalachia*. Cleveland, OH: Belt Publishing, 2018.

Clapp, Elsie. *Community Schools in Action*. New York: Viking Press, 1939.

Clark, Amy D. "Letters from Home: The Literate Lives of Appalachian Women." *Appalachian Journal* 41 (Fall 2013–Winter 2014): 54–76.

Clark, Amy, Alana Johnson, and Dalena Mathews. "The Gendered Language of Gravestones: A Comparison of Northern and Central Appalachian Cemeteries." In *Handbook of the Changing World Language Map*, edited by Stanley Brunn and Roland Kehrein, 1839–1851. New York: Springer, 2020.

Collins, Gail. *America's Women: 400 Years of Dolls, Drudges, Helpmates, and Heroines*. New York: Perennial, 2003.

Colombo, Gary, Bonnie Lisle, and Sandra Mano. *Frame Work: Culture, Storytelling, and College Writing*. Boston: Bedford, 1997.

Conley, Summer. "Commentary: What My Mamaw Has Taught Me about Women's Labor and the Appalachian Matriarchy." 100 Days in Appalachia, August 19, 2021. https://www .100daysinappalachia.com/2021/08/commentary-what-my-mamaw-has-taught-me -about-womens-labor-and-the-appalachian-matriarchy/.

Connors, Robert J. *Composition-Rhetoric: Backgrounds, Theory, and Pedagogy*. Pittsburgh: University of Pittsburgh Press, 1997.

Cooper, Marilyn. "Rhetorical Agency as Emergent and Enacted." *College Composition and Communication* 62, no. 3 (February 2011): 420–449.

Delpit, Lisa, and Joanne Kilgour Dowdy, eds. *The Skin That We Speak: Thoughts on Language and Culture in the Classroom*. New York: The New Press, 2002.

Derreth, R. Tyler, and David S. Guthrie. "Presbyterians and Higher Education." In *The Oxford Handbook of Presbyterianism*, edited by Gary Scott Smith and P.C. Kemeny, 579–580. Oxford: Oxford University Press, 2019.

Donahue, Patricia, and Bianca Falbo. "(The Teaching of) Reading and Writing at Lafayette." In *Local Histories: Reading the Archives of Composition*, edited by Patricia Donahue and Gretchen Flesher Moon, 38–57. Pittsburgh: University of Pittsburgh Press, 2007.

Donawerth, Jane. *Conversational Rhetoric: The Rise and Fall of a Women's Tradition, 1600–1900*. Carbondale: Southern Illinois University Press, 2012.

Donehower, Kim. "Rhetorics and Realities: The History and Effects of Stereotypes about Rural Literacies." In *Rural Literacies*, edited by Kim Donehower, Charlotte Hogg, and Eileen Schell, 37–76. Carbondale: Southern Illinois University Press, 2007.

Edbauer, Jenny. "Unframing Models of Public Distribution: From Rhetorical Situation to Rhetorical Ecologies." *Rhetoric Society Quarterly* 35, no. 4 (Fall 2005): 5–24.

Eicholz, Hans L. "A Closer Look at 'Modernity': The Case of William Findley and Trans-Appalachian Political Thought." In *The Whiskey Rebellion and the Trans-Appalachian Frontier*, edited by W. Thomas Mainwaring, 57–72. Washington, PA: Washington and Jefferson College, 1994.

Enoch, Jessica. "A Woman's Place Is in the School: Rhetorics of Gendered Space in Nineteenth- Century America." *College English* 70, no. 3 (2008): 275–295.

Eschbach, Elizabeth. *The Higher Education of Women In England and America, 1865–1920*. New York: Routledge, 1993.

Faragher, John, and Florence Howe, eds. *Women and Higher Education in American History*. New York: Norton, 1988.

Ferrence, Matthew. *Appalachia North: A Memoir*. Morgantown: West Virginia University Press, 2019.

Fisk, William. "Muskingum College: Persistence and Success." In *Cradles of Conscience: Ohio's Independent Colleges and Universities*, edited by John William Oliver Jr., James Hodges, and James O'Donnell, 324–337. Kent, OH: Kent State University Press, 2003.

Fleming, Cynthia G. "Knoxville College: A History and Some Recollections of the First Fifty Years, 1875–1925." *East Tennessee Historical Society's Publications* 58–59 (1986–1987): 89–111.

"Franklin College (New Athens)." Ohio History Connection. Accessed July 19, 2022. https:// ohiohistorycentral.org/w/Franklin_College_(New_Athens).

Gaston, Joseph. *Portland, Oregon, Its History and Builders: In Connection with the Antecedent Explorations, Discoveries, and Movements of the Pioneers that Selected the Site for the Great City of the Pacific*. Chicago: S. J. Clarke Pub. Co., 1911.

Giffen, Heather, William Kerrigan, and Ryan Worbs. *Muskingum College*. Charleston: Arcadia Publishing, 2009.

Golden, James, and Edward P. J. Corbett. *The Rhetoric of Blair, Campbell, and Whately*. Carbondale: Southern Illinois University Press, 1990.

Guernsey County Genealogical Society. *Guernsey County Community & Family History Book*. Evansville, IN: MT Pub. Co., 2008.

Haaga, John, "Educational Attainment in Appalachia." Population Reference Bureau, July 1, 2004. https://www.arc.gov/report/educational-attainment-in-appalachia/.

Hall, Edith. "Intellectual Pleasure and the Woman Translator in Seventeenth- and Eighteenth-Century England." In *Women Classical Scholars: Unsealing the Fountain from the Renaissance to Jacqueline de Romilly*, edited by Rosie Wyles and Edith Hall, 103–131. Oxford: Oxford University Press, 2016.

Hanna, William. *History of Greene County, Pa*. Published by the author, 1882. https://archive .org/details/historyofgreenec00hann/mode/2up.

Harding, Thomas. "College Literary Societies: Their Contribution to the Development of Academic Libraries, 1815–76." *The Library Quarterly* 29, no. 1 (January 1959): 1–26.

Harmon, Sandra. "'The Voice, Pen and Influence of Our Women Are Abroad in the Land': Women and the Illinois State Normal University, 1857–1899." In *Nineteenth-Century Women Learn to Write*, edited by Catherine Hobbs, 84–102. Charlottesville: University Press of Virginia, 1995.

Harney, Will. "A Strange Land and a Peculiar People." *Lippincott's Magazine* 12 (1873): 430–438.

Hayes, Amanda. *The Politics of Appalachian Rhetoric*. Morgantown: West Virginia University Press, 2018.

Henderson, John McLenahan. *The John McLenahan Folk*. Pittsburgh, PA: The United Presbyterian Board of Publication, 1912. https://archive.org/details /johnmcclenahanfo00byuhend.

Hendrickson, Katie. "Student Resistance to Schooling: Disconnections with Education in Rural Appalachia." *High School Journal* 95, no. 4 (2012): 37–49.

Hobbs, Catherine. "Introduction." In *Nineteenth-Century Women Learn to Write*, edited by Catherine Hobbs, 1–33. Charlottesville: University of Virginia Press, 1995.

Holmes, Andrew. *The Irish Presbyterian Mind: Conservative Theology, Evangelical Experience, and Modern Criticism, 1830–1930*. Oxford: Oxford University Press, 2018.

Horner, Winifred Bryan. *Nineteenth-Century Scottish Rhetoric: The American Connection*. Carbondale: Southern Illinois University Press, 1993.

Jones, Loyal. *Appalachian Values*. Ashland, KY: The Jesse Stewart Foundation, 1994.

Kitzhaber, Albert. *Rhetoric in American Colleges, 1850–1900*. Dallas, TX: Southern Methodist University Press, 1990.

Lerner, Neal. "Archival Research as a Social Process." In *Working in the Archives: Practical Research Methods for Rhetoric and Composition*, edited by Alexis Ramsey, Wendy B. Sharer, Barbara L'Eplattenier, and Lisa S. Mastrangelo, 195–205. Carbondale: Southern Illinois University Press, 2010.

Locklear, Erica Abrams Locklear. *Negotiating a Perilous Empowerment: Appalachian Women's Literacies*. Athens: Ohio University Press, 2011.

Lutz, Alma. *Emma Willard: Pioneer Educator of American Women*. Westport, CT: Greenwood Press, 1964.

Mattingly, Carol. *Well-Tempered Women: Nineteenth-Century Temperance Rhetoric*. Carbondale: Southern Illinois University Press, 1998.

McCarthy, Margaret. *History of Higher Education in America*. New York: Peter Lang, 2011.

McCrumb, Sharyn. *Sharyn McCrumb's Appalachia: A Collection of Essays on the Mountain South.* Waverly, TN: Oconee Spirit Press, 2011.

McCumber, John. "How Humanities Can Help Fix the World." *Chronicle of Higher Education* 63, no. 6 (October 2016). https://www.chronicle.com/article/how-humanities-can-help -fix-the-world/.

Mercer County Historical Society and Henderson County Historical Society. *History of Mercer and Henderson Counties: Together with Biographical Matter, Statistics, Etc.* Chicago: H. H. Hill and Co., 1882. https://archive.org/details/historyofmercerh00merc.

Miami County Kansas History. "Miss Flora." Accessed May 28, 2021. http://thinkmiami countyhistory.com/Miss-Flora.html.

Moore, Marat. *Women in the Mines: Stories of Life and Work.* Woodbridge, CT: Twayne Publishers, 1996.

NeCamp, Samantha. *Literacy in the Mountains: Community, Newspapers, and Writing in Appalachia.* Lexington: University Press of Kentucky, 2019.

Nelson, Adam R. "Public Education in the Old Northwest: Legacies of Ohio's First Land Grant." In *Settling Ohio: First Peoples and Beyond*, edited by Timothy Anderson and Brian Schoen, 219–236. Athens: Ohio University Press, 2023.

Officers and Students of the Ohio University. *Annual Catalogue of the Officers and Students of the Ohio University, Athens, Ohio, for 1871–72.* Athens, OH: Athens Messenger Office, n.d. https://archive.org/details/ohiouniversitybu1872ohio/mode/2up.

O'Snodaigh, Padraig. *Hidden Ulster: Protestants and the Irish Language.* Belfast: Lagan Press, 1995.

Parker, Patsy. "The Historical Role of Women in Higher Education." *Administrative Issues Journal* 5, no. 1 (Spring 2015): 3–14. https://dc.swosu.edu/aij/vol5/iss1/3/.

Payne, Ruby. *A Framework for Understanding Poverty.* 3rd ed. Highlands, TX: Aha! Process, Inc., 1996.

Porter, Lorle. *A People Set Apart: Scotch-Irish in Eastern Ohio.* Zanesville, OH: New Concord Press, 1998.

Ricks, Vickie. "'In an Atmosphere of Peril': College Women and Their Writing." In *Nineteenth-Century Women Learn to Write*, edited by Catherine Hobbs, 59–83. Charlottesville: University Press of Virginia, 1995.

Rivers, Nathaniel, and Ryan Weber. "Ecological, Pedagogical, Public Rhetoric." *College Composition and Communications* 63, no. 2 (December 2011): 187–218.

Rothermel, Beth Ann. "'Our Life's Work': Rhetorical Preparation and Teacher Training at a Massachusetts State Normal School, 1839–1929." In *Local Histories: Reading the Archives of Composition*, edited by Patricia Donahue and Gretchen Flesher Moon, 134–158. Pittsburgh, PA: University of Pittsburgh Press, 2007.

Rousculp, Tiffany. *Rhetoric of Respect: Recognizing Change at a Community Writing Center.* Urbana, IL: National Council of Teachers of English, 2014.

Royster, Jacqueline Jones. *Traces of a Stream: Literacy and Social Change among African American Women.* Pittsburgh, PA: University of Pittsburgh Press, 1994.

Royster, Jacqueline Jones, and Geza Kirsch. *Feminist Rhetorical Practices: New Horizons for Rhetoric, Composition, and Literacy Studies.* Carbondale: Southern Illinois University Press, 2012.

Ruggles, Steven. "Marriage, Family Systems, and Economic Opportunity in the United States since 1850." University of Minnesota Population Center Working Paper No. 2014–11, 2014. https://pop.umn.edu/research/working-papers.

Scott, John. *Hugh Scott: An Immigrant of 1670, and His Descendants.* Published by the author, 1895. https://archive.org/details/hughscottimmigra00scot/.

Shepley, Nathan. "Places of Composition: Writing Contexts in Appalachian Ohio." *Composition Studies* 37, no. 2 (2009): 75–90.

Shuman, Amy. *Storytelling Rights.* Cambridge: Cambridge University Press, 1986.

Sicherman, Barbara. "College and Careers: Historical Perspectives on the Lives and Work Patterns of Women College Graduates." In *Women and Higher Education in American History*, edited by John Faragher and Florence Howe, 130–164. New York: Norton, 1988.

Sigourney, Lydia. *Letters to My Pupils*. New York: Carter & Brothers, 1851.

————. *Letters to Young Ladies*. New York: Harper & Brothers, 1837.

Snyder, Thomas. *120 Years of American Education: A Statistical Portrait*. Washington, DC: US Department of Education Office of Educational Research and Improvement, 1993. https://nces.ed.gov/pubs93/93442.pdf.

Snyder, Todd. *The Rhetoric of Appalachian Identity*. Jefferson, NC: McFarland, 2014.

Sohn, Katherine Kelleher. *Whistlin' and Crowin' Women of Appalachia*. Carbondale: Southern Illinois University Press, 2006.

Spring, Joel. *The American School*. 5th ed. Boston: McGraw-Hill, 2001.

————. *Deculturalization and the Struggle for Equality: A Brief History of the Education of Dominated Cultures in the United States*. New York: Routledge, 2021.

Teets, Sharon. "Education in Appalachia." In *A Handbook to Appalachia*, edited by Grace Toney Edwards, JoAnne Aust Asbury, and Ricky L. Cox, 119–142. Knoxville: University of Tennessee Press, 2006.

Traister, Rebecca. *All the Single Ladies: Unmarried Women and the Rise of an Independent Nation*. New York: Simon & Schuster, 2016.

Trigiani, Adriana. "The Origin Project." Accessed October 24, 2023. https://adrianatrigiani.com/the-origin-project/.

Turpin, Andrea. *A New Moral Vision: Gender, Religion, and the Changing Purposes of American Higher Education, 1837–1917*. Ithaca, NY: Cornell University Press, 2016.

"Viola Doudna Romans." Ohio Statehouse, January 2, 2022. https://www.ohiostatehouse.org/museum/ladies-gallery/viola-doudna-romans.

Wallace, H. F. *A Busy Life: A Tribute to the Memory of the Rev. David A. Wallace*. Greeley, CO: N.p., 1885. https://archive.org/details/busylifetributet00wall.

Webb-Sunderhaus, Sara. "'Keep the Appalachian, Drop the Redneck': Tellable Student Narratives of Appalachian Identity." *College English* 79 (2016): 11–33.

Welch, John. *A Plea for Small Colleges: An Address to the Professors and Students of Franklin College, New Athens, Harrison County, Ohio, Delivered June 28, 1876*. Cadiz, OH: W. V. Kent, 1876.

Welsch, Kathleen. "Thinking Like *That*: The Ideal Nineteenth-Century Student Writer." In *Local Histories: Reading the Archives of Composition*, edited by Patricia Donahue and Gretchen Flesher Moon, 14–37. Pittsburgh, PA: University of Pittsburgh Press, 2007.

Whately, Richard. *Elements of Rhetoric*. Boston, MA: James Munroe and Company, 1844.

Wigginton, Eliot. *Sometimes a Shining Moment: The Foxfire Experience*. New York: Anchor, 1986.

Wilder, Craig Steven. *Ebony and Ivy: Race, Slavery, and the Troubled History of America's Universities*. New York: Bloomsbury Press, 2013.

Willard, Emma. *An Address to the Public Particularly to the Members of the Legislature of New York Proposing a Plan for Improving Female Education*. Middlebury, VT: J. W. Copeland, 1819.

Wolfe, William. *Stories of Guernsey County*. Published by the author, 1943.

Wright, Christina. "Becoming to Remain: Community College Students and Post-Secondary Pursuits in Central Appalachia." *Journal of Research in Rural Education* 27, no. 6 (2012): 1–11.

Wright, Elizabethada, and S. Michael Halloran. "From Rhetoric to Composition: The Teaching of Writing in America to 1900." In *A Short History of Writing Instruction: From Ancient Greece to Modern America*, edited by James Murphy, 213–246. Mahwah, NJ: Hermagoras Press, 2001.

Young, Vershawn Ashanti, and Aja Y. Martinez, eds. *Code-Meshing as World English: Pedagogy, Policy, Performance*. Urbana, IL: National Council of Teachers of English, 2011.

Index

---

small colleges and, 29, 59–162
small stories and, 48–49
teachers' institutes and, 40–41
See also Antrim, Ohio; cultural context,
shared regional; Gaston, Mollie
and Elma; religion; Smith, Mary
(m. Wherry); Stockdale, Mary
Catherine Hixon
composition teachers, 169n8
Condit, Samantha Knox, 89
Conley, Summer, 172n34
Connors, Robert, 52, 53, 73
consolidation of schools, 125
consumption (tuberculosis), 44–45
Cooper, Marilyn, 175n34
correctness (goodness), 56, 61–62, 125, 131
cost of college
author's personal stories and, 120, 127
COVID and, 160
farmers and, 144
Findley Sr. on, 130
funding of college and, 147
mothers' influence and, 175n3
Muskingum and, 176n14
present-day choices and, 118, 147, 160,
175n3, 176n14
Coulter, Cora (Bell's niece), 89–90
Coulter, Isabell "Bell," 88–90
Coulter, Jane and Robert, 88
Coulter, Margaret, 89
Coulter, Nancy, 89
Coulter, Sara Bell (Bell's grand-niece)
(m. Heinz), 90
Coulter, Thomas Benton, 88, 89
County Antrim (Ireland), 1
COVID pandemic, 156–157, 160
cows, women compared to, 172n25
Craig, Nancy and William, 67–68
Craig, Sue (m. Suydam), 67–68
Craig family, 107
critical imagination, 13–14, 16
critical localized imagination, 13–14
critical reading and writing, 84
critical thinking, 130–131, 158
Crumbaker, Kate, 49
cultural context, American, 12, 18, 31, 61, 128,
132, 175n22
cultural context, shared regional
academic knowledge and, 134
Appalachian identity and, 92–93
author's sources and, 14–15, 63
Blair and, 54
colonization of, 56–57
critical localized imagination and, 13–14
Elements of Rhetoric and, 15
families and, 129–130
gender and, 92
gravestones and, 14–15
immigration and, 92
"literature" and, 56–57
Madison prejudices and, 129–132
Madison women and, 120

mothers' influence on children's education
and, 80
pleasure in education and, 96
present-day, 85, 121–124
rhetoric and, 15, 58
stereotypes of Appalachia and education
and, 124–133
stories and, 8–9, 63
cultural homogenization, 83
cultural "other," 17
current events, 167n25
curricula, 5, 32–33, 124, 133, 177n11
See also rhetoric (speaking/writing)
Custer, George Armstrong, 140

dancing, 97
Davis, Frances Elliot, 114
Davis, Rebecca Harding, 140
deaths of students at Madison, 35, 44–45
decentralization, 131
delicacy and correctness, 56
Delpit, Lisa, 165n1
democracy, 30–31, 79
Demorest, William Jennings and Demorest
Contests, 66
DeRosier, Linda Scott, 121–122, 123, 158
Derry, Ireland, 28
dialects, 54, 58, 63, 169n24
discourse of power, 61
divorce, 90, 135
doctors (physicians), 1, 42, 45, 88, 90–91,
96–97, 127, 141, 142, 147
See also Gaston, Rachel Perry; "granny
women"; professional development and
careers; Vincent, Charity
domestic violence/abuse, 101
Donawerth, Jane, 53, 169n8
Donehower, Kim, 122, 158, 169n29, 170n33
Doudna, Viola (m. Romans), 103–105,
149–150
Dover, Ohio, 137
Dowdy, Joanne Kilgour, 165n1
Downard, Cordelia (m. C. C. Smith), 87–88
Downard, Elizabeth and Daniel, 87–88
Duncan, James, 37–38

Eastern Europeans, 27
Eastern Ohio Teacher's Association, 153
East Guernsey Local School District, 25
Edbauer, Jenny, 172n38
1854 Catalogue of Madison, 31–35, 51
Eliza B. Wallace Hospital, 114
Ellis, Peter Berresford, 93
Emerson, Ralph Waldo, 52, 67
empowerment, 16, 62–63, 82, 83, 99, 104,
105–106, 109, 110–115, 308
See also rights for women
England, 93
English Anglican Church, 166n8
English Protestant immigrants, 26–27